Sociology

A Student–Centred Approach for A–Level

PAUL TROWLER

Unwin Hyman

To my wife

Published by
UNWIN HYMAN LIMITED
15–17 Broadwick Street
London W1V 1FP

© Paul Trowler 1987
Copyright of extracts is as listed in the
Acknowledgements
Reprinted 1988

British Library Cataloguing in Publication Data

Trowler, Paul
    Active sociology: a student–centred approach
    for A-level.
    1. Sociology
    I. Title
    301   HM66

ISBN 0–7135–2694–7

Typeset in Great Britain by
Latimer Trend & Company Ltd, Plymouth
Printed in Great Britain at the University Press, Cambridge

 Preface

In the selection of extracts for this book I have tried to ensure that the student is presented with as wide a variety of the 'flavours' of sociology as possible. Some are from recent publications while others are from well-known works by the founding fathers of sociology. Both empirical and theoretical works have been chosen. Where the extract is from an empirical study, details of the methodology are given and there are usually questions designed to foster a critical awareness of this aspect of sociological work. Each of the major perspectives in the discipline has a representative here and the chapters are structured in such a way as to encourage the student to explore the comparative strengths and weaknesses of these perspectives. For this reason, the groups of questions have been designed to cover, where possible, the educational objectives in Bloom's cognitive taxonomy (see B. S. Bloom (ed.), *Taxonomy of Educational Objectives: The Classification of Educational Goals Handbook 1: the Cognitive Domain*, D. McKay and Co. Inc., New York 1956.) The tasks for the student in the cognitive domain (that covered here) are in order of level of task involved. The later ones in the list are at a higher cognitive level and will be more demanding. The affective domain is not dealt with here. See also C. Kissock and P. Iyortsuun, *A Guide to Questioning: Classroom Procedures For the Teacher*, Macmillan, London 1982.

Active Sociology is designed to be used as a resource for reinforcement of work already done in class and as a supplement to the more traditional form of textbook. The extracts can be handled in a number of ways, depending on circumstances and the preferences of the teacher and students. In the classroom students can work individually or in small groups tackling the exercises together. A later plenary session for comparison and discussion of answers may be helpful if this is done. Another possibility is to allocate different extracts on the same topic to small groups within the class so that later comparisons can be made by the class as a whole. This should elicit maximum exchange of information between students and encourage them to articulate their ideas more fully. Alternatively the passages could be studied in the quiet and privacy of home.
Whichever approach is chosen, however, it is advisable to ensure that the introduction to the relevant chapter is read before the extracts are tackled.

No doubt students will find some of the passages taxing. A few are written in the kind of prose which has gained sociology its unenviable reputation for obfuscation. Others are written in a refreshingly clear style. The exercises are there to encourage an *active* reading technique which, with perseverence and the help of the glossary sections, should help decipher even the most tortuous English.

Note to Student

This book presents a number of extracts from both modern and classical sociological works. Some of the pieces selected summarise theories, others illustrate perspectives, while some have been selected mainly because they are interesting in their own right.

At the beginning of each chapter an introduction puts the extracts into context. In some chapters, readings are grouped into subjects within that chapter's broad topic area. For example, in the Sociology of Education chapter, one group of two extracts concerns perspectives on education and a second group of five extracts concerns reasons for educational underachievement among certain categories of students. Key words and terms are underscored in each extract and definitions given in the glossary that follows it. Questions also follow each extract and, where appropriate, there are questions after groups of extracts. The questions are designed to help you develop the following skills:

Knowledge Simple recall of information in the text. Knowledge of the terminology used.

Comprehension and interpretation Differentiation between concepts. Comparing/contrasting/rephrasing/explaining ideas. Understanding in addition to recall of ideas.

Application Using relevant information and ideas in the passage to solve problems.

Analysis Understanding of the whole theory, not merely individual parts of it.

Synthesis Understanding of how different perspectives on the same topic relate to each other and to the subject. (Such questions are asked after two or more extracts.)

Evaluation Assessing the quality of ideas, theories and perspectives. (Evaluation questions follow individual questions and groups of questions).

The following set of questions, drawn from various sections in the book, demonstrates these objectives:

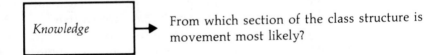

Knowledge → From which section of the class structure is movement most likely?

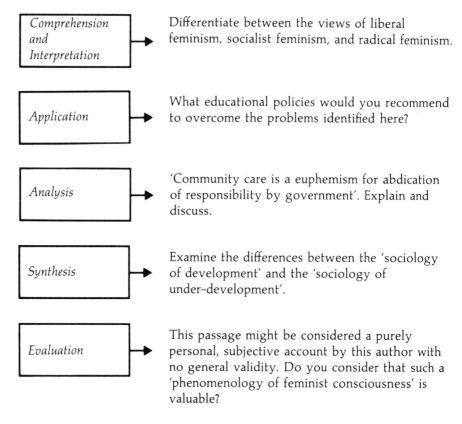

Comprehension and Interpretation →	Differentiate between the views of liberal feminism, socialist feminism, and radical feminism.
Application →	What educational policies would you recommend to overcome the problems identified here?
Analysis →	'Community care is a euphemism for abdication of responsibility by government'. Explain and discuss.
Synthesis →	Examine the differences between the 'sociology of development' and the 'sociology of under-development'.
Evaluation →	This passage might be considered a purely personal, subjective account by this author with no general validity. Do you consider that such a 'phenomenology of feminist consciousness' is valuable?

It is advisable to read the introduction to each chapter before tackling any of the extracts. It is also recommended that you read the extracts in the order in which they appear since questions on later extracts sometimes assume knowledge of previous ones.

Each chapter ends with a bibliography, giving full details of the source of extracts, further reading, and details of any references made in the introduction and extracts themselves. The page numbers given at the head of each extract refer to the edition cited in the bibliography.

Contents

The Sociology of Race

The Sociology of Deviance

The Sociology of the Mass Media

The Sociology of Stratification

The Sociology of Gender

Methodological Techniques

The Sociology of Development

The Sociology of the Family

Social Policy

The Sociology of Youth Culture

The Sociology of Work

The Sociology of Politics

The Sociology of Education

◪ The Sociology of Race

Introduction   This chapter is divided into three sections. The first section presents
extracts from and about well-known sociological studies of race which
have attempted to examine the relationship between race, class,
prejudice and exploitation. The second section concerns the official
response to one particular problem concerning racial or ethnic groups:
their schooling in Britain. The third section contains evidence on racial
discrimination from the most recent available studies on that subject.

The first extract, from Rex and Tomlinson's *Colonial Immigrants in a
British City* presents the basic elements of their 'underclass' thesis. This
was developed on the basis of empirical evidence collected during a
four-year study of the Handsworth district of Birmingham and updates
and extends the earlier work done by Rex and Moore in the
Sparkbrook area, reported in *Race, Community and Conflict*. Despite
Rex and Tomlinson's use of the term 'underclass', with its Marxist
overtones, their perspective is more akin to Weber's than that of
Marx. Rex and Tomlinson are concerned to examine how the
potentially distinct categories of status and class interact; in this case
status is derived from racial characteristics and class from market
situation. The study discovered evidence of inequalities in immigrant,
as compared to white, groups in the following areas: occupational
distribution; unemployment; support from trades unions in times of
crisis; housing, and, finally, schooling (especially among West Indians).
The Asian and West Indian groups in Handsworth felt that these
multiple disadvantages were the result of discrimination against them.
The authors write that:

> Since we have argued that the so-called new poor, deprived and disadvan-
> taged, form a special class in British society, which fails to enjoy the full
> advantages of trade union protection and the welfare state, it would seem
> that the classification of all immigrants as part of the disadvantaged means
> that they are set apart from, and below, the mainstream working class.

The second extract, from Miles' *Racism and Migrant Labour* presents
a summary of three theses about the class position of immigrants from
the New Commonwealth to Britain. These include Rex and
Tomlinson's Weberian argument and two Marxist ones. He rejects all
three and wishes to replace them with an alternative Marxist account.
This is not dealt with in the extract and so the following is a brief
summary of it.

Miles believes that:

> The process of racial categorisation, and its effects, should ... always be
> analysed as occurring within a particular historical and material context ...
> racism as an ideology must always be analysed as a particular historical
> construction.

His analysis of the British case runs like this:

1 Immigration from the Caribbean and India was encouraged because of demand in Britain for wage labour. This meant that the majority of migrants to Britain in the 50s and 60s were destined to become members of the proletariat:

> It is therefore a nonsense to argue that 'immigrants' were prevented from 'entering' the working class by racial discrimination practised by employers and workers [as Rex and Tomlinson do].

2 There was only a demand for labour in some sections of the economy—those where there were low wages, unsocial hours and unskilled work.

3 Immigrants entered a climate of negative stereotypes which resulted from the loss of empire. They met pre-formed negative images about the type of people they were.

Miles suggests that:

> The result of these three characteristics ... is that the migrants occupy a structurally distinct position in the economic, political and ideological relations of British capitalism, but within the boundary of the working class. They therefore constitute a fraction of the working class, one that can be identified as a racialised fraction.

The second section begins with selections from a *Times Educational Supplement* article on the 1985 Swann Report. This contained the findings and recommendations of the Swann Committee (known as the Rampton Committee before a change of chairman). Set up in 1979 by the Labour Government, its remit was to examine the situation of ethnic minority education in Britain and to make proposals to improve it. An interim report was published in 1981 and the final report in 1985.

The second extract in this section, from *The Empire Strikes Back* by the Birmingham University Centre for Contemporary Cultural Studies (the CCCS) gives a critical appraisal of the Committee's interim report (the findings of which are much the same as those of the final report summarised in the first extract in this section). The authors suggest that implementing the report would result in a reworking of 'multiculturalist ideology'. This term refers to an approach to ethnic minorities in Britain which encourages cultural diversity rather than trying to eliminate differences between ethnic minorities and the dominant British culture. Multicultural education tries to provide a curriculum suited to all ethnic groups in the school. In the past, though, multicultural programmes which have been offered have been criticised for not meeting the needs of West Indians, who were thought not to have a distinct culture at all. Moreover, such educational schemes are usually seen as an optional extra—'icing on the cake'—rather than being an integral part of the school's approach across the whole curriculum. A final criticism of multicultural education, at least as it has been put into practice up to now, is that syllabuses do not recognise the desire of blacks to maintain their diversity and to stress the opposition and conflict that exists between white society and ethnic minorities within it. West Indian teachers, students and parents, particularly, have increasingly rejected multiculturalism and demanded that Black Studies be taught in schools, a much more radical proposal altogether. Rex and Tomlinson's evidence shows that there are groups in Birmingham which seek to obtain acceptance for the following propositions:

> That the class position of the black immigrant from the West Indian islands is only understood if it is recognised that he is part of a people who were taken into captivity.
> That captivity meant not only slavery but cultural castration.
> That if he is to recognise his manhood the West Indian must assert that he is proud to belong to an African culture.
> That since this culture cannot be fully recaptured he must start building it anew, though a first stop in that direction must be denial of the culture which has been imposed on him. And that the revolution of the Third World, and particularly the African part of it, is his revolution and one with which he should be identified in every way.

This is far from the liberal doctrine of multicultural education, yet such attitudes are completely ignored by the Rampton report, despite their prevalence, argue the authors of *The Empire Strikes Back*.

The two extracts in the third and last section both come from Policy Studies Institute publications. They are *Black and White Britain* and *Racial Discrimination*. The first describes the results of a nationwide interview and questionnaire survey of a nationally representative sample of 5,001 black adults and 2,305 white adults, conducted in 1982. The first set of tables selected here refers to experiences of discrimination against West Indians and Asians and the attitudes held by those groups about discrimination in Britain. The second set compares the findings of a different PSI study, conducted in 1984/5, with those of similar ones conducted in 1973/4 and 1977/9 by the Political and Economic Planning Group (PEP, PSI's predecessor) and the Nottingham Community Relations Council (CRC) respectively. Each of these three studies made bogus applications for jobs in order to test how employers would react to candidates who were similar in all respects except ethnic background. The 1984/5 PSI tests involved three candidates: one white, one West Indian and one Asian. The CRC study did the same while the PEP study used only two candidates (one white and one coloured). The more recent study was carried out in London, Birmingham and Manchester and covered a range of jobs, which are listed in the table.

J. Rex and S. Tomlinson

Colonial Immigrants in a British City: a Class Analysis, 1979, pp. 275–6
(Chapter 9, 'Working Class, Underclass and Third World Revolution')

What we set out to do in the empirical studies reported in this book was to discover something of the relationship between West Indian and Asian immigrants, and their children and the class structure (or class struggle) in British society. We wished to see how far they appeared, from what we could discover of their employment, housing and educational histories, to have attained the same position as other working–class people, and how far they identified with or participated in working–class organisations. The concept of underclass was intended to suggest the alternative possibility, namely that these minorities were systematically at a disadvantage compared with working–class whites and that, instead of identifying with working–class culture, community and politics, they formed their own organisations and became in effect a separate underprivileged class. The third term in our title, however, draws attention to the possibility that this underclass need not be seen as simply having negative qualities, namely those which follow from being left out of the native working class, but might be thought of as presenting, within the content of British politics, a wider political conflict, arising from the restructuring of a formerly imperial society.

To state briefly at the outset the conclusions which we propose to spell out in more detail in this chapter, what we shall argue are the following points:

1 That, although there is some considerable overlap between the experience of West Indians and Asians and their white working–class neighbours, this is not sufficient to justify the expectation that within, say, a generation, the minorities will have been absorbed into and have equal rights with the working class.

2 That the differences between the minorities and the working class are not simply quantitative but qualitative and structural, with the immigrant situation being characterised by a different kind of position in the labour market, a different housing situation, and a different form of schooling.

3 That during the period of immigrant settlement, while the immigrant minorities have tried to adjust to British society and have established their own security in it to the extent of having obtained regular employment and their own housing, they have also been stigmatised as an unwanted and threatening element in that society.

4 That the question of the absorption of immigrant minorities into the working class has been settled against absorption, with the native working class rejecting black immigrants and uniting with other indigenous classes against them.

5 That the immigrant minorities have been forced in this situation to begin organising themselves for self–defence, developing their own political strategies separately from those of the working class.

6 That this process of organisation takes a different form in the two minority communities: in the Asian communities it takes the form of defensive organisation within which individuals may aim at capital accumulation and social mobility; in the West Indian community it may take the form of withdrawal from competition altogether with emphasis upon the formation of a black identity, even though a small minority might achieve, and a larger might continue to aspire towards, assimilation.

7 That the conflicts with British society in which immigrants and their children find themselves engaged may come to be understood in terms of a wider perspective of the readjustment of classes, groups and segments, which occurs with the collapse of the imperial social structure. For the West Indians this is clearest in that their ideologies will emphasise an end to the period of captivity which they believe their people to have suffered. For the Asians it may involve a reconsideration of the rather more favourable position which they have had within the empire, and, particularly, whether they could still find themselves a role as 'the Jews' of post–imperial society.

The underlying theme which runs through all of these points is that of increasing polarisation in the relation between the West Indian and Asian minorities on the one hand and the British cultural, social and political organisations on the other.

Glossary

Underclass a class of workers whose economic situation puts them below the working class in terms of income, status, life chances, etc.

Stigmatised not approved of, branded as bad.

Assimilation complete absorption so that distinctive characteristics are lost.

Questions

1 Summarise Rex and Tomlinson's conclusions in your own words.
2 What sort of evidence would need to be collected in order to support Rex and Tomlinson's 'underclass' thesis?
3 In what sense is Rex and Tomlinson's a *Weberian* analysis?
4 Do you consider that increasing separation between the white working class, the West Indian and the Asian communities represents a 'social problem' either now or for the future? Justify your answer.
5 What social policies should be put into effect, if any, as a result of these findings?

R. Miles

Racism and Migrant Labour, 1982, pp. 151–53

Migration and Class Structure: Some Theories

Within both sociological and Marxist literature concerned with the class structure of Britain, recognition is given to the fact of migration to Britain from the New Commonwealth. Within this literature, the following distinct theses can be distinguished. The first and third of these arguments can be described as Marxist, while the second is sociological and is based upon Weberian premises and assumptions.

(i) Unitary working class thesis
This claims that 'coloured immigrants' to Britain share with the indigenous working class the dependent conditions of exploited wage labour and that the practice of racial discrimination only serves to increase the impact upon these 'immigrants' of those otherwise common disadvantages. From this perspective, 'immigrants' are an integral part of the working class (Westergaard and Resler, 1976, pp. 356–60)[1].

(ii) Underclass thesis
This claims that the impact of discrimination is crucial in allocating 'immigrants' to a specific class position apart from the working class. It is argued that 'immigrants' do not share the same experience as the working class because of the impact of discrimination upon their position in the employment, education and housing markets. Discrimination ensures that they occupy an inferior position in these three markets, with the consequence that they are not and cannot be assimilated into the working class. They therefore constitute a class beneath the working class by virtue of their inferior circumstances and life chances, an interpretation which is captured in the concept of 'underclass' (Rex and Tomlinson, 1979, pp. 275–6)[2].

(iii) Divided working class thesis
This claims that class position is determined by the position in the relations of production and that in Britain, this leads to the identification of two main classes, the bourgeoisie and the working class. Both 'immigrant' and indigenous workers, it is claimed, constitute the working class by virtue of their identical position in production relations. To this point in the argument, there is agreement with the unitary working class thesis. However, it is then argued that, because of their lower incomes and inferior social conditions, 'immigrants' occupy a distinct economic position within the working class and that this is paralleled by a subjective division within the same class. Consequently, the working class is conceived of as being divided into two distinct strata (Castles and Kosack, 1973, p. 477[3]; cf. Moore, 1977)[4].

These three theses are mutually exclusive by virtue of their different interpretations of the impact of racial discrimination upon the class structure. They are, therefore, unsatisfactory for different reasons. The unitary working class thesis is partly founded upon empirical claims which are contradicted by the available evidence (see Phizacklea and Miles, 1980, pp. 17–20)[5] and is mistaken in claiming that discrimination creates no 'special disabilities' for 'immigrants'. For example, immigration law has placed New Commonwealth migrants in a quite distinct and disadvantaged position in political and legal relations (with the result, for example, that they are often required to produce their passports to demonstrate their right to live in Britain: see *The*

Guardian, 30 May 1980; *The Sunday Times*, 17 August 1980), while racial discrimination places specific economic constraints upon migrants which are not placed upon indigenous labour (for example, by limiting promotion opportunities: Smith, 1977, pp. 182–90)[6]. The underclass thesis mistakenly assumes that discrimination is the sole factor determining the position of migrants in what are defined as the three different markets which come to constitute the determinants of class position. It attributes no explanatory significance to the status of being migrants (Phizacklea and Miles, 1980, p. 227). Additionally, by defining class in subjectivist terms at the level of distribution of resources via markets, it rules out consideration of the significance of relations of production. Finally, the divided working class thesis makes the unwarranted assumption of there being a homogeneous working class which is 'divided' only by 'immigration'. In fact, the working class is fractured by many political and ideological divisions, and these divisions existed prior to migration from the New Commonwealth. Moreover, it operates with an economistic definition of class, a position that is now largely rejected within Marxist analysis.

[1-6] See Bibliography

Glossary

New Commonwealth West Indies, India, African countries, etc. Generally ex–colonies in the Third World. They are contrasted with the Old Commonwealth, which includes Australia, New Zealand and Canada.

Indigenous belonging to that area.

Explanatory significance having importance in explaining something.

Subjectivist terms in terms of the ideas of the people involved (as opposed to objectively).

Relations of production class relations: bourgeoisie and proletariat in capitalism, for example.

Homogeneous uniform, all of the same kind.

Economistic definition of class a definition based only on economic criteria (for example, ownership of the means of production).

Questions

1 Express the three arguments about the position of immigrants in the class structure in your own words.
2 Why does Miles refer to the first and third theories as Marxist?
3 What 'special disabilities' are suffered by immigrants other than those mentioned in the passage?
4 Choose one of the three theories and list the sorts of evidence you would need to collect to support it.

Question on Rex and Tomlinson, and Miles extracts

Complete this table, summarising the views represented:

	Rex and Tomlinson	Miles
Main cause of racial disadvantage		
Best solution to racial disadvantage		
Predictions for the future of race relations in Britain		

The Times Educational Supplement
'The Swann Report', 15 March 1985

The Swann Committee says that its report is 'concerned primarily to change behaviour and attitudes'. While the education system must not be expected to carry the whole burden of change, schools are uniquely well-placed to take a lead, it says.

'We believe that everyone in Britain has a direct interest in ensuring that those institutions and the attitudes which inform them, change to take full account of the pluralism which is now a marked feature of British life.' While recognising that society and institutions seldom change rapidly, the committee 'cannot emphasise too strongly the urgency of the need for change where attitudes to the ethnic minorities are concerned'.

The committee says it has not been possible to prepare any detailed costings for its recommendations but adds 'it is clear that a number will carry resource implications and we would urge the Government to demonstrate its commitment to the development of "education for all" by ensuring that the necessary additional resources are made available.'

Society is faced with a dual problem: eradicating discriminatory attitudes of the white majority and evolving an educational system which ensures that all pupils achieve their full potential.

In the short term, the first of these problems is a matter for the law, the Government, housing authorities, employers, unions, the Commission for Racial Equality and many others. But in the long run it is a matter for schools to bring about this much-needed change in attitudes.

The second problem is specifically one for the education system. A start has been made in recent years, but there is still a long way to go before schools bring out the full potential of all their pupils, particularly their ethnic minority ones.

The essential steps of the argument for 'education for all' are:

● The fundamental change that is necessary is the recognition that the problem facing the education system is not how to educate children of ethnic minorities, but how to educate all children.

● Britain is a multiracial and multicultural society and all pupils must be enabled to understand what this means.

● This challenge cannot be left to the independent initiatives of education authorities and schools: only those with the experience of substantial numbers of ethnic minority pupils have attempted to tackle it, though the issue affects all schools and all pupils.

● Education has to be something more than the reinforcement of the beliefs, values and identity which each child brings to the school.

● It is necessary to combat racism, to attack inherited myths and stereotypes and the ways in which they are embodied in institutional practices.

● Multicultural understanding has also to permeate all aspects of a school's work. It is not a separate topic that can be welded on to existing practices.

● Only in this way can schools begin to offer anything approaching equality of opportunity for all pupils.

Language and language education

☐ A good command of English is essential to equality of opportunity, academic success and to participation on equal terms as a full member of society. This first priority in language learning by all pupils, therefore, must be given to the learning of English.

☐ English taught as a second language must be provided in mainstream schools, not in separate language centres.

☐ Pre-school provision should be given priority as it is particularly helpful for children from homes where English is not the first language.

☐ All teachers in schools with substantial numbers of pupils for whom English is not their first language have a responsibility to help them and should be given support and training to do this.

☐ Although the linguistic, religious and cultural identities of ethnic minority pupils should be fostered, bi-lingual education should not be introduced in maintained schools.

☐ Mainstream schools should not provide mother tongue maintenance; this should be left to community groups. But l.e.a.s should help these groups by providing premises, materials and in-service training for teachers.

☐ Minority languages should be included in the language curriculum of secondary schools where there is sufficient demand. All pupils should be encouraged to think of studying them.

☐ The Government should ensure that teachers of ethnic minority languages get appropriate training, support and recognition. These teachers must be fully proficient in English.

Religion and the role of the school

☐ The committee favours a non-denominational and undogmatic approach to religious education as the best means of enabling all pupils to understand the nature of religious belief, the religious dimension of human experience and the plurality of faiths in contemporary Britain.

☐ The Government should, in consultation with religious and education bodies, look afresh at the relevant provisions of the 1944 Education Act to see whether alterations are needed.

The separate schools debate

☐ Although ethnic minority communities have the right to establish their own voluntary aided schools, the committee believes that the demand to exercise this right would diminish if the policies of 'education for all' were adopted.

☐ The establishment of separate schools would fail to tackle many of the underlying concerns of the communities and might exacerbate the very feelings of rejection which they are seeking to overcome.

☐ L.e.a.s with multiracial school populations should consider keeping or re-establishing a single-sex school as an option.

☐ Schools should respond more to the needs of Muslim pupils; they should ensure there is respect and understanding between teachers and parents and that the demands of the school do not place a child in conflict with the requirements of his faith.

Teacher education

☐ All courses should take account of Britain's pluralistic society.

☐ All students should gain some practical experience of a multiracial school.

☐ In-service training should reflect the multiplicity of cultures, faiths and languages in Britain.

☐ The DES should fund an independent evaluation of the content and effectiveness of the various racism awareness training programmes.

☐ Grants should be available for authorities to release teachers for in-service courses relating to 'education for all'.

☐ The DES should fund a scheme for teacher exchanges between multiracial and all-white schools to foster greater understanding of our society.

The employment of ethnic minority teachers

☐ The DES should ask all training institutions to collect statistics on the ethnic origin of all students training to be teachers and it should record and publish ethnic statistics on all employed teachers.

☐ 'We regard the under-representation of ethnic minorities in the teaching profession as a matter of great concern, which calls for urgent attention.'

☐ Ethnic minority teachers are still subject to racial prejudice and discrimination both in gaining employment and in advancing their careers. 'While we do not support positive discrimination in the form of quotas, and do not wish to see any diminution of standards, we urge both the CRE and those involved in making appointments, to devote far greater efforts to identifying and overcoming racist obstacles to employing and promoting ethnic minority teachers.'

☐ Access courses which offer a second chance for entry to higher education should be expanded.

Swann stresses the following points if the principle of 'education for all' is to be implanted:

● The response of schools, both 'multiracial' and 'all white', to cultural diversity has to be seen as a central feature of the current debate on the balance and breadth of the school curriculum. The Secretary of State should focus on this issue when considering responses to DES Circular 8/83 and in any further statements that he may make and any agreements that he may seek about the curriculum; . . . .

● All l.e.a.s should declare their commitment to the principles of 'education for all', to the development of a pluralist approach to the curriculum, and to countering the influence of racism;

● Every l.e.a. should have at least one adviser and perhaps a senior officer with responsibility to promote the policies we have put forward, to act as a catalyst to encourage teachers and other advisers to adopt a pluralist perspective in their work;

● HM Inspectorate should issue clear guidance on the practical implications of adopting a pluralist approach to the curriculum and on ways of countering the influence of racism on schools;

● The School Curriculum Development Committee should review existing materials which reflect a pluralist approach. The committee should consider how these materials may be

made more widely known and how the production of further such resources may be stimulated;
● Examining Boards should reflect cultural diversity in the syllabuses they offer and in their working practices;
● The Secondary Examinations Council should co-operate with the School Curriculum Development Committee to ensure that initiatives to broaden the school curriculum are reflected by parallel developments within the examinations system;
● All l.e.a.s should expect their schools to produce clear policy statements on 'education for all' and monitor their implementation;
● All schools should adopt clear policies to combat racism;
● The DES should organise a series of regional conferences for elected members of l.e.a.s, teachers and other educationalists to discuss the implications of this report; . . . .
● The DES should implement the recommendations of our interim report relating to the collection of ethnically-based statistics within education. . . .

Achievement and underachievement

The chapter concludes that: 'There is no doubt that West Indian children, as a group, and on average, are underachieving, both by comparison with their school fellows in the white majority, as well as in terms of their potential, notwithstanding that some are doing well.' . . .

The school leaver survey carried out by the DES for the committee—a repeat of the exercise done for the interim report published in 1981—showed a slight improvement in the relative performance of West Indian leavers, over the period. But they are still doing markedly less well than their fellows from other groups.
● In all CSE and GCE O level exams, 6 per cent cent of West Indians obtained five or more higher grades compared with 17 per cent of Asians and 19 per cent of all other leavers;
● In CSE English and O level English language 15 per cent of West Indians got higher grades compared with 21 per cent of Asians and 29 per cent others;
● In CSE and O level maths, 8 per cent of West Indians scored higher grades compared with 21 per cent Asians and 21 per cent others;
● At A level, 5 per cent got one or more pass compared with 13 per cent Asians and 13 per cent other leavers;
● One per cent of West Indians went on to

university compared with 4 per cent of Asians and 4 per cent others;
● One per cent of West Indians went on to full-time degree courses in further education, compared with 5 per cent Asians and 5 per cent of all other leavers.

But the survey also showed that:
● In all CSE and GCE O levels, the percentage of West Indians obtaining five or more higher grades has increased from 3 per cent in 1978–79 to 6 per cent in 1981–82;
● In English, the percentage obtaining higher grades increased from 9 to 15 per cent;
● In maths, the percentage increased from 5 to 8;
● At A level, the percentage for West Indians obtaining one pass increased from 2 to 5.

The committee hopes that these improvements might be due to some extent to increased sensitivity on the part of schools, but believes they offer scant grounds for complacency.

On Asian achievement, the school leaver survey shows that they do about as well as white children except in English language. Bangladeshis do markedly less well than all groups, majority and minority.

The interim report, says the committee, was criticised on two matters in particular, first that it failed to consider IQ, held by many to be responsible for West Indian underachievement, and second that it paid too little attention to social class and socio-economic factors, long known to be closely related to achievement among white children.

On IQ, the report says it has been able to make an important contribution 'thanks to an impressive research paper commissioned from Professor Nicholas Mackintosh and Dr Mascie-Taylor' (from Cambridge University).

These authors show that the often quoted gap between West Indian and white IQ scores is sharply reduced when account is taken of socio-economic factors.

'IQ has long been a sensitive and emotive issue. We hope that it can now cease to be so.'

On the second point of social class and status, it is clear that ethnic minority children suffer from an extra element of social and economic deprivation over and above that of the white majority. This is due mainly to prejudice and discrimination in employment and housing.

But there is no easy answer as to what proportion of West Indian underachievement is due to these social and environmental factors, nor do they explain all of the picture. . . .

The conclusions on Asians are even less complete. Again, IQ is not the answer to why Asians do about as well as whites despite more economic and social deprivation and as much discrimination to face as blacks.

But racial prejudice does not have identical effects on every minority, and white attitudes vary towards different groups.

However, two suggestions are offered as to why Asians manage to surmount direct racial prejudice.

Asians are given to 'keeping their heads down and adopting a low profile', thereby making it easier to succeed in a hostile environment. West Indians are given to 'protest' and a high profile with the reverse effect. But this is a stereotype judgement and must be viewed with caution.

A second explanation lies in the particularly tight-knit nature of the Asian community and family.

'Wherever the truth may lie, the reasons for the very different school performance between Asians and West Indians seem likely to lie deep within their respective cultures.' ...

Glossary

Pluralism having a number of distinct groups which form the whole.

L.e.a. local education authority.

Non-denominational belonging to no particular Church.

Undogmatic not imposing views without reasoned argument.

Exacerbate to make worse.

DES Department of Education and Science (government department).

CRE Commission for Racial Equality.

Access courses courses for adults to enable them to go on to higher education.

DES Circular 8/83 entitled 'The School Curriculum', asked L.e.a.'s to send details of curriculum developments to the DES.

Catalyst something which helps a change to take place.

IQ intelligence quotient, a measure of intelligence.

Emotive causing emotions to be aroused.

Questions

1 Briefly summarise the recommendations of the Report, using the same headings as used in the extract.

2 Why, according to the extract, might it be mistaken to simply point to ethnic background to explain the underachievement of West Indians relative to whites and Asians?

3 On the basis of the general recommendations made in the report, make some specific proposals as to how schools and colleges should be changed in order to implement them (discuss specific changes in the curriculum and syllabuses, ways to ensure a greater proportion of black teachers are employed, etc.)

Centre for Contemporary Cultural Studies

The Empire Strikes Back: Race and Racism in Seventies Britain, 1982, pp. 206–08

Racism as it exists and functions today cannot be treated simply from a sociological perspective: it has to be located historically and in terms of the wider structures and relations of British society. The historical roots of racist practices within the British state, the British dominant classes, and the 'British' working class, go deep and cannot be reduced to simple ideological phenomena. They have been conditioned, if not determined, by the historical development of colonial societies which was central to the reproduction of British imperialism. This process generated a specific type of 'nationalism' pertinent in the formation of British classes long before the 'immigration' issue became a central aspect of political discourse.

The Rampton Committee was set up in 1979 in order to look at 'the educational needs and attainments of children from ethnic minority groups taking account, as necessary, of factors outside the formal education system relevant to school performance, including influences in early childhood and prospects for school leavers'. In practice, however, its terms of reference in no way suggested that racism itself had to be analysed in order to explain the 'underachievement' of black pupils. In its submission to the Committee the Institute of Race Relations pointed out that:

'Your terms of reference are concerned with the "educational needs and attainments of children from all ethnic minority groups", particularly West Indian children. We feel, however, that an ethnic or cultural approach to the educational needs and attainments of racial minorities evades the fundamental reasons for their disabilities — which are the racialists' attitudes and the racist practices in the larger society and in the educational system itself.'

The first interim report of the Committee was published in June 1981, under the title 'West Indian children in our schools'. By then, however, the Chairman had been replaced by a person thought more amenable to routine policy analysis, and the Government had made it clear that social and political questions were not the main concern of the revamped Committee. These changes were a response to attempts by black members of the Committee to consider the place of racism as central to its considerations.

This is no place to consider the impact of the Rampton report, or the forthcoming Swann reports on the Asian communities, in policy and practice. The early signs are that the main result will be a reworking of the multiculturalist ideology and its further institutionalisation in the educational system. There is little likelihood, however, that governments are going to take seriously the view of blacks themselves that racism *is* the central issue. At one point in the Rampton report we find the following statement:

'Many West Indians insisted to us that the major reason for the underachievement of their children at school was racism (racial prejudice and discrimination), and its effects both in schools and in society generally. Many other people who gave evidence mentioned racism as a contributory factor.'

But such ideas are not discussed in the body of the report itself, and they seem to have had little impact on the formulation of policy alternatives. By implication the report seems to be saying that with increased special provision and more multiculturalism the problem of racism will disappear, at least from schools. In addition, by locating the source of racism in schools in the attitudes of teachers, Rampton failed to face up to the thorny problems of looking at the racism inherent in all state institutions. . . .

Multiculturalists had visions of classrooms as microcosms of a race relations paradise. Proponents of community policing strategies are concerned to reap a harvest of information from the seed–beds of schools and youth clubs. Meanwhile, black youth recognise liberal dreamers and the police for what they are and act. They determine the terrain on which the next struggle will be fought—the street, the day. Intensive policing of all areas of black life, domestic, public, social and educational testifies to the political strength and resilience of black culture. Black communities as a whole have withdrawn their consent to being governed in an increasingly authoritarian and racist way. Black youth have led the way in the redefinition of who's got the problem.

Glossary

Ideological phenomena things which are only in the realm of ideas.
Conditioned strongly influenced by something.
Microcosms miniature representations of something.

Questions

1 What is the Centre for Contemporary Cultural Studies' main criticism of the Rampton (Swann) Report's analysis of the causes of racial disadvantage in Britain?

2 What is the Centre for Contemporary Cultural Studies' view of its recommendations?

3 On the basis of the evidence given here, what would you say the Centre for Contemporary Cultural Studies' position on the causes of these problems is?

Question on The Times Educational Supplement and Centre for Contemporary Cultural Studies extracts

1 'Racial prejudice, discrimination and disadvantage can best be tackled in schools'. Explain and discuss.

C. Brown
Black and White Britain: The Third PSI Survey, 1984, p.218

Table 116:
Experience of racial discrimination in employment

Column percentages

	Men West Indian	Men Asian	Women West Indian	Women Asian
Have you yourself ever been refused a job for reasons which you think were to do with race or colour?				
Yes	26	10	23	8
No	45	32	49	33
Other/DK	29	57	28	59
Have you ever been treated unfairly at work with regard to promotion or a move to a better position, for reasons which you think were to do with race or colour?				
Yes	11	8	5	3
No	84	76	91	79
Other/DK	5	16	5	19

Table 117
Belief in racial discrimination in employment

Column percentages

	White	Men West Indian	Men Asian	White	Women West Indian	Women Asian
Do you think there are employers in Britain who would refuse a job to a person because of their race or colour?						
Yes	73	77	48	69	77	29
No	23	7	25	28	5	15
Other/DK	4	16	28	4	18	56
If yes, how many?						
Most	5	14	8	3	15	5

About half	14	22	14	14	26	10
Fewer than half	32	31	19	29	28	10
Hardly any	18	4	2	16	2	2
Other/DK	5	6	3	7	6	3

Do you believe there are firms
or organisations in Britain
where *promotion* is less likely
for Asian or West Indian
people than for white people,
even though their experience
and qualifications are the
same?

Yes	55	78	57	49	73	34
No	28	8	17	30	8	12
Other/DK	17	15	26	21	19	60

C. Brown and P. Gay

Racial Discrimination: Seventeen Years after the Act, PSI, 1985, p. 26–27

Table 8

Comparisons between tests in 1973/4, 1977/9 and 1984/5. Correspondence tests only

Column percentages

	1973/4 PEP study		1977/9 CRC study		1984/5 PSI study	
	All jobs	Comparison group	All jobs	Comparison group	All jobs	Comparison group
No discrimination	58	64	46	44	54	56
Discrimination against black applicant	36	30	48	49	38	37
Discrimination against white applicant	6	7	6	7	8	7
Number of vacancies covered by tests	234	138	103	59	267	229

Notes: (1) The percentages for the 1977/9 and 1984/5 studies are calculated using the paired test model.
(2) The job categories for the three studies are as follows:

	1973/4	1977/9	1984/5
'All jobs':	Junior clerk (M)	Junior clerk (M)	Junior clerk (F)
	Junior clerk (F)	Junior clerk (F)	Sales rep. (M)
	Salesman (M)	Shop Asst. (F)	Clerk (F)
	Accountant (M)	Salesman (M)	Secretary (F)
	Management trainee (M)	Secretary (F)	
	Secretary (F)		

'Comparison group': Junior clerk (F)
Sales rep. (M)
Secretary (F)

Table 9

Column percentages

Comparisons between tests in 1973/4, 1977/9 and 1984/5: individual job categories

	1973/4 PEP	1977/9 CRC	1984/5 PSI
Sales Rep (male)			
No discrimination	60	29	52
Discrimination v. black	32	65	38
Discrimination v. white	8	6	10
No. of vacancies covered by tests	66	23	99
Secretary (female)			
No discrimination	79	60	60
Discrimination v. black	19	35	33
Discrimination v. white	2	5	6
No. of vacancies covered by tests	36	20	89
Junior Clerk (female)			
No discrimination	56	47	51
Discrimination v. black	33	44	44
Discrimination v. white	11	9	5
No. of vacancies covered by tests	36	16	41
Skilled Manual (male)			
No discimination	76	n.a.	70
Discrimination v. black	22	n.a.	27
Discrimination v. white	2	n.a.	3
No. of vacancies covered by tests	65	n.a.	68

Note: The percentages for the 1977/79 and 1984/5 studies are calculated using the paired test model.

Glossary

Correspondence test one where only written application was made.
Paired test because the CRC and PSI studies tested employers' responses to three applicants and the PEP only used two applicants, comparison is made difficult. The authors solved this problem by treating each three applicant tests as a pair of two applicant tests: that is to say the Asian–white element of the test and the West Indian–white element are treated as separate tests. Thus they get two results for each employer tested in the CRC and PSI tests.

Questions on the tables

1 Tables 116 and 117 compare West Indians and Asians in terms of:
   (a) experience of racial discrimination in employment
   (b) beliefs about the extent of racial discrimination in employment.
   What reasons might there be for the differences which exist between the racial groups as far as these issues are concerned?
2 What problems might be associated with asking the sorts of questions found in Tables 116 and 117?

3 Put into words the changes there have been in racial discrimination between 1973 and 1985 as demonstrated by Table 8.

4 From Table 9, in which job category was there most discrimination against the black applicant? Why do you think this might be?

5 On the basis of the evidence presented in Tables 8 and 9, are the number of cases of racial discrimination in employment increasing or decreasing in Britain? What reasons would you suggest there are to explain this?

6 What criticisms have you of the PSI's method of testing employers' attitudes on race by having researchers pretend to be applicants for jobs? Do you consider the results of such a test to be valid?

Bibliography

Source of extracts

J. Rex and S. Tomlinson, *Colonial Immigrants in a British City: A Class Analysis*, Routledge & Kegan Paul, London, 1979

R. Miles, *Racism and Migrant Labour*, Routledge & Kegan Paul, London, 1982

The Times Educational Supplement, 15 March, 1985

Centre for Contemporary Cultural Studies, *The Empire Strikes Back: Race and Racism in Seventies Britain*, Hutchinson, London, 1982

C. Brown, *Black and White Britain: The Third PSI Survey*, Heinemann, London, 1984

C. Brown and P. Gay, *Racial Discrimination: Seventeen Years After the Act*, PSI, London 1985

Reference in the Introduction

J. Rex and J. Moore, *Race, Community and Conflict*, Oxford University Press, Oxford, 1967.

References in Miles extract

1 J. Westergaard and H. Resler, *Class in a Capitalist Society*, Penguin, Harmondsworth, 1976.

2 J. Rex and S. Tomlinson, *Colonial Immigrants in a British City*, Routledge & Kegan Paul, London, 1979.

3 S. Castles and J. Kosack, *Immigrant Workers and Class Struggle in Western Europe*, Oxford University Press, Oxford, 1973.

4 R. Moore, *Migrants and the Class Structure of Modern Europe*, 1977, in R. Scase (ed.), *Industrial Society: Class, Cleavage and Control*, Allen & Unwin, London, 1977.

5 A. Phizacklea and R. Miles, *Labour and Racism*, Routledge & Kegan Paul, London, 1980.

6 D. J. Smith, *Racial Discrimination in Britain*, Penguin, Harmondsworth, 1977.

Further reading

P. Cohen and C. Gardner, *It ain't 'alf racist Mum*, Comedia, London, 1983

C. Husband, *Race in Britain*, Hutchinson, London, 1982

M. Kettle and L. Hodges, *Uprising: The Police, the People and the Riots in Britain's Cities*, Pan, London, 1982

Z. Layton–Henry, *The Politics of Race in Britain*, Allen & Unwin, London, 1984

The Open University, *Class, Race and Immigration* D207, Block 2, Study Section 14, Open University Press, Milton Keynes, 1980

◪ The Sociology of Deviance

Introduction   This chapter is divided into two sections. The first contains extracts from work which illustrates some of the important perspectives in the sociology of deviance. The second includes critical comments on a number of these approaches to the subject and hence is an 'answer' to the first.

The following is a brief summary of the main perspectives. Among the earliest sociological work on deviance is Durkheim's (especially in *The Rules of the Sociological Method*) which gives a functionalist view that crime and deviance is inevitable in society and is functional for it (i.e. useful in maintaining society). He argues that even in a society of saints there would be deviance. Although it would be of a sort which would appear incredibly minor to us, to the saints it would seem scandalous. This is because not everyone is as strongly socialised into the norms of society as others. This is just as well because if deviance did not exist society would be completely static. 'To make progress, individual originality must be able to express itself,' argues Durkheim. Furthermore, punishment of crime and deviance makes it clear to all in society where the boundaries of behaviour lie. By establishing the boundaries, the crime and its punishment help to strengthen them.

Later, functionalists moved away from Durkheim's apology for the existence of crime in society. R. K. Merton in *Social Theory and Social Structure* introduces the concept of *dysfunction*, i.e. the case where an institution or other social phenomenon has a harmful effect on society. Merton, like Durkheim, believes that society is based on shared values and goals. However, Merton recognises that when some individuals fail to achieve these goals they may be forced to deviate from the normal patterns of behaviour. This deviance (which may include crime) can be harmful, or dysfunctional, for society as a whole. In the extract presented here, Merton outlines the alternative reactions which may result from failure to achieve the goals set by society.

Merton's approach was extended by Cloward and Ohlin's *Delinquency and Opportunity* which suggested that there exist 'illegitimate opportunity structures', i.e. structured (but illegitimate) ways of achieving social goals which are available to the criminal in the same way that 'legitimate opportunity structures'—education, a career, etc.—are available to ordinary citizens. While Merton concentrates on the *individual* deviant, Cloward and Ohlin show that deviant subcultures may help predispose people towards choosing illegitimate means of achieving their desires, such as burglary and other forms of crime. Cloward and Ohlin argue that there are 'three major types of delinquent subculture typically encountered among adolescent males in lower class areas of large urban centres'. These are:

The criminal pattern, in which criminals teach 'apprentices' how to cooperate with others in criminal activity and in which the young develop hostility and distrust towards the larger society.

The conflict pattern, in which gangs, based on values of toughness and aggression are the context of socialisation for the young.

The retreatist pattern, in which addictive drugs are consumed both on an individual basis and with others. The dominant ethos here is neither committing criminal acts upon nor conflict with the larger society but retreating from it into a world of drugs. The search for ecstatic experiences is one of the driving motives of life.

Cloward and Ohlin's identification of subgroups with deviant norms and values was a theme taken up by many other writers who could be said to comprise the 'subcultural' school of deviance. They include E. Sutherland, G. Sykes, D. Matza, A. Cohen and W. B. Miller. Linked to this approach was the Chicago school of deviance, an example is C. R. Shaw and H. D. McKay's *Juvenile Delinquency in Urban Areas*, which argued that crime and deviance is often found in inner city areas because there one finds little or no community. This lack of community is due to the high population turnover and the consequent weakening of norms and values and decline in the social control which sustains them. While the subcultural approach stresses the presence of alternative norms and values the Chicago school points to the absence of 'normal' ones.

A very different approach to the sociology of deviance came with the development of the interactionist approach within sociology. Writers in this school include E. Lemert, A. Cicourel and E. Goffman (see pp. 148–50 for an extract from Goffman's *Asylums*). Here, however, I have included an extract from H. Becker's influential *Outsiders*. Interactionism concentrates its attention on the way people and groups become labelled by others and on the effect this labelling has upon their behaviour. Becker argues that labelling does not occur at random; there are set rules whose infraction can cause the label to be applied. These rules are the products of initiatives by people that Becker terms 'moral entrepreneurs'. There are two related types: rule creators and rule enforcers. The first are crusading reformers who are disturbed by some aspect of the existing rules. Prohibitionists and abolitionists (of slavery) are examples cited by Becker. Mrs Whitehouse is a contemporary British example. Rule enforcers include the police or, to continue the Whitehouse example, the British Board of Film Censors. They represent the institutionalisation of the moral crusade. In the passage included here, Becker discusses how labels are applied to those who infringe the rules established by moral entrepreneurs and the effect this has on them.

Related to interactionism, or the 'labelling approach' as it is sometimes called, is the ethnographic approach, popular particularly in America in the 1960s and 1970s. Ethnographic studies document the lives and 'world views' of a variety of deviants, the information having been gained through close contact with them, usually participant or non-participant observation. The literature is full of accounts of prostitutes' lives, of lesbians, skid row culture, deliquent gangs, pool hustlers and so on. Such work usually limits itself to describing the particular culture being examined, avoiding trying to make any general statements or provide any 'explanations', especially not ones which would not be obvious to the subjects of the study. The extract included here concerns American gays who pick up truck drivers and the methods they employ. Conducted by Corzine and Kirby in 1974, the study employed non–participant observation from parked cars or nearby picnic tables. Some conversations and semi–structured interviews were held to gain deeper understanding of the behaviour of the subjects. The researchers describe the opening gambits, midgames and resolutions of the encounters between cruisers and truckers. Only the first two have been reprinted here.

The next two extracts illustrate a very different approach to deviance than previous ones. F. Pearce, adopting a Marxist perspective, states that 'real' crime is committed by corporations and by the state. He quotes an early entrepreneur, Daniel Drew:

> Law is like a cobweb; it's made for flies and smaller kinds of insects, so to speak, but lets the big bumblebees break through. When technicalities of the law stood in my way, I have been able to brush them aside easy as anything.

Examples of such lawbreaking include avoiding anti–trust legislation (laws designed to stop companies achieving a monopoly or near monopoly in the market place and hence having too much power compared to consumers), the making of illegal excess profits through coordinating supposedly secret bids for government work, violation of labour laws and so on. The short extract which follows the one from Pearce's *Crimes of the Powerful* is presented as contemporary evidence from Britain to illustrate his point. It comes from an article in *The Observer*, 1 December 1985.

Section 2 of this chapter presents some critical comments on the literature of the sociology of deviance. Liazos attacks interactionist and ethnographic approaches to the study of deviance. He suggests that such studies uncritically accept dominant stereotypes of deviants as being 'perverts' of one sort or another. In so doing they ignore the hidden crime of large corporations and the state and so fulfil an ideological function. Liazos' perspective is close to that of Pearce. The extract from Lea and Young, on the other hand, while also being written from a left–wing perspective, is critical of Marxist and radical theory for having ignored working class crime, even of excusing it. Writers like Pearce have neglected such crime and hence have not articulated explanations of it. However, Heidensohn's extract points out that *female* crime and deviance has been ignored by sociologists of deviance of all sorts. Her book *Women and Crime* seeks to explain this omission and move towards a sociology of female crime, or at least a sociology which can adequately explain the relative lack of involvement of women in crime. She writes from a feminist perspective.

R. K. Merton

Social Structure and Anomie, in R. S. Denisoff,
Sociology: Theories in Conflict, 1972, pp. 99–105

The conceptual scheme to be outlined is designed to provide a coherent, systematic approach to the study of socio-cultural sources of deviate behaviour. Our primary aim lies in discovering how some social structures *exert a definite pressure* upon certain persons in the society to engage in nonconformist rather than conformist conduct. The many ramifications of the scheme cannot all be discussed; the problems mentioned outnumber those explicitly treated.

Among the elements of social and cultural structure, two are important for our purposes. These are analytically separable although they merge imperceptibly in concrete situations. The first consists of culturally defined goals, purposes, and interests. ... The second phase of the social structure defines, regulates, and controls the acceptable modes of achieving these goals. Every social group invariably couples its scale of desired ends with moral or institutional regulation of permissible and required procedures for attaining these ends. ...

An effective equilibrium between the two phases of the social structure is maintained as long as satisfactions accrue to individuals who conform to both constraints, viz., satisfactions from the achievements of the goals and satisfactions emerging directly from the institutionally canalised modes of striving to attain these ends. Success, in such equilibrated cases, is twofold. Success is reckoned in terms of the product and in terms of the process, in terms of the outcome and in terms of activities. Continuing satisfactions must derive from sheer *participation* in a competitive order as well as from eclipsing one's competitors if the order itself is to be sustained. The occasional sacrifices involved in institutionalised conduct must be compensated by socialised rewards. The distribution of statuses and roles through competition must be so organised that positive incentives for conformity to roles and adherence to status obligations are provided *for every position* within the distributive order. Aberrant conduct, therefore, may be viewed as a symptom of dissociation between culturally defined aspirations and socially structured means. ...

The extreme emphasis upon the accumulation of wealth as a symbol of success in our own society militates against the completely effective control of institutionally regulated modes of acquiring a fortune. Fraud, corruption, vice, crime, in short, the entire catalogue of proscribed behaviour, becomes increasingly common when the emphasis on the *culturally induced* success-goal becomes divorced from a coordinated institutional emphasis. This observation is of crucial theoretical importance in examining the doctrine that antisocial behaviour most frequently derives from biological drives breaking through the restraints imposed by society. The difference is one between a strictly utilitarian interpretation which conceives man's ends as random and an analysis which finds these ends deriving from the basic values of the culture.

Our analysis can scarcely stop at this juncture. We must turn to other aspects of the social structure if we are to deal with the social genesis of the varying rates and types of deviate behaviour characteristic of different societies. ...

Table 1

	Culture goals	Institutionalised means
I. Conformity	+	+
II. Innovation	+	−
III. Ritualism	−	+
IV. Retreatism	−	−
V. Rebellion*	±	±

*This fifth alternative is on a plane clearly different from that of the others. It represents a *transitional* response which seeks to *institutionalise* new procedures oriented toward revamped cultural goals shared by the members of the society. It thus involves efforts to *change* the existing structure rather than to perform accommodative action *within* this structure, and introduces additional problems with which we are not at the moment concerned.

In every society, Adaptation I (conformity to both culture goals and means) is the most common and widely diffused. Were this not so, the stability and continuity of the society could not be maintained. ... It is this fact alone which permits us to speak of a human aggregate as comprising a group or society.

Conversely, Adaptation IV (rejection of goals and means) is the least common. Persons who 'adjust' (or maladjust) in this fashion are, strictly speaking, *in* the society but not *of* it. Sociologically, these constitute the true 'aliens'. Not sharing the common frame of orientation, they can be included within the societal population merely in a fictional sense. In this category are *some* of the activities of psychotics, psychoneurotics, chronic autists, pariahs, outcasts, vagrants, vagabonds, tramps, chronic drunkards and drug addicts. These have relinquished, in certain spheres of activity, the culturally defined goals, involving complete aim–inhibition in the polar case, and their adjustments are not in accord with institutional norms. ...

Be it noted that where frustration derives from the inaccessibility of effective institutional means for attaining economic or any other type of highly valued 'success', that Adaptations II, III and V (innovation, ritualism and rebellion) are also possible. The result will be determined by the particular personality, and thus, the *particular* cultural background, involved. Inadequate socialization will result in the innovation response whereby the conflict and frustration are eliminated by relinquishing the institutional means and retaining the success-aspiration; and extreme assimilation of institutional demands will lead to ritualism wherein the goal is dropped as beyond one's reach but conformity to the mores persists; and rebellion occurs when emancipation from the reigning standards, due to frustration or to marginalist perspectives, leads to the attempt to introduce a 'new social order.'

Glossary

Ramifications subdivisions of a complex structure.
Institutionally canalised formally set–out routes.
Aberrant straying from a moral standard.
Militates against prevents something from being true or something from happening.
Utilitarian based on the usefulness something has.
Mores accepted and enforced standards of behaviour.

Questions

1 The following phrase is an important summary of Merton's views on why some people adopt deviant behaviour. Explain it in your own words: 'Aberrant conduct, therefore, may be viewed as a symptom of dissociation between culturally defined aspirations and socially structured means'. (line 44)

2 Give one example each of forms of deviance which illustrate the innovative, ritualistic, retreatist and rebellious forms of deviance. What factors, according to Merton, will influence which of these options an individual will choose?

3 The rise of the Mafia among Italian immigrants to America could be used to illustrate Merton's theory. Show how this could be done.

4 Merton's theory explains how *individuals* become deviants. Cloward and Ohlin (see the introduction to this section) concentrate on deviant groups and subcultures within society. In your view is the individual or the group approach to deviance the best one and why?

H. S. Becker
Outsiders, 1963, pp. 8–11

The sociological view I have just discussed defines deviance as the infraction of some agreed–upon rule. It then goes on to ask who breaks rules, and to search for the factors in their personalities and life situations that might account for the infractions. This assumes that those who have broken a rule constitute a homogeneous category, because they have committed the same deviant act.

Such an assumption seems to me to ignore the central fact about deviance: it is created by society. I do not mean this in the way it is ordinarily understood, in which the causes of deviance are located in the social situation of the deviant or in 'social factors' which prompt his action. I mean, rather, that *social groups create deviance by making the rules whose infraction constitutes deviance*, and by applying those rules to particular people and labelling them as outsiders. From this point of view, deviance is *not* a quality of the act the person commits, but rather a consequence of the application by others of rules and sanctions to an 'offender'. The deviant is one to whom that label has successfully been applied; deviant behaviour is behaviour that people so label.

Since deviance is, among other things, a consequence of the responses of others to a person's act, students of deviance cannot assume that they are dealing with a homogeneous category when they study people who have been labelled deviant. That is, they cannot assume that these people have actually committed a deviant act or broken some rule, because the process of labelling may not be infallible; some people may be labelled deviant who in fact have not broken a rule. Furthermore, they cannot assume that the category of those labelled deviant will contain all those who actually have broken a rule, for many offenders may escape apprehension and thus fail to be included in the population of 'deviants' they study. Insofar as the category lacks homogeneity and fails to include all the cases that belong in it, one cannot reasonably expect to find common factors of personality or life situation that will account for the supposed deviance. ...

Malinowski discovered the usefulness of this view for understanding the nature of deviance many years ago, in his study of the Trobriand Islands:

'One day an outbreak of wailing and a great commotion told me that a death had occurred somewhere in the neighbourhood. I was informed that Kima'i, a young lad of my acquaintance, of sixteen or so, had fallen from a coco–nut palm and killed himself. ... I found that another youth had been severely wounded by some mysterious coincidence. And at the funeral there was obviously a general feeling of hostility between the village where the boy died and that into which his body was carried for burial.

Only much later was I able to discover the real meaning of these events. The boy had committed suicide. The truth was that he had broken the rules of exogamy, the partner in his crime being his maternal cousin, the daughter of his mother's sister. This had been known and generally disapproved of but nothing was done until the girl's discarded lover, who had wanted to marry her and who felt personally injured, took the initiative. This rival threatened first to use black magic against the guilty youth, but this had not much effect. Then one evening he insulted the culprit in public—accusing him in the hearing of the whole community of incest and hurling at him certain expressions intolerable to a native.

For this there was only one remedy; only one means of escape remained to the unfortunate youth. Next morning he put on festive attire and ornamentation, climbed a coco–nut palm and addressed the community, speaking from among the palm leaves and bidding them farewell. He explained the reasons for his desperate deed and also launched forth a veiled accusation against the man who had driven him to his death, upon which it became the duty of his clansmen to avenge him. Then he wailed aloud, as is the custom, jumped from a palm some sixty feet high and was killed on the spot. There followed a fight within the village in which the rival was wounded; and the quarrel was repeated during the funeral. ...

If you were to inquire into the matter among the Trobrianders, you would find ... that the natives show horror at the idea of violating the rules of exogamy and that they believe that sores, disease and even death might follow clan incest. This is the ideal of native law, and in moral matters it is easy and pleasant strictly to adhere to the ideal—when judging the conduct of others or expressing an opinion about conduct in general.

When it comes to the application of morality and ideals to real life, however, things take on a different complexion. In the case described it was obvious that the facts would not tally with the ideal of conduct. Public opinion was neither outraged by the knowledge of the crime to any extent, nor did it react directly—it had to be mobilised by a public statement of the crime and by insults being hurled at the culprit by an interested party. Even then he had to carry out the punishment himself. ... Probing further into the matter and collecting concrete information, I found that the breach of exogamy—as regards intercourse and not marriage—is by no means a rare occurrence, and public opinion is lenient, though decidedly hypocritical. If the affair is carried on *sub rosa* with a certain amount of decorum, and if no one in particular stirs up trouble—'public opinion' will gossip, but not demand any harsh punishment. If, on the contrary, scandal breaks out—everyone turns against the guilty pair and by ostracism and insults one or the other may be driven to suicide[1].'

Whether an act is deviant, then, depends on how other people react to it. ...

[1] See Bibliography

Glossary

Infraction violation, breaking (of a rule).

Homogeneous of the same kind (opposite of heterogeneous—all different). The noun is homogeneity.

Exogamy a custom compelling marriage with a partner outside one's own tribe or group.

Sub rosa in confidence, with a pledge of secrecy (actual or implied).

Ostracism exclusion from society.

Questions

1 In what sense do 'social groups create deviance by making the rules whose infraction constitutes deviance'?

2 Becker rejects the view that criminals have something in common with each other just because they have committed the same crime. Why does he believe this to be mistaken?

3 By the use of the Trobriand Island example, Becker implies that ordinary people are no different from deviants (both break the rule of exogamy in this case). The only difference is that deviants are the ones who get labelled. What arguments/evidence/examples can you think of to:
(a) confirm
(b) refute
this view?

4 Taking the example of the crime of shoplifting committed by two different people, what factors about them or their situation may lead one to become publicly labelled as a shoplifter and the other not to be so labelled? Consider why one may be caught and the other not *and* why, if both are caught, the crime of one may become public knowledge and the other not.

5 Give two criticisms of the labelling approach to deviance.

J. Corzine and R. Kirby
'Cruising the Truckers: Sexual Encounters in a Highway Rest Area',
Urban Life, Vol. 6, No. 2, 1977

Opening gambits
The majority of cruisers prefer to make the initial approach in sexual encounter while the driver is sitting in his parked truck. Frequently, a cruiser will first park his car at John's Diner or a rest area where he can observe individuals entering or leaving the buildings in order to look over prospective sex partners. Others prefer to drive slowly by the parked trucks until they see someone who interests them. When this happens the cruiser will stop his car along the driver's side of the truck cab and roll down his window. If the driver rolls down his window or it is open, the cruiser initiates the conversation, usually with the question: 'Do you have the time?' An approach style which is used less frequently is described by Roger, a cruiser who has no car and hitchhikes to and from the rest areas.

'I wait in a rest area and look for a truck driver to leave his truck to go into the restroom. If his appearance appeals to me, I go into the restroom and ask him if he wants to get it on. That's the only method I use. . . . I do not go anyplace with the driver but the tearoom. . . . I'm not going to get myself into a situation that I can't get myself out of.'

However, not all truck drivers who are interested in sex sit in their trucks and wait to be approached. Most cruisers with whom we have talked during the study reported they had been involved in a sexual encounter where the truck driver had made the initial approach. The first time he engaged in sexual activity with a truck driver, Greg was the one who was approached. 'Actually I became aware of it through a truck driver. I was stopped at a traffic light next to a truck and I was looking at the driver. He motioned me to pull over past the intersection. When I pulled over, he asked me if I had time for a little action. I've been doing it ever since.'

This type of initiation to the possibility of cruising truck drivers was reported by one other respondent. However, the most frequent pattern is for the cruiser to make the initial approach.

A more complex type of approach, called 'running a truck' by cruisers, is employed primarily during daytime or early evening hours when few trucks are parked for the night. The cruiser drives toward one of the rest areas in the inside lane of the interstate and allows other traffic to pass him. If he sees a truck driver who interests him, he will change lanes and pull his car to within a few feet of the rear of the truck. Depending on whether it is day or night, he honks the horn or flashes the lights to get the truck driver's attention. The cruiser then passes the truck and when his car is even with the cab waves at the driver. After the truck is passed, the cruiser pulls back into the outside lane and flashes his lights three times. When the cruiser reaches the rest area, he pulls into the entrance and parks his car. If the truck follows, the same approach technique is used as when a truck is initially parked. Although running a truck is a secondary technique and somewhat dangerous on a crowded highway, a few cruisers prefer its almost exclusive use because it virtually eliminates the possibility of approaching a driver who is uninterested in sexual activity.

Midgames
The answer to 'Do you have the time?' or other ambiguous opening questions such as 'Do you have a match?' determines whether an attempted pickup is made or the encounter is abruptly terminated. A response with a *double entendre* or indefinite meaning such as 'I could find some time,' or 'that's not all I've got,' is perceived by the cruiser as a cue that the driver may be interested in a sexual exchange or as it is usually called, 'action'. If the response is a direct answer to the question—'it's eight o'clock'; or indicates a hostile attitude—'turn on the radio,' the cruiser will terminate the conversation and leave the setting. After the cruiser and driver have a chance to look each other over more closely, sometimes one or both will terminate the encounter because the other is not considered physically attractive. Those cruisers active in the gay subculture share a set of common expectations concerning the characteristics of a 'normal' encounter with truck drivers. When actual events differ from what is expected, the result is often confusion, indecisiveness, or the termination of the encounter. These can result when a number of unexpected situations occur including

the presence of two men driving for a company which usually employs one man and, ironically, meeting a driver who is not heterosexual.

'I was on my way home from work shortly before midnight. I commuted from a small town and the trip was about thirty minutes. I was cruising a truck with ———— plates and flashed my lights several times. When the driver also flashed the truck lights, I pulled into the rest area. It was not well lighted and when the driver got out I could see tits under the clothing and almost left. When the driver got closer I could see it was a man wearing falsies. When we got into the truck sleeper I found that he was wearing women's underwear. I had never run into anything like that before. He told me that he dressed like that a lot late at night when he was on the road.'

Because of our limited number of interviews with truck drivers, we are uncertain if they share a similar set of expectations as to what constitutes a normal encounter. As there is an apparent lack of communication between drivers who frequent the sexual marketplace, they may evaluate emerging encounters more on the basis of past personal experience than by reference to a set of shared subcultural expectations.

If the encounter continues, a difference in styles emerges between individual cruisers. A few favour a rather direct approach and soon follow the opening question with a rather explicit proposition. More often the subsequent conversation is indirect and ambiguous. One or both participants interject statements into the conversation which contain vaguely disguised sexual innuendos—'I'm getting hungry, how about you?' or 'I'm sure you know what I'm here for.' If the driver has previous experience in the sexual marketplace, he usually understands the cruiser's true purpose. Although frequently no identifying information is exchanged during the encounter, the cruiser and driver may exchange first names which are often fictitious during the midgame stage.

We did not observe the body and eye signals reported by researchers in other gay settings (Hooker, 1967[1]; Humphreys, 1975[2]). Interaction during the approach and midgame stages of the encounter is almost exclusively verbal. Although most encounters occur at night when nonverbal communication is impractical, more important as an explanation for the reliance on verbal communication is that neither group is familiar with the slang or nonverbal gestures which have meaning in the other's subculture. Verbal communication and a rather direct approach also serve to insure that, most of the time, both participants will understand when an agreement for an exchange of sexual services has been reached.

Most cruisers report they will end the conversation with a driver if no agreement can be reached in approximately 10 minutes. Encounters often end in midgame because one or both participants are suspicious of the other's intentions. Most drivers carry large sums of cash and/or credit cards to pay travel expenses. As a result, they are often on guard against the threat of robbery. Cruisers are aware of the threat of physical violence if they offend a driver. These suspicions are intensified when more than one individual is in either vehicle. The presence of the extra person usually becomes a point of contention in the conversation. Although group sex is reported to occur sometimes when three or more persons are present, a more common outcome is that the lone individual will not leave or trust someone to enter his vehicle. It was this problem which led us to abandon the practice of riding with cruisers. Assurances that we were friends of the cruiser who were 'wise' and would remain in the car were not successful in allaying the suspicions of the driver. . . .

[1–2]See Bibliography

Glossary

Gambit opening moves in chess (also used for an opening move in a discussion).

Cruiser someone looking for a short-term, physical, homosexual relationship.

Double entendre word or phrase deliberately used to have a double meaning.

Questions

1 Summarise the findings of this piece of research in a paragraph.
2 The authors say that they conducted 'a limited number of interviews with truck drivers'. In fact they interviewed only two. Why do you think they obtained such a small sample? Is evidence obtained from two people permissible in sociology?
3 Is it possible to distinguish this sort of sociology from journalism? If so, what are the differences? If not, what is the point of sociologists doing such research?
4 Comparing this study to Merton's, which is the best, would you say, and why?

F. Pearce
Crimes of the Powerful, 1976, pp. 158–60

Within sociology, and particularly within criminology, the serious study of the state and its agents and of the activities of the ruling class is virtually non-existent. A start has been made by scholars like Poulantzas and Miliband, but nevertheless most of what has been written has been administratively oriented or meritocratic in its inspiration. On the other hand, endless surveys and reports have been compiled on crime, racial disturbance, working-class militancy, drug 'abuse', etc. This book has also been concerned with crime, but in a different way. In it I have looked at the state, the ruling class and organised crime and have described the criminal conspiracy so often tying them together during this century. The intention in using a Marxist approach has been to rescue the study of organised crime from the moralising empiricism of journalists and the political naivety of corporate liberals. By relating the varying fortunes of gangsters to the needs of the ruling class, the subordinate status of the former has become clear as has the need for an analysis of the mode of production of which the ruling class is an element. Only by understanding the development of monopoly capitalism within a world context is it possible to make sense of the development of syndicated crime in American and other countries. Furthermore, the distance between rhetoric and action becomes manifest when contrasting the publicly stated purpose of legislation and the actual targets in mind when it was framed and implemented.

The material in Parts 2 and 3 of this book shows that the most important practitioners of 'organised crime' within a national and international context are not the Capones, Lanskys or Lucia-nos of the world but the American corporations and their agent, the American state. However, whilst this may be true, much more work is needed on this topic. We know that many of the major American fortunes were made illegally (Russell Sage, for example, made his money from criminal fraud and then set up a foundation which sponsored studies of crime in the New York and Pittsburgh slums). Again many British fortunes have been built on the terrorisation of colonial peoples as earlier the aristocracy had become rich through forced enclosures. But we do not have enough detailed work on either the present activities or the growth of the major corporations. The same, of course, applies to the repressive apparatus of the state. (Police violence in Britain during the General Strike and against the Hunger Marchers has almost been forgotten and is rarely mentioned in academic texts.)

Part 3 of this book is only indicative, more in the nature of development of a theoretical framework for analysing the problem than a completed piece of work in itself. One topic certainly worth investigating is the relationship between the American political parties and organised crime. A number of writers have already pointed to the strong evidence linking ex-President Nixon with organised crime, so it seems fitting to end with a quotation from him:

'The organised criminal relies on physical terror and psychological intimidation, on economic retaliation and political bribery, on citizens' indifference and government acquiescence. He corrupts our governing institutions and subverts our democratic processes.'—Richard Nixon, 24 April 1969

Glossary

Criminology the study of criminal behaviour. It includes elements of sociology, psychology, psychiatry and law. It tends to be oriented towards making law enforcement more efficient through the study of criminality, studying modes of punishment and their effectiveness and so on.

Moralising empiricism used here the phrase means that journalists concentrate their attention only on those crimes that are evident 'on the street', so to speak, and they are damning about them and the people who commit them.

Corporate liberals well-meaning individuals who are attached to some institution (for example, a university). They are said by Pearce to be politically naive because they do not appreciate the way in which the powerful are able to use their power to hide their misdemeanours from the public gaze.

Mode of production a Marxist term referring to the nature of a particular economy and the class relations within it.

Monopoly capitalism a capitalist economic system which has reached a stage of development in which the economy is dominated by just a few very large corporations which, as a result, have great power.

Questions

1 According to Pearce, what was the problem with much of the previous work in criminology and the sociology of deviance? What contribution does he believe he has made to these subjects?
2 What reasons would a Marxist give for the fact that much sociological and criminological work has concentrated on racial disturbances, working class militancy, drug abuse, etc?

R. Hall, D. Leigh and A. Harris
'Exposed: JMB Multi–Million Swindle', *The Observer*, 1 December 1985

Evidence that the collapsed Johnson Matthey and other City of London banks were involved in gigantic currency swindles linking Britain and Nigeria have been uncovered by *The Observer*.

The rackets, which cost Nigeria more than £5 billion during President Shagari's corrupt regime, were referred by the Fraud Squad last week to the Director of Public Prosecutions.

We have also established that the bank itself knew at least one of its officials was involved in taking bribes in June 1984 just before the crash. The Bank of England, however, attempted a quiet rescue and did not call in the Fraud Squad.

'We regarded it as immaterial because the opportunity for fraud was created by bad banking practice which was the cause of the collapse,' said a spokesman yesterday.

The main purpose of the African swindles was to get hard currency out of Nigeria during its oil boom years. Leading figures in the ruling party amassed fortunes, then sought the help of Asian traders and shippers to smuggle the money to London.

This was done by bogus imports. Sterling would be made available to import sugar, and other commodities. They even included toothpicks, because the lack of import duty simplified the paperwork. Nigerian politicians helped speed the grant of import licences.

JMB's role was to pay out sterling in London on loans backed by Nigerian banks, once it had proof, from bills of lading and inspection certificates, that the goods were actually embarked on a ship.

Often these were forged, or one among several shipments would be bogus. Sometimes the cargoes left, but went elsewhere. At the other end, import duty would be paid on imaginary cargoes, and customs officials bribed to say they had seen the goods landed. Some Asian traders collected vast pay–offs, and the politicians had their money to spend on buying houses, cars and other assets in Britain.

Sometimes containers listed as holding expensive machinery or consumer goods were found packed with scrap metal and waste paper. A Swiss surveillance company employed by the Nigerian Government struggled to stop such cargo frauds. In August 1984—coincidentally, the time when JMB was collapsing—its contract was cancelled and the job given to three other inspection companies.

A leading Western banker with Nigerian connections told *The Observer* yesterday: 'The directors of JMB would have had to be incredibly naive not to know what was going on. Any banker in his right mind would have checked the information.'

As the scale of corruption behind the collapse began to emerge last week, the head of the special team of lawyers, accountants and police investigating the affair revealed that his staff feel 'concern and frustration' about their 'monstrous caseload' of City scandals.

Dorian Williams, the DPP assistant director heading the newly launched fraud investigation group into JMB, said in a letter to *The Times*: 'Fraud is a significant destructive factor in our national life. It gives birth to a deep and corrosive cynicism. As it flourishes, honesty is less and less practised.' He made clear his department has too few resources. ...

When JMB teetered on the edge of collapse, in April 1984, bribery of a senior offical in the banking department was reported to JMB itself, over deals with shippers.

The man was allowed to resign in June but not prosecuted. The Bank of England accepted the situation when it nationalised the bank. In its report on JMB nearly a year later, this discovery was played down: 'No evidence of fraud by the directors or staff of JMB has been discovered, except in one case dealt with before and immaterial to the collapse.'

Glossary   Director of Public Prosecutions (DPP) a barrister or solicitor who undertakes proceedings in cases of murder and other crimes of importance.

Questions   1 What was the nature of the alleged fraud by JMB officials?
2 This article is used to illustrate Pearce's argument about organised crime within the capitalist system. Do you think that it gives his ideas credibility or not (for example, does the fact that it has become front page news undermine the argument?)?
3 What criticisms have you got of Pearce's Marxist approach to the sociology of deviance?

A. Liazos

The Poverty of the Sociology of Deviance, in M. Fitzgerald *et al., Welfare In Action,* 1977, pp. 37–41

I examined sixteen textbooks in the field of 'deviance', eight of them readers, to determine the state of the field. ...

The omissions from these lists [of types of deviants] are staggering. The covert, institutional forms of 'deviance' are nowhere to be found. Reading these authors, one would not know that the most destructive use of violence in the last decade has been the war in Vietnam, in which the US has heaped unprecedented suffering on the people and their land; more bombs have been dropped in Vietnam than in the entire World War II. Moreover, the robbery of the corporate world—through tax breaks, fixed prices, low wages, pollution of the environment, shoddy goods, etc.—is passed over in our fascination with 'dramatic and predatory' actions. Therefore, we are told that 'while they certainly are of no greater social importance to us than such subjects as banking and accounting [or military violence], subjects such as marijuana use and motorcycle gangs are of far greater interest to most of us. While it is only a coincidence that our scientific interests correspond with the emotional interest in deviants, it is a happy coincidence and, I believe, one that should be encouraged'. . . .

An effort is made to transcend this limited view and substantive concern with dramatic and predatory forms of 'deviance'. Becker (1964)[1] claims that the new (labelling) sociology of deviance no longer studies only 'delinquents and drug addicts, though these classical kinds of deviance are still kept under observation.' It increases its knowledge 'of the processes of deviance by studying physicians, people with physical handicaps, the mentally deficient, and others whose doings were formerly not included in the area.' The powerful 'deviants' are still left untouched, however. This is still true with another aspect of the new deviance. Becker claims that in the labelling perspective 'we focus attention on the other people involved in the process. We pay attention to the role of the non-deviant as well as that of the deviant.' But we see that it is the ordinary non-deviants and the low-level agents of social control who receive attention, not the powerful ones (Gouldner, 1968)[2].

In fact, the emphasis is more in the *subculture* and *identity* of the 'deviants' themselves rather than on their oppressors and persecutors. To be sure, in varying degrees all authors discuss the agents of social control, but the fascination and emphasis are on the 'deviant' himself. Studies of prisons and prisoners, for example, focus on prison subcultures and prisoner rehabilitation; there is little or no consideration of the social, political, economic, and power conditions which consign people to prisons. Only now are we beginning to realise that most prisoners are *political prisoners*—that their 'criminal' actions (whether against individuals, such as robbery, or conscious political acts against the state) result largely from current social and political conditions, and are not the work of 'disturbed' and 'psychopathic' personalities. This realisation came about largely because of the writings of political prisoners themselves: Malcolm X (1965), Eldridge Cleaver (1968), and George Jackson (1970), among others[3-5]. . . .

The collection of memoirs and apologies of 'deviants' in their own words, (McCaghy *et al.*,

1968)[6] covers the lives and identities of 'pervert deviants': prostitutes, nudists, abortionists, criminals, drug users, homosexuals, the mentally ill, alcoholics, and suicides. For good measure, some 'militant deviants' are thrown in: Black Muslims, . . . and a conscientious objector. But one wonders about other types of 'deviants': how do those who perpetuate the covert institutional violence in our society view themselves? Do they have identity problems? How do they justify their actions? How did the robber barons of the late 19th century steal, fix laws, and buy politicians six days of the week and go to church on Sunday? By what process can people speak of body counts and kill ratios with cool objectivity? On these and similar questions, this book (and all others) provides no answers; indeed, the editors seem unaware that such questions should or could be raised. . . .

Because of these biases, there is an implicit, but very clear, acceptance by these authors of the current definitions of 'deviance'. It comes about because they concentrate their attention on those who have been *successfully labelled as 'deviant'*, and not on those who break laws, fix laws, violate ethical and moral standards, harm individuals and groups, etc., but who either are able to hide their actions, or, when known, can deflect criticism, labelling, and punishment. . . .

Furthermore, the essence of the labelling school encourages this bias, despite Becker's (1963: 14)[7] assertion that 'insofar as a scientist uses "deviant" to refer to any rule-breaking behaviour and takes as his subjects of study only those who have been *labelled* deviant, he will be hampered by the disparities between the two categories.' But as the following statements from Becker and others show, this is in fact what the labelling school does do.

Deviance is 'created by society . . . *social groups create deviance by making the rules whose infraction constitutes deviance*, and by applying those rules to particular people and labelling them as outsiders' (Becker, 1963: 8–9). Clearly, according to this view, in cases where no group has labelled another, no matter what the other group or individuals have done, there is nothing for the sociologist to study and dissect.

'Rules are not made automatically. Even though a practice may be harmful in an objective sense to the group in which it occurs, the harm needs to be discovered and pointed out. People must be made to feel that something ought to be done about it (Becker, 1963: 162).'

'What is important for the social analyst is not

what people are by his lights or by his standards, but what it is that people construe one another and themselves to be for what reasons and with what consequences (Lofland, 1969: 35).'[8]

'... deviance is in the eyes of the beholder. For deviance to become a social fact, somebody must perceive an act, person, situation, or event as a departure from social norms, must categorise that perception, must report the perception to others, must get them to accept this definition of the situation, and must obtain a response that conforms to this definition. Unless all these requirements are met, deviance as a social fact does not come into being (Rubington and Weinberg, 1968: v).'[9]

The implication of these statements is that the sociologist accepts current, successful definitions of what is 'deviant' as the only ones worthy of his attention. To be sure, he may argue that those labelled 'deviant' are not really different from the rest of us, or that there is no act intrinsically 'deviant', etc. By concentrating on cases of successful labelling, however, he will not penetrate beneath the surface to look for other forms of 'deviance'—undetected stealing, violence, and destruction. When people are not powerful enough to make the 'deviant' label stick on others, we overlook these cases. But is it not as much a *social fact*, even though few of us pay much attention to it, that the corporate economy kills and maims more, is more violent, than any violence committed by the poor (the usual subjects of studies of violence)? By what reasoning and necessity is the 'violence' of the poor in the ghettoes more worthy of our attention than the military bootcamps which numb recruits from the horrors of killing the 'enemy' ('Oriental human beings', as we learned during the Calley trial)? But because these acts are not labelled 'deviant', because they are covert, institutional, and normal, their 'deviant' qualities are overlooked and they do not become part of the province of the sociology of deviance. Despite their best liberal intentions, these sociologists seem to perpetuate the very notions they think they debunk, and others of which they are unaware.

[1-9]See Bibliography

Glossary

Corporate world the world of multi–national corporations.
Substantive concerning the substance, not, e.g., the methodology.
Agents of social control groups and institutions in society which enforce the norms of behaviour, e.g. the police, schools, the family.
Covert secret or hidden (the opposite of overt).

Questions

1 What is Liazos' criticism of Becker and the labelling school?
2 Explain the phrase 'Deviance is in the eyes of the beholder' (line 132).
3 What is Liazos' argument that leads to the conclusion 'most prisoners are political prisoners' (line 60)? Do you agree with the argument?
4 Does reading this extract make you reconsider your comments on the validity of the study of cruisers and truckers?

Questions on Merton, Becker, Pearce, and Liazos extracts

1 Complete this table, summarising the views represented:

	Merton (Functionalist)	Becker (Interactionist)	Pearce and Liazos (Marxist)
Characteristics of deviants			
Cause of deviance			
In sociological studies attention should be focused on...			

2 Imagine you are Pearce. Bearing in mind his comments on much of the previous work in sociology and criminology, what criticisms have you of Merton's approach?

3 Imagine you are Becker. Taking into account his comments that deviants have little in common with each other, what criticisms would you make of Merton?

4 Essay question: Critically assess the contribution which labelling theory has made to the sociological understanding of deviance.

J. Lea and J. Young
What is to be Done about Law and Order?, 1984, pp. 11–12; 226–27

We are caught between two opposing views on crime: the mass media and a substantial section of right-wing opinion are convinced that the crime rate is rocketing, that the war against crime is of central public concern and that something dramatic must be done to halt the decline into barbarism. The left, in contrast, seeks to minimise the problem of working-class crime; left-wing criminology has—with a few notable exceptions—spent most of the last decade attempting to debunk the problem of crime. It has pointed to the far more weighty crimes of the powerful, stressing how the working class has much more pressing problems. It sees the war against crime as a side-track from the class struggle, at best an illusion invented to sell news, at worst an attempt to make the poor scapegoats by blaming their brutalising circumstances on themselves. A new left realism about crime must seek to navigate between these two currents. It must neither help fan moral panic nor must it make the serious political mistake of neglecting discussion of crime—leaving the running to the conservative press. But it must be objective and try to assess the actual threat of crime: its impact, its relative

impact compared with other social problems, and who its targets are.

We have chosen to focus largely on what are conventionally thought of and defined as crimes, but not because we are unaware of the severe and perhaps greater impact of crimes committed by the upper and middle classes. Thus we will consider assault against the person rather than crimes at work due to violation of safety regulations; burglary rather than income tax evasion; theft of motor cars rather than corporate criminality. Our emphasis on official crime is not accidental—it aims to redress the balance in radical thinking.

Radical criminology and exposé journalism, over the last two decades, have done a vital job in showing up the calculated violence and cupidity of the powerful. But in their attempt to counter the mass media they have evolved a blind spot about the crimes which most of the population see as worrying. Even more problematically, they have suggested that these public concerns are creations of the media. We will argue to the contrary that there is an only too real problem of crime in this country. ... Our analysis has centred around the ideas of marginality and relative deprivation. We have argued that the progressive economic marginalisation of a generation of young people, among whom the ethnic minorities are heavily represented, coupled with a high degree of relative deprivation, has produced a youth subculture. This subculture, manifested in different ways among black and white youth and within different groups of black and Asian youth, is an attempt to come to terms with lack of achievement and denial of opportunity—that is, with relative deprivation. Such a subculture is contradictory: it combines the attempt to sustain dignity and solidarity with a highly individualistic predatory streak. It faces both ways, in the direction of a petty criminality that wears down the community, and in the direction of a unity and solidarity in the face of adversity.

Thus one consequence of economic marginality and relative deprivation is a rise in crime rates.

This has become bound up with the vicious circle of the drift to military policing in the inner city which has become one of the central grievances of young people, blacks in particular, and ranks alongside socioeconomic deprivation like housing and unemployment as one of the main ingredients of the riots of summer 1981. In particular, the drift to military policing emphasises the solidarity of the community and tends to direct it against the police. Finally, the frustrations of the young and the black community reached breaking point, in the form of riot, because of the lack of any other effective channels whereby their grievances could be formulated and represented in the political system. This political marginality, we have argued, has been one of the consequences of economic marginality in a society in which the forms of political group formation are based on participation in the production process.

Glossary

Debunk remove a false reputation.
Moral panic a wave of hysteria in a country about a 'social problem'.
Cupidity greed for gain.
Relative deprivation a feeling of being poor compared to other groups or categories of people which one sees as comparable to oneself.

Questions

1 How do Lea and Young explain the rise in the crime rates?
2 What do the authors mean by 'military policing' (line 73)? What evidence is there that there has been a 'drift to military policing'?
3 How would an interactionist (like Becker) view Lea and Young's acceptance of the idea that an increase in working-class crime, as reflected in the statistics, is a problem in society?
4 Would you agree, on the limited evidence of the passage from Pearce, that he (amongst other left-wing writers) 'seeks to minimise the problem of working-class crime'?

F. Heidensohn

Women and Crime, 1985, pp. 11–12

Finding a place for female crime

If we were to try to draw a portrait of a 'typical' female offender at this stage she would be a young girl, a first offender charged with shoplifting, and her likely destiny would be a caution or a non-custodial sentence. There are, of course, small groups of women who deviate from this: the regular drunk with a string of convictions, or

the prostitute regularly fined for soliciting, as well as a sprinkling of women convicted of serious crimes such as murder, and offences associated with terrorism. However, while a very few female offenders have attracted unusual popular attention ... the picture is not on the whole an exciting one. 'Monster' murderers or big-time gangsters are scarcely found amongst the ranks of women offenders. There is little evidence of the drama of juvenile gang activity between girls of the kind which has excited the interest of several generations of sociologists.

It is because of their lack of glamour as well as their low social threat, that as several commentators have suggested, female criminals have received so little consideration in the immense literature from sensational to serious which has been generated on the topic of crime (Smart, 1977[1]; Millman, 1982[2]). Yet I believe this cannot be the complete explanation. Even though women criminals may have seemed boring under-achievers compared with their male counterparts, the pattern of sex crime ratios — that is, the relative share of males and females in crime — was far too serious an issue to ignore for so long (Heidensohn, 1968[3]; Harris, 1977[4]). Baldly, no theory of criminality which ignores the overwhelming importance of gender can be valid. *Sex differences in criminality are so sustained and so marked as to be, perhaps, the most significant feature of recorded crime.*

In later chapters of this book I shall examine why female crime was neglected for so long and how, in the end, a feminist approach was necessary to free it from this invisible state. At this stage I simply want to point out that, paradoxically, an examination of female criminality and unofficial deviance suggests that we need to move away from studying infractions and look at conformity instead, because the most striking thing about female behaviour on the basis of all the evidence considered here is how notably conformist to social mores women are. There is no evidence that this is somehow innate in women, a feature of their sweeter 'better' natures, nor as the nursery rhyme has it that little girls are 'sugar and spice and all things nice' while boys are 'snaps and snails and puppy dogs tails'. In fact some women can and do commit offences of the same kind as men, save where legal or technical barriers exist, but they do so in very much smaller numbers, at less serious levels and far less often. In consequence, there are far more men than women in prison.

I shall therefore devote some space in this book to the pressures to conform and the patterns of social control experienced by women and to show how these are related to female crime. It is at this point that I think the wider relevance of female criminality to women in general can be seen. Only a few women are ever defined as criminal, but the control system which subtly, and with their compliance, inhibits the rest affects most women. Criminologists and even the more broadly interested sociologists of deviance have been uncomfortable with the study of female criminality because, logically, it leads to the superficially dull topic of conformity and not to the excitements of deviance.

The growth of a feminist appreciation of social divisions and forces enables a reappraisal. It is possible to break conventional moulds and link different approaches to the topic, it also means that we no longer take for granted long-current assumptions about the world. Thus I have used feminist analyses of family life to show how these have a bearing on the social constraints experienced by women. In what follows I have deliberately mixed résumés of scholarly researches with more direct descriptions by individuals and popular accounts. Crime is not just for experts who have, in any case, no purpose to their existence if they cannot convey their findings to wider and less specialised audiences. At times, therefore, the argument I convey is direct and simple. It is meant to be challenging, and I hope, arresting. There are, of course, reservations and caveats as with all such contentions: real life is far more complicated than any description or analysis can reasonably portray. The main aims that I have followed have been to convey as fully and faithfully as possible the experiences undergone by women offenders through their own and society's reactions and in the courts and prison. The questions raised by these experiences are then analysed and as far as possible, answered in a coherent fashion. There should be here something of interest and relevance and certainly to argue about for professionals who encounter female offenders and for students.

[1-4]See Bibliography

Glossary   Infraction violation, breaking (of a rule).
Mores accepted and enforced standards of behaviour.
Résumé summary.
Caveat proviso. A qualification to a statement or argument.

Questions   1 What reasons are there for the absence of female criminals from the literature on crime, according to this passage?

2 Currently the criminal statistics show that women commit far fewer crimes than men generally. What factors may lead to inaccuracy in the statistics in this respect?

3 What 'pressures to conform and patterns of social control' are experienced by women more than men? Use personal descriptions and anecdotes as well as 'theory'.

4 Heidensohn wishes to see a redirection in the sociology of deviance so that it studies conformity as well as deviance. Explain why this is the case and give some examples of the kind of subject–matter such a sociological enterprise might examine.

Bibliography

Source of extracts

R. K. Merton, *Social Structure and Anomie*, in R. S. Denisoff, *Sociology: Theories in Conflict*, Wadsworth Publishing Inc, California, 1972

H. S. Becker, *Outsiders*, Glencoe Free Press, New York, 1963

J. Corzine and R. Kirby, 'Cruising the Truckers: Sexual Encounters in a Highway Rest Area', originally in *Urban Life*, Volume 6, Number 2, 1977, Sage Publications; reprinted in D. H. Kelly (ed.), *Deviant Behaviour*, St Martin's Press, New York, 1979

F. Pearce, *Crimes of the Powerful*, Pluto Press, London, 1976

R. Hall *et al.*, article on JMB in *The Observer*, 1 December, 1985

A. Liazos, *The Poverty of the Sociology of Deviance*, in M. Fitzgerald *et al.*, *Welfare in Action*, Routledge & Kegan Paul, London and Open University Press, Milton Keynes, 1977

J. Lea and J. Young, *What is to be Done about Law and Order?*, Penguin, Harmondsworth, 1984

F. Heidensohn, *Women and Crime*, Macmillan, London, 1985

References in the Introduction

E. Durkheim, *The Rules of the Sociological Method*, New York Free Press, New York, 1938

R. A. Cloward and L. E. Ohlin, *Delinquency and Opportunity*, Glencoe Free Press, New York, 1961

E. Sutherland and D. Cressey, *Differential Association Theory*, in D. H. Kelly (ed.), *op cit.*

G. Sykes and D. Matza, *Techniques of Neutralisation*, in M. E. Wolfgang *et al.* (eds), *The Sociology of Crime and Delinquency*, John Wiley and Sons, New York, 1962

D. Matza, *Delinquency and Drift*, John Wiley and Sons, New York, 1964

A. Cohen, *Delinquent Boys*, Glencoe Free Press, New York, 1955

W. B. Miller, *Lower Class Culture as a Generating Milieu of Gang Delinquency* in Wolfgang *et al.*, *op cit.*

C. R. Shaw and H. D. McKay, *Juvenile Delinquency in Urban Areas*, University of Chicago Press, Chicago, 1942

E. Lemert, *Human Deviance, Social Problems and Social Control*, Prentice Hall, Englewood Cliffs, 1972

E. Cicourel, *The Social Organisation of Juvenile Justice*, Heinemann, London, 1976

E. Goffman, *Asylums*, Penguin, Harmondsworth, 1968

Reference in Becker extract

B. Malinowski, *Crime and Custom in Savage Society*, Humanities Press, New York, 1926

References in Corzine and Kirby extract

1 E. Hooker, *The Homosexual Community* in J. H. Gagnon and W. Simon (eds), *Sexual Deviance*, Harper & Row, New York, 1967
2 L. Humphreys, *Tearoom Trade: Impersonal Sex in Public Places*, Aldine, Chicago, 1975

References in Liazos extract

1 H. Becker, *The Other Side*, Free Press, New York, 1964
2 A. Gouldner, 'The Sociologist as Partisan', *American Sociologist*, 3(2), 1968
3 Malcolm X, *The Autobiography of Malcolm X*, Grove Press, New York, 1965
4 E. Cleaver, *Soul on Ice*, McGraw–Hill, New York, 1968
5 G. Jackson, *Soledad Brother*, Bantam Books, New York, 1970
6 C. McCaghy *et al.* (eds), *In Their Own Behalf*, Appleton Century–Crofts, New York, 1968
7 H. Becker, *Outsiders*, Free Press, New York, 1963
8 J. Lofland, *Deviance and Identity*, Prentice Hall, Englewood Cliffs, New Jersey, 1969
9 E. Rubington and M. S. Weinberg (eds), *Deviance: the Interactionist Perspective*, Macmillan, New York, 1968

References in Heidensohn extract

1 C. Smart, *Crime and Criminology*, Routledge & Kegan Paul, London, 1977
2 M. Millman, *Images of Deviant Men and Women*, in M. Evans, 'The Women Question', Fontana, London, 1982
3 F. M. Heidensohn, 'The Deviance of Women: a Critique and an Enquiry', *British Journal of Sociology*, Vol. XIX, No 2, 1968
4 A. Harris, 'Sex and Theories of Deviance', *American Sociological Review*, Vol. 42:1, 1977

Further reading

S. Box, *Deviancy, Reality and Society*, Holt, Rinehart & Winston, London, 1981

S. Box, *Power, Crime and Mystification*, Tavistock, London, 1983

P. Carlen, *Women's Imprisonment*, Routledge & Kegan Paul, London, 1983

D. Downs and P. Rock, *Understanding Deviance*, Clarendon Press, Oxford, 1982

M. Hough and P. Mayhew, *The British Crime Survey*, Home Office Research Study No 76, HMSO, London, 1983

I. Taylor, *Law and Order*, Macmillan, London, 1982

I. Taylor *et al.* (eds), *Critical Criminology*, Routledge & Kegan Paul, London, 1975

The Sociology of the Mass Media

Introduction   The four extracts in this chapter concern the influence of the mass media upon attitudes. We can classify three theories which represent the main views which exist on this topic: *manipulative* theory, *hegemonic* theory and *market* theory. Each of these is represented by at least one extract.

Manipulative theory argues that the capitalist class use the media to propagate pro–capitalist ideology and to suppress or ridicule any other points of view. Thus they manipulate, in a very deliberate way, both the content of the media and the responses of the audience to it. Such theorists (who are usually Marxists) point to the concentration of ownership of the press in the hands of a few companies which are often dominated by one man. Examples of such men are 'Tiny' Rowland, Robert Maxwell and Rupert Murdoch. Marxists argue that such men often deliberately acquire loss–making newspapers *not* in order to make a profit but as a tool for use in pushing their political and social beliefs. They believe that advertisers also use their position in funding the press to control content, at least in an indirect way. This is done by withholding business from papers or journals which the advertisers disapprove of. ... Manipulative theory can be applied to the broadcasting media as well as the press, although the arguments here are more complicated due to the fact that the BBC and IBA are not privately owned. The BBC is a public corporation set up by the Government and funded from television licence fees. Its Board of Governors is appointed by the Government and its operations are controlled by a Charter, which is subject to Government renewal every few years. This sets limits on the BBC's output (for example, the Corporation's Charter states that there must not be a political complexion to reporting of news). Although the commercial television and radio channels *are* privately owned, they are controlled by the IBA (Independent Broadcasting Authority) which is governed by Act of Parliament. Supporters of manipulative theory argue that the theory can be applied even in these two institutions, despite the absence of any capitalist owners, because both the Board of Governors of the BBC and the IBA are members of 'The Establishment'. They are:

> men and women drawn from the list of the 'good' and the 'great' kept in Whitehall by the Director of the Public Appointments Unit ... [this list] contains the names of those 4,000 citizens who have been recommended to successive governments as trustworthy enough to be called on to accept duty on offical and semi–official bodies. (S. Hood, *On Television*)

On those rare occasions when it becomes necessary, the Boards are subject to direct influence by the Government. Two examples from 1985 could be used to illustrate this. The 'Real Lives' programme which was cancelled during the summer of that year included interviews with individuals said to be involved with terrorism in Northern Ireland. It was not shown on the instructions of the Home Secretary, it was alleged, and was only subsequently shown (though in a modified form) after a public outcry and a strike by television journalists. The second example comes from the autumn of 1985 when it was discovered that MI5, the internal security department, had an office in the BBC and was involved in the selection of staff applying for production and journalists' posts. MI5 would examine applicants' backgrounds and effectively veto any who appeared to have radical associations. Hence manipulation was occurring through careful selection of the type of people allowed to occupy positions of influence within the broadcasting media. For the Marxist, such direct influence by Government or its agencies is done in the interests of the capitalist class because the Government is 'the ruling committee of the bourgeoisie'. The first extract presented here articulates the manipulative theory and it comes from R. Miliband's *The State in Capitalist Society*.

Hegemonic theorists are less extreme in their claims about bias in the media. According to this theory biased media output does not result from deliberate manipulation by the capitalist class, either directly or through the Government. Instead the theory suggests that media personnel are middle class, affluent people who tend to take a 'reasonable', consensus–oriented view on most issues. Thus they will generally be pro–SDP, 'wet' Conservative and moderate Labour (i.e. the middle–ground of politics), and against extremism in any form. Usually they will accept the establishment line on most issues and be unable to sympathise with minority points of view (e.g. those of black activists, Greenham Common peace protestors, striking miners, etc.). This natural inclination is reinforced by secondary socialisation into the culture of the press and broadcasting media. They learn how events such as strikes 'should' be treated; for example, on TV, rather than filming studio discussions of the issues involved ('talking heads') footage is shown of the effect of strikes. Journalists learn that some 'angles' on strikes will not meet the approval of senior people and so may not be included on the programme or in the newspaper. Thus the choice of alternative points of view being expressed is strictly limited. The content of virtually all the media reflects the perspective of the dominant group in society: white, male and middle class. Their hegemony (i.e. the dominance of their ideas over those of others) is reinforced by media output: other, 'minority', views are seen as odd or peripheral. In fact, of course, white male and middle class people are as much a minority as females, blacks, peace campaigners, gays, etc. The Glasgow Media Group adhere to this perspective on the media. In *More Bad News* they summarise their view on this as follows:

> Our argument, then, is that the world view of journalists will prestructure what is to be taken as important or significant. It will do this in two ways. First it will affect the character and content of specific inferential frames used in the news. ... Second it will set general boundaries on where news is looked for, and on who are the significant individuals, the 'important' people to be interviewed, etc.

However, in their more recent *War and Peace News*, the Glasgow Media Group seem to have added some elements of the manipulative theory to their analysis of media bias. In this book they also stress the pressures on broadcasting journalists to put the establishment line, even if it does not accord with their own views. Sometimes, however, journalists can escape these pressures and present a critical point of view or even an anti–establishment line. Jonathan Dimbleby is mentioned as an example of a TV journalist whose views are 'out of the ordinary'. He has been able to use the media to express them. Thus: 'Those who produce media output may be conditioned by powerful forces but they are not totally determined by them'. The extract from *War and Peace News* selected here concentrates on the nature rather than the causes of media bias, using the example of the presentation of the Greenham Common women's peace campaign.

The extract from Fiske and Hartley's *Reading Television*, also written from the point of view of hegemonic theory, applies it to fictional programmes rather than to broadcast news. The authors use semiotic analysis (i.e. the systematic reading of symbols for hidden meanings) in their study of television. Their argument is that the media, being run by members of the dominant class, propagate the dominant ('hegemonic') value system. This is not an obvious process, though. Values are encapsulated in signs or codes in television plays and elsewhere. One can read these signs and decode the message, given enough experience. In the extract presented here they 'decode' the fictional television programme about the flying squad—*The Sweeney*.

Market theorists agree that there is bias in the media. For example, most newspapers are pro–Conservative, they treat women as sex objects, concentrate on crimes of sex and violence, tend to sensationalise and trivialise important matters, and so on. The broadcast media take a generally middle–of–the–road and pro–establishment stance in news and current affairs programmes. They too tend to personalise and trivialise issues, the market theorist would argue. However, this is not because of deliberate manipulation by the capitalist class or due to journalists' world views. It is because this is what the public wants. The media are merely responding to market demand. Most people want to hear an 'establishment' view expressed because this is the one most people agree with. The majority of the population want to read about sex and violence because these are exciting and interesting subjects. There *are* alternatives in the media for those with minority tastes; for example, in the press there is *The Morning Star* for communists, *Spare Rib* for feminists and on television there are programmes like 'Ebony' for ethnic minorities. There are also access programmes, i.e. programmes which cover subjects suggested by ordinary members of the public or pressure groups and which are made under their direction rather than that of professional media personnel. We, the public, can choose those parts of the media we agree with and ignore others. As a result there is no influence on our attitudes other than the reinforcement of beliefs which we held already. Even when we are exposed to media messages which are contrary to our own beliefs we do not simply accept them. We perceive them as misguided, misinformed or simply as lies. We tend, also, to pay most attention to those messages which are consonant with our own ideas, tending to quickly forget any discordant views. Market theorists, then, stress that the audience is not an homogeneous body, injected with a single message and reacting to it like a patient injected by a hypodermic syringe (this simple view is aptly called the 'hypodermic' model of media influence). Instead the audience is recognised as being a disparate group of people who use the media in different ways and for different reasons (an approach known as the 'uses and gratifications' model of media influence). According to the market theorist there is no cause for concern about the influence of the media. The manipulative and hegemonic theorists consider the audience to be gullible and easily influenced by messages which are really alien to them. However, as we have seen, an audience practises:

Selective exposure They only tend to allow themselves to be exposed to messages in the media with which they agree.
Selective perception They react to media messages differently, depending on whether they strike a concordant or discordant note.
Selective retention (or remembering) They are likely to retain in the memory only those messages which are considered valid or true.

The extract selected here to represent the market model comes from John Whale's *The Politics of the Media*.

R. Miliband
The State in Capitalist Society, 1973, pp. 203–08, 210

The nature of the contribution which the mass media make to that political climate is determined by the influences which weigh most heavily upon them. There are a number of such influences—and they all work in the same conservative and conformist direction.

The first and most obvious of them derives from the ownership and control of the 'means of mental production'. Save for state ownership of radio and television stations and of some other means of communications, the mass media are overwhelmingly in the private domain (and this is also true of most radio and television stations in the United States). . . .

Rather obviously, those who own and control the capitalist mass media are most likely to be men whose ideological dispositions run from soundly conservative to utterly reactionary; and in many instances, most notably in the case of newspapers, the impact of their views and prejudices is immediate and direct, in the straightforward sense that newspaper proprietors have often not only owned their newspapers but closely controlled their editorial and political line as well, and turned them, by constant and even daily intervention, into vehicles of their personal views. . . .

However, it is not always the case that those who own or ultimately control the mass media do seek to exercise a direct and immediate influence upon their output. Quite commonly, editors, journalists, producers, managers, etc. are accorded a considerable degree of independence, and are

even given a free hand. Even so, ideas do tend to 'seep downwards', and provide an ideological and political framework which may well be broad but whose existence cannot be ignored by those who work for the commercial media. They may not be *required* to take tender care of the sacred cows that are to be found in the conservative stable. But it is at least *expected* that they will spare the conservative susceptibilities of the men whose employees they are, and that they will take a proper attitude to free enterprise, conflicts between capital and labour, trade unions, left-wing parties and movements, the Cold War, revolutionary movements, the role of the United States in the world, and much else besides. The existence of this framework does not require total conformity; general conformity will do. This assured, room will be found for a seasoning, sometimes even a generous seasoning, of dissent. . . .

A second source of conformist and conservative pressure upon newspapers and other media is that exercised, directly or indirectly, by capitalist interests, not as owners, but as advertisers. The direct political influence of large advertisers upon the commercial media need not be exaggerated. It is only occasionally that such advertisers are able, or probably even try, to dictate the contents and policies of the media of which they are the customers. But their custom is nevertheless of crucial importance to the financial viability, which means the existence, of newspapers and, in some but not all instances, of magazines, commercial radio and television. That fact may do no more than *enhance* a general disposition on the part of these media to show exceptional care in dealing with such powerful and valuable interests. . . .

A third element of pressure upon the mass media stems from government and various other parts of the state system generally. That pressure, as was noted earlier, does not generally amount to <u>imperative dictation</u>. But it is nevertheless real, in a number of ways.

For one thing, governments, ministries and other official agencies now make it their business, even more elaborately and systematically, to supply newspapers, radio and television with explanations of official policy which naturally have an apologetic and <u>tendentious</u> character. The state, in

other words, now goes in more and more for 'news management', particularly in times of stress and crisis, which means, for most leading capitalist countries, almost permanently; and the greater the crisis, the more purposeful the management, the evasions, the half-truths and the plain lies. . . .

There *are* of course a good many such people working in and for the mass media, who suffer various degrees of political frustration, and who seek, sometimes successfully, often not, to break through the <u>frontiers of orthodoxy</u>. But there is little to suggest that they constitute more than a minority of the 'cultural workmen' employed by the mass media. The cultural and political <u>hegemony</u> of the dominant classes could not be so pronounced if this was not the case. . . .

Glossary   <u>Means of mental production</u> techniques used to affect the way people think about things and the subjects they think about.
<u>Ideological dispositions</u> sets of beliefs which are firmly held.
<u>Imperative dictation</u> instructions to do something.
<u>Tendentious</u> designed to promote a particular viewpoint.
<u>Frontiers of orthodoxy</u> the limits of what is considered normal.
<u>Hegemony</u> the dominance of a particular set of ideas.

Questions   1 Miliband suggests that there are three forms of influence on the content of the mass media. What are they?
2 Ideas are said to 'seep downwards' from the owners and the controllers of the mass media to the journalists and editors. These ideas are described as the 'sacred cows' of conservatism. Miliband gives some examples of the kind of topics these cover: free enterprise, conflicts between capital and labour, etc. Elaborate on the kinds of views which will be expressed on these issues and suggest other media sacred cows.
3 Do you agree that those in the media will 'show exceptional care' when dealing with the interests of the powerful? Can you think of any examples to confirm or refute the idea that these interests are dealt with in a different way than those of other sections of the community?
4 What criticisms have you of the general notion that the content of the media is controlled, directly or indirectly, by the capitalist class?

Glasgow University Media Group
War and Peace News, 1985, pp. 198–201

We analysed the coverage of six women's peace demonstrations that appeared on the news between December 1982 and December 1983, in a total of thirty eight bulletins; and compared it with other reports including some from the women who participated. We found that many features central to the camp were not covered in the news. First, why is the camp all-women? This is a fairly obvious question, asked by many visitors to the camp except apparently TV journalists; it does not seem to be prevalent in news reports and was not explained or raised in any of the coverage in our sample. How is the camp run? The women's peace movement has developed its own form of organising, based on collective decision-making and individual responsibility, run without leaders or any formal structure of bureaucracy. It's an exceptional method, quite distinct from the way CND, for example, or any political party works; but again the TV did not tell us about it. Instead, it gave the impression that the women's peace camp is run by the better-known disarmers of CND:

'At Greenham Common today women peace protesters have started a five-day attempted blockade. It's one of a number of events organised by CND to coincide with US 4th July celebrations.'
BBC2, 19.35, 4.7.83

'Once again demonstrators from all over Britain converged on Greenham Common, and CND's hopes of a big turnout were fully realised.'
BBC1, 22.15, 11.12.83

The camp has always been independent from CND, and there are many differences between the two.

A further question is, what exactly is the political protest the camp is making? The broadcasters have grasped the fundamental idea that the camp is opposed to Cruise missiles—although even this is not always made clear. Coverage on the two ITV evening bulletins and BBC2's *Newsnight* of the opening of the five-day blockade at Greenham Common avoided giving any reason at all for the women's action. The full BBC2 report ran:

'Women peace campaigners have been trying without success to prevent workers entering or leaving Greenham Common air base. Police were there in strength and cleared a passage to allow workers in and out. There was one arrest. The protest began today on American Independence Day and is expected to continue until Friday.'
BBC2, 22.25, 4.7.83

On ITN the newscaster began: 'At Greenham Common police broke up an attempted blockade by women peace protesters' (ITN, 17.45, 4.7.83); and the correspondent concentrated on how the women were dragged away rather than why they were there. The BBC1 news did state that the protest was against Cruise. This is the full text of a BBC1 report:

'American Independence Day has been marked by more protests *against the siting of Cruise missiles* in Britain. The largest demonstration was at Greenham Common air base. Several dozen women tried to block coaches carrying base workers into the compound. There have been no reports of arrests.
Correspondent: There are fewer protesters than previously at Greenham. Too few to succeed in their aim of blockading the base. A large force of police is apparently prepared if many more arrive as the five-day protest goes on. The main aim is publicity which helps explain the choice of today, American Independence Day.'
BBC1, 17.45, 4.7.83

Note the claim that 'the main aim is publicity'. The same point was made on International Women's Day for Disarmament: 'The women were more interested in putting across their anti-nuclear message than in inconveniencing the public'. (BBC1, 21.00, 24.5.83).

The news does not give any publicity to the women's *case*. Opposition to Cruise is mentioned, and some 'anti-nuclear message' is referred to, but the women have no chance to explain exactly *why* they oppose Cruise, *why* they are anti-nuclear. In particular, the broader anti-militarism of the women's peace movement, and the links they make between male supremacy, male violence, and nuclear weapons, are buried. Of course 'putting across their anti-nuclear message' is not the broadcasters' job; but they are falling down on the job of providing informative reporting if they cover the demonstrations without explaining (or allowing the demonstrators to explain) what they are trying to say.

Moreover the broadcasters *do* find space to give a full and proper explanation of the official pro-Cruise message. The BBC2 news story *Countdown to Cruise* on 9 November 1983 reports on:

'1. (50 secs.) Mrs Thatcher's speech in Bonn urging the Soviet Union to accept the "zero option".
2. (18 secs.) The 24-hour peace camps set up at all the 102 US bases in Britain (though the newscaster adds that "the government says they got their sums wrong and there are only 74").
3. (27 secs.) "The effort of a group of Greenham women to take their action to the other side of the Atlantic" with their court case against President Reagan for acting illegally in deploying Cruise.
4. (30 secs.) The visit of fourteen Labour MPs to the Greenham peace camp "to show solidarity".

5. (10 secs.) The government announcement that policing Greenham had cost £1.5 million over the past year.
6. (12 mins. 25 secs.) The correspondent's own story of how "this morning I went down to Greenham to look as it were behind the wire".'

This is the background he gives to the decision to site Cruise in Europe:

'These missiles, planned for Britain, Holland, Belgium, Germany and Italy, are intended to tell the Russians: Just in case you are tempted to try any attack, the West can now strike back from European soil, at selected military targets as far away as Kiev and Minsk, without having to risk certain annihilation by calling in America's intercontinental strategic system.

So the argument runs, these new Cruise missiles here at Greenham Common will actually make war *less* likely, by demonstrating to the Russians that if they attempted to lop off Western Europe from America, there would actually be a credible and still very demanding Western nuclear response.

Well, there's debate about the cogency of that nuclear strategy.'

BBC2, 23.00, 9.11.83

At this point the reporter goes into the technical details of deployment: the training and organisation of missile crews, the composition of missile convoys, the construction of missiles, the timetable for deployment:

'If all goes well, and all these tests are successfully passed, then the 501st will be awarded its Initial Operational Capability, its IOC. By the end of the year, Greenham will be a fully active nuclear weapons base.'

BBC2, 23.00, 9.11.83

This is followed by the use of the silos, and the programme for convoy dispersal. Finally, he interviews a military specialist in a wood—'an extremely good dispersal area'—about how the missiles would be fired. The official justification for Cruise—resting on the assumption of a Soviet threat ('to tell the Russians: "Just in case you're tempted to try any attack"'), and the deterrence arguments ('these new Cruise missiles here at Greenham will make war *less* likely')—presented in detail as 'news'.

This is scarcely in neutral terms, using such phrases as '*if all goes well* ... Greenham will be a fully active nuclear weapons base'. Meanwhile, the case *against* Cruise is reduced to the single sentence: 'Well, there's debate about the cogency of that nuclear strategy'—even though the whole item is based on reports of active *opposition* to Cruise. In all, 1 minute and 15 seconds are devoted to the protest, and 12 minutes and 25 seconds to the 'technical background'. If it were not for the peace camp, the Greenham Common base would probably not be news at all, yet the political reasoning of the camp is virtually silenced. . . .

Glossary

Greenham Common United States military base near Newbury, Berkshire. Nuclear missiles are stored there.

Cruise missiles American nuclear missiles. They are designed to be extremely mobile and are therefore able to avoid being destroyed before they have been launched.

Zero option the possibility of abolishing *all* nuclear weapons.

Deterrence arguments primarily the view that the possession of nuclear weapons will deter any aggressor from attacking the country which has them. The alternative view is that the possession of such weapons makes a country a threat and thus more likely to become a target.

Questions

1 There is, according to the Glasgow University Media Group, a tendentious use of words in television news broadcasts. For example, words like 'ransom', 'trouble', 'made idle', 'radical', 'Scargill surcharge', etc., have been used in reporting industrial relations and they all contain assumptions and negative connotations. Give some examples from this passage.

2 The Glasgow University Media Group argue that there is a hierarchy

of access to the media; i.e. that members of the 'establishment' get more coverage in the media for their views and their interpretation of the facts than do 'ordinary' members of the public. Give an example from the passage of this hierarchy of access in operation.

3 The Glasgow University Media Group suggest that the media 'set the agenda' of political debate. This means that the public are told which are the important issues to think and talk about. They are also given a general framework within which the discussion should take place. An example from the field of industrial relations would be:

Important issue: strikes at British Leyland

Framework of debate: the disruptive influence of trade unions on British industry and competitiveness abroad.

Give an example from the passage of the agenda–setting function of the media in operation.

4 Would you agree that the anti–nuclear case has not been given any publicity and, more generally, that the media only present one 'angle' on current issues? Support your answer with examples from current news reporting.

5 The research technique adopted by the Glasgow University Media Group is 'content analysis' of tape-recorded news programmes. This involves the measurement of the content of news broadcasts—type of item, length of time devoted to it, who was interviewed in what circumstances, and so on—in order to establish the presence of bias in the output. What are:

(a) the advantages

(b) the disadvantages of this technique?

J. Fiske and J. Hartley
Reading Television, 1978, pp. 186–88

The television of <u>recession</u>

The Sweeney's world is not one where 'white hat' restores the accepted moralities by the mere act of shooting 'black hat'. Their world is unpredictable, episodic, present-tense. They react to events rather than manipulating them—just as British frigates react to Icelandic gunboats and the British army to the IRA. Their domestic life is not the stable scholastic comfort which Ironside enjoys. When off duty (or even when on duty) *The Sweeney*'s male is either marking time, drinking, or attempting to pull a bird—often in competition with one of his colleagues. On the rare occasions when Regan is shown at home he does not sit, he stands. The home is merely another location where he can keep in contact with the real world of the streets—the foregrounded feature is the phone, together with the beer-stocked fridge and the electric kettle. His home-life is not stressed, but sketchy details are given. These enrich the series' unglamorous <u>verisimilitude</u> by hinting at

domestic troubles to match Regan's professional ones. The overall mythology which emerges is one where perceptions of social permanency are constantly challenged, but where a man with internal motivation and skill can carve out an acceptable set of personal relations and professional achievements. Hostility is expected from and shown to both the higher reaches of the authoritarian institution and the external world.

The relations between individuals and their institutions is in fact one of *The Sweeney*'s most complex elements. The villains, for example, are rarely if ever individuals acting alone—usually they are surrounded by accountants, lawyers and women as well as the usual henchmen. This increases their legitimacy as targets in a world where bourgeois security is regarded with a jaundiced eye. The deviant 'aping' of legitimate business enterprise confers the impersonal powers of the business institution on the villains, who act not only as criminals but as criminal bosses. This enables the audience to identify more easily with Regan and Carter in a society where the overwhelming majority of the people have no share in the ownership and control of the institutions they work for.

But the focus of attention is Regan's relationship with Carter. It is not the same kind of relationship as that between Starsky and Hutch. The latter is one of equality—their rank in the police force is the same. They are more boyish; there are fraternity-based codes underlying much of their dialogue, which is, however, less important than their non-verbal behaviour: they exchange meaningful looks (which not only cement their friendship but set them apart from the characters who are excluded from the looks), there is much body contact, signalling an unselfconscious affection, and their stance is relaxed. Their cognitive processes are basically the same—'are you thinking what I'm thinking?' The American myth of a social dissonance between college graduates and non-college men is introduced as a potential tension to their relationship, but only one to be overcome. For instance, when both are trapped in a building which is airtight, college-boy Hutch starts using maths to compute how long they can survive while practical Starsky starts looking around the given setting for a means to escape. The manual non-college man, who is the team's driver and Jewish, just as Ironside's driver and action-man is black, is married to his more intellectual counterpart in a fruitful relationship which works because it transcends the dissonance: their differing methods make the team as a whole more efficient.

Carter, however, is not Regan's equal, he is his sergeant. Their relationship is one of fruitful friendship too, and they compete equally with each other for women, jokes and theories about the current case. Carter has even been shown competing for Regan's status by trying for the rank of inspector. In personal terms there is no distinction between the two. But in professional terms there is. The camera is 'focused' on Regan and while he is constrained in his freedom of action only by the police hierarchy, Carter is constrained by his own identity, which is defined in subordination to Regan. Hence Regan can be anti-authoritarian, since that suggests a stance towards an external social pressure. Carter shares this stance, but he cannot be anti-authoritarian in the same way, since his superior authority is Regan. Regan relies on Carter to back him up, and uses both Carter and his own anti-authoritarian stance as positive and helpful means by which he creates his personal living space. *The Sweeney* tells us that in a period when 'real life' offers us wage-restraint, inflation and a fall in living standards, there is no need for class hostility. The Regan/Carter relationship personalises for the television audience a point of view which places two 'classes' in a hostile environment and shows how working together can produce individual satisfaction for both—though *not* equality for the subordinate 'class'. Hence *The Sweeney* presents a society where class divisions are overcome because both 'classes'—Regan and Carter—share the same outlook on life, methods and language. They do not share the same status, but are presented as finding no tension in this position. Carter is presented as being fully satisfied in his subordination, a subordination that is acceptable because of the personal value discerned in Regan (whose language and behaviour codes are themselves working-class in mode). Thus *The Sweeney* shares with *Starsky and Hutch* and *Ironside* the 'personalisation' of status relationships, in much the same way as the other version of reality—news reporting—personalises the social forces which produce the events reported.

Glossary

Recession a period when a country's economy slows down so that production and consumption of goods are at a low level and unemployment increases.

The Sweeney fictionalised television programme about the flying squad (Cockney rhyming slang: Sweeney Todd = flying squad).

Verisimilitude degree of closeness to the truth.

Fraternity group of males in a brotherly relationship with each other. In American universities there are male clubs called fraternities.

Dissonance a lack of harmony or similarity.

Questions

1 In your own words summarise Fiske and Hartley's 'reading' of *The Sweeney*.

2 Give your 'reading' of any television programme you know.
3 What criticisms have you of this sort of semiotic analysis of television programmes?

J. Whale
The Politics of the Media, 1977, pp. 84–5

The tastes of a body of readers may alter over the years. They change as the prevailing climate of ideas changes and as a result of what they discover to be appearing in rival newspapers. The *Daily Mirror* would never have begun (in the 1970s) to show photographs of naked women, or to lead the paper with stories like 'I married the monster who raped Miss X', if the *Sun* had not led the way after its change of ownership in 1969. Once the *Sun* had demonstrated that its readers liked that kind of approach, the *Mirror* adopted it too, and the decline in the *Mirror*'s circulation was at least checked. Yet it was not an expedient which was open to *The Times*, struggling for new readers at much the same time. Existing readers of *The Times* would have been outraged at being addressed in that way. The loss would have far outweighed the gain.

It is readers who determine the character of newspapers. The *Sun* illustrates the point in its simplest and saddest form. Until 1964 the *Daily Herald*, and between 1964 and 1969 the broadsheet *Sun*, had struggled to interest working people principally through their intellect. The paper had declined inexorably. Murdoch gave up the attempt and went for the baser instincts. Sales soared. By May 1978, selling just under 4 million copies, the *Sun* was reckoned to have overtaken the *Mirror*—which had held the lead since winning it from the *Express* in 1949—as the biggest-selling national daily paper. At the *Express*, the message was received. The year before, after a struggle between assorted financiers, the Beaverbrook empire had passed to a shipping and property concern named Trafalgar House. The new chairman was Victor Matthews; and in November 1978 Matthews launched, from Manchester, a paper called the *Daily Star* which extended the *Sun* formula even further downmarket. At the London *Evening Standard* (another

Beaverbrook paper) Matthew's dismissal of a cultivated editor, Simon Jenkins, in the same month presaged a similar approach there. These were owners' decisions, certainly; but they would have meant nothing without the ratification of readers.

That, in the end, is the answer to the riddle of proprietorial influence. Where it survives at all, it must still defer to the influence of readers. The policy of the *Daily Telegraph*, its selection and opinion of the news it reports, is decided by the editor and his senior colleagues. But there is a regulatory force which keeps the paper's policy from straying too widely or suddenly from preordained paths; and that force is not the proprietor but the readers. They chose the paper for qualities they expect to see continued.

The press is thus predominantly conservative in tone because its readers are. If any substantial number of people seriously wanted the structure of society rebuilt from the bottom, the *Morning Star* would sell more copies than it does. The reason why national newspapers fall tidily into two bundles—popular and posh, with the popular ones all physically smaller than the posh (since the *Daily Express* joined the other tabloids in January 1977) but selling five times as many copies—is that British life remains similarly and obstinately divided. The steady lessening of the economic differences between classes has done nothing to narrow the cultural gap. Certainly there are people who read both a posh and a popular paper, just as there are gradations between the popular papers: both the *Mirror* and the *Sun* aim at readers who are more squarely working–class than the *Express* and the *Mail* do. These things show the complexity of the class pattern, without denying its general lines. The broad shape and nature of the press is ultimately determined by no one but its readers.

Glossary   Inexorably relentlessly, in a way that cannot be stopped.
Presaged gave a forewarning of something.

Ratification approval.

Proprietorial influence influence by the proprietor or owner of
something.

Questions

1 What reasons does Whale give for the character of the *Sun* today?
2 Why are newspapers divided into 'the popular and the posh'
according to Whale?
3 Whale is only discussing the press in this extract. Apply the same
sort of analysis to the broadcast media.
4 What criticisms have you got of Whale's 'market theory'?

**Questions on
all the extracts**

1 Fill in this table, summarising the theories represented:

	Market	Manipulative	Hegemonic
Cause of bias in the media			
Nature of media's effect on the audience			
View on the nature of society			
Best 'solution' to media bias			

2 'The ability to control the content of the mass media is crucial to the
maintenance of the power of the elite.' Discuss.
3 Examine the relationship between the patterns of ownership and
control of the mass media and their content.
4 Discuss the view that the reporting of 'news' must be biased.

Bibliography

Source of extracts

R. Miliband, *The State in Capitalist Society*, Quartet Books, London 1973,
first published 1969

Glasgow University Media Group, *War and Peace News*, Open
University Press, Milton Keynes, 1985

J. Fiske and J. Hartley, *Reading Television*, Methuen, London, 1978

J. Whale, *The Politics of the Media*, Fontana, London, 1977

References in the Introduction

S. Hood, *On Television*, Pluto Press, London 1980

Glasgow University Media Group, *More Bad News*, Routledge & Kegan
Paul, London 1980

Further reading

S. Cohen and J. Young, *The Manufacture of News*, Constable, London
1981, first published 1973

J. Curran *et al.* (eds), *Mass Communications and Society*, Edward Arnold,
London 1977

J. Curran and J. Seaton, *Power Without Responsibility*, Fontana, London,
1981

Glasgow University Media Group, *Bad News*, Routledge & Kegan Paul,
London, 1976

Glasgow University Media Group, *Really Bad News* Writers and
Readers, London, 1982

P. Golding and P. Elliott, *Making the News*, Longman, London, 1979

A. Hetherington, *News, Newspapers and Television*, Macmillan, London,
1985

D. McQuail (ed.), *Sociology of Mass Communications*, Penguin,
Harmondsworth, 1979, first published 1972

C. Seymour–Ure, *The Political Impact of the Mass Media*, Constable,
London, 1974

J. Tunstall, *The Media in Britain*, Constable, London, 1983

◪ The Sociology of Stratification

Introduction   The first section of this chapter concerns the theory of proletarianisation and presents two extracts from recent texts on the subject. The Marxist concept of proletarianisation refers to the view that the middle class are becoming like the working class in terms of pay, conditions of work, attitudes, and so on. The reason for this is the fact that the middle class, who do not own the means of production, are really in the same class position as the manual working class. As technology advances and capitalism reaches a more mature stage, this fact will become increasingly apparent. The jobs of the middle class will become as routinised as manual work. Unemployment will affect non–manual occupations as well as manual ones. The search for profit will mean a restriction of the salaries of the middle class and increasing supervisory control of their work. Eventually, runs this Marxist argument, the middle class will become aware of their true interests and ally themselves with the working class as a revolutionary force.

The first extract, from T. May's *Middle Class Unionism* discusses the nature of middle class unionism and its political consequences. The statistics about unionism among the middle class seem to lend credence to the proletarianisation thesis. Between 1971 and 1975 nearly 600,000 additional white–collar workers were affiliated to the TUC. Their overall share of TUC membership was thus raised from 27 per cent to 31.5 per cent. This would appear to indicate increased militancy among the middle class and a willingness to adopt traditionally working class forms of action. However, May casts doubt on this conclusion. While he recognises the growth of middle class unionism and the greater willingness now of the middle class to strike, he suggests that, despite appearances, these phenomena are not symptoms of proletarianisation.

The second extract on this topic, from Crompton and Jones' *White Collar Proletariat* (the methodology and general description of which can be found in the introduction to the chapter 'The Sociology of Work', p. 173) addresses the question of the proletarianisation of the clerical worker in particular. In this they are following in the steps of D. Lockwood's famous *The Blackcoated Worker*. Lockwood studied clerical workers' market situation (financial rewards for work), work situation (nature of the job they do), and status situation (the prestige awarded to workers by society) both at the time he was writing and in the last century. While he saw some evidence of a movement towards working class characteristics in each of these, he concluded that there were still important differences between the market, work and status situations of clerical workers and those of the working class. Moreover, clerical workers saw themselves as different from the working class and this fact cannot be shrugged off, as some Marxists try to do, as simply 'false consciousness' on the part of the clerical worker. This study was published in 1958 and so is not only now out of date but, like many other studies of the time and later, ignores the importance of *gender* in clerical work (despite the fact that Lockwood acknowledges that clerical workers are now mainly 'white bloused' rather than 'blackcoated' he retains the latter title for his book). Crompton and Jones find this aspect to be crucial in their study of bank, insurance and local government employees. They argue that even if the pay, work and status of clerical workers has deteriorated over the years this would be relatively inconsequential if these workers find it relatively easy to gain promotion to managerial and supervisory posts, where conditions are better. Such promotion possibilities would limit the social and political consequences of proletarianisation lower down the scale. In analysing whether this is or is not the case Crompton and Jones find that *gender* is an important determining factor in promotion prospects, but that it is one that is now changing in its impact. These issues are elaborated on in this extract.

The second section of this chapter deals with the concept of embourgeoisement. This represents the contrary view to proletarianisation, suggesting that the working class are becoming increasingly like the middle class in terms of income, lifestyle, values, life chances and so on. The theory was prevalent in the 1950s and '60s both in Britain and the USA, a time of economic boom in both countries. The theory has since come under much critical fire. One of the most famous refutations of it was Goldthorpe and Lockwood's study of three factories in Luton: Vauxhall Motors, Skefco Ballbearings and Laporte Chemicals. Luton was chosen because it was considered to be a place where conditions were ripe for embourgeoisement to occur. It had modern industries, management were enlightened, new housing was available, workers were well paid and so on. Many of the workers in its factories had moved from older traditional working class areas, thus proving themselves to be aspiring to 'better things' and cutting themselves off from the old working class culture and communities. If embourgeoisement were not occurring in Luton then it would not be occurring anywhere, Goldthorpe and Lockwood's argument ran. The three companies chosen for special study by Goldthorpe and Lockwood represent different types of production technology (production line, machine–minding and process production). The idea was to see whether technology had any influence on embourgeoisement—it didn't. The authors interviewed 229 manual workers in different types of jobs and 54 non–manual workers for comparison. As is now well known, Goldthorpe and Lockwood claim to have refuted the embourgeoisement thesis but also to have discovered important differences between the 'affluent workers' they studied and the traditional working class. Hence they claim to have identified a 'new working class'. The extract gives a summary of the most important results of the study.

The second extract in this section, from Davis and Cousins' *The 'New Working Class' and the Old*, examines Goldthorpe and Lockwood's findings and suggests that they are sadly lacking in a number of ways. From specific criticisms, Davis and Cousins move to general comments about the route that sociology as a discipline should be taking and express their belief that studies like Goldthorpe and Lockwood's are taking the discipline up a blind alley. This extract concludes the section on embourgeoisement.

The next selection, which stands alone, is from Heath's book, *Social Mobility*. Anthony Heath was one of the participants in the Nuffield Mobility Study, conducted in 1972 and led by J. Goldthorpe of Nuffield College, Oxford. This involved questioning 10,000 adult males between the ages of 20 and 64 years in England and Wales about their social background and current occupations. In 1974 there was a follow-up study in which some of the sample were asked questions about their attitudes, rather than just factual questions. The aim of the study as a whole was to identify the patterns of social mobility among a representative cross-section of all males, and so achieve an understanding of these patterns in Britain as a whole. Heath summarises the results of this study and also uses information from the General Household Survey and other sources, especially to gather data about the mobility of women, excluded from direct study in the Nuffield survey.

Both the Nuffield Mobility Study and Heath use a typology of social stratification which is summarised below:

Class
1 Higher-grade professionals (self employed and salaried), administrators, managers, large proprietors.
2 Lower-grade professionals, administrators, higher-grade technicians and supervisors of non-manual employees.
3 Routine clerical, sales personnel, other rank and file non-manual workers.
4 Farmers, small proprietors and self-employed workers. The 'petty bour-geoisie'.
5 Supervisors of manual workers and lower-grade technicians.
6 Skilled manual workers who have served apprenticeships or other forms of industrial training.
7 Semi- and unskilled manual workers in industry, plus agricultural workers.

The final extract, which like Heath's, stands alone, is from A. Gorz's *Farewell to the Working Class*. It considers the changes that have occurred in the class structure of the advanced industrial societies and what the future might hold for them in this respect. He suggests that the working class as we once knew it has now virtually disappeared as a result of technological change. New social groups are forming, particularly what Gorz calls the 'non-class' or the 'neo-proletariat'. However, while 'technology' creates the circumstances for this 'non-class' to develop, largely as a result of the unemployment it creates, Gorz considers it necessary for *people* to recognise the nature of the social and economic changes being effected and to seize the opportunities they present for a better way of living. We should not emphasise the negative aspects of unemployment and the loss of traditional skills, but see the exciting possibilities which the new situation presents. Gorz should not be mistaken for a Marxist, despite apparent similarities between his view of society and that of Marxists. Gorz does not consider class conflict and revolution to be central to social change. Self-determination within the context of evolving technology is central to this theory. Gorz rejects Marx's view of human behaviour as determined by technological developments—Marx's 'technological determinism' as it is often called. Gorz writes:

> The working class defined by Marx or Marxists derives its theological character from being perceived as a subject transcending its members. It makes

history and builds society through the agency of its unwitting members, whatever their intentions. . . . The non–class of those who are recalcitrant to the sacralisation of work [i.e. who reject work as the be all and end all], on the contrary, is not a 'social subject'. It has no transcendent unity or mission. . . . It is not the harbinger of a new subject–society offering integration and salvation to its individual members. Instead it reminds individuals of the need to save themselves and define a social order compatible with their goals and autonomous existence.

T. May
'Middle Class Unionism', in R. King and N. Nugent, *Respectable Rebels*, 1979, pp. 121–23

This examination of middle class unionism has been concerned with three main questions—how far are the middle class unionised, what is the nature of that unionism, and what are the wider consequences for the political parties and the TUC?

The answer to the first question is bedevilled by difficulties of definition and the absence of important information. The discussion has equated middle class with non–manual workers while being well aware that this may lead to some individuals being seen as middle class who certainly do not regard themselves in that way. Again, so far as unionism is concerned we have chosen to define the term fairly widely and to regard any association which has 'the regulation of relations between workers and employers' as a manifestation of unionism. This definition obviously entails a concern with staff associations and some of the activities of professional groups as well as bodies that call themselves unions and affiliate to the TUC. While it is not possible with this kind of approach to measure precisely the impact of unionism upon non–manual workers there is little doubt . . . that it has increased. But the increase— or, to be more precise, the increase in density, which is the important measure—dates from the middle 1960s and has not been a phenomenon of the mid–1970s as have some of the other examples of 'revolt' discussed in this book. Neither is there much indication of an appreciable quickening of pace during the post–1974 period. The consideration of the reasons for the increase of unionism takes us directly to the second of the major questions—the nature or character of such unionism.

The tactic we adopted here was to assume that an individualist ethic characterised the middle class and had kept them away from the economic collectivism of associations and unions. If they were now joining such groups this would seem to imply that an important social change was taking place. We discussed this hypothesis by examining four different objections to it. This discussion suggested three main conclusions. Firstly, that a small element of middle class unionism can be described as 'proletarianisation'. It is clear that some non–manual workers identify with the working class and, like them, join trade unions in order to make advances collectively since the chances of individual mobility appear slight or non–existent. What we do not know is whether this category is growing. Even if we assume that there is a fairly close connection between subjective consciousness and objective circumstances, it does not take us much further, for we would need to know what the prospects are for the continued expansion of non–manual employment and in what areas and at what levels future growth will take place. The 1972 Nuffield Mobility Survey indicated that substantial expansion in non–manual employment since 1945 was an important reason for the continuing possibility of upward career mobility.

The second conclusion emphasises the important role that increasing government and employer recognition has had in promoting non–manual unionism and the fertile soil that has been created for such recognition through changes in employment conditions. So far as government is concerned, the expansion in the public sector workforce and successive laws have been the most important factors. Though it has not yet passed into law, the very prospect of the introduction of industrial democracy in which employee representation would be through trade unions has led many managers to consider joining a trade union in order not to be left out. Changes in the size of companies and in the size of work units has encouraged recognition procedures to be used. The doubts, hesitations and reservations that are displayed by many, especially about embracing unions affiliated to the TUC, are illustrated by the continued existence of many staff groups and the attempts at building an alternative peak organisation to the TUC.

The final conclusion to emerge from the discussion of the character of middle class unionism was that while many of the middle class belonged to organisations which were quite prepared to use the tactics of 'traditional' unions, including the full-scale strike, such tactics were not being used as a gesture of solidarity but for precisely the opposite reason—in order to re-assert differentials with manual workers. It is here that one finds the closest correspondence to the kinds of 'revolt' described in other chapters in this book. The impact of very high levels of inflation, increases in taxation and highly restrictive pay policies have fuelled a sense of resentment on the part of many salaried workers. The differences that marked them off from the bulk of manual workers are less clear, and in turning to unionism they are adopting the apparently successful techniques of manual workers to reclaim advantages that they see as being unjustifiably reduced.

The third section of the chapter examined some of the consequences of increased unionism. It was argued that, despite the conservatism of the TUC, some changes have been made and others appear likely in order to satisfy the demands of the increasingly strong non-manual element within it. With the affiliation of all the major public-sector non-manual unions the TUC's claim to representativeness has been enhanced, but, as with any body spanning a range of diverse interests, the problems of designing viable policies are considerable.

Nevertheless in 1975–6 and 1976–7 the TUC committed itself to two stages of incomes policy which, in contrast to previous attempts, were successful in that all affiliates kept to them in their pay settlements. Beyond the desire for improvements in representation and consultation and some concern about the effects of flat-rate pay policies on differentials, it was not possible to see white collar unions displaying much unity. Such unity as has been evident is further limited by the fact that there are a small but significant number of unions and associations representing non-manual unionists who do not wish to affiliate to the TUC. . . .

There are also divided views on the relationship with the political parties. Most non-manual unions have chosen not to affiliate to the Labour Party and among the minority who do (such as ASTMS) nearly two-thirds of the members do not pay the political levy. With the decline in the membership of a number of traditional unions, barely half the TUC's membership is now affiliated to the Labour Party. This development enhanced the importance of the TUC/Labour Party Liaison Committee as the major formal channel through which the Labour Party during 1972–4 and the Labour Government after 1974 conducted relations with the trade unions. In principle the growing gap between the trade union movement in the Labour Party and the trade union movement in the TUC should make the Conservative Party's relationship with the TUC easier, since the latter has always emphasised its role as a negotiator with whatever party currently forms the Government. However, there were few signs, as the Conservatives took office in May 1979, that this would necessarily be the case.

Glossary

TUC Trades Union Congress. May describes the TUC as a 'peak' organisation, meaning that it operates at a higher level than the individual unions of which it is composed.

Affiliate become an associated member of.

Individualist ethic concentration upon one's own life and interests rather than on those of the group or groups to which one belongs.

Hypothesis an assumption about the cause of something.

Mobility (here) referring to social mobility and the survey conducted by John Goldthorpe of Nuffield College, Oxford. See the extract from Heath in this chapter.

Public-sector national or local government, nationalised industries and associated employers, i.e. those which are not privately owned.

Incomes policy a policy, usually initiated by central government, which sets limits on wage increases.

Effects of flat–rate pay policies on differentials this refers to the fact that a flat–rate (i.e. lump sum) increase has the effect of eroding differentials between different levels of income, i.e. the gap between the lower-paid and the higher-paid declines. Percentage pay increases have the opposite effect.

ASTMS The Association of Scientific, Technical and Managerial Staff.

Political levy money charged to union members when they pay their union subscription fees. The cash is often used to support the Labour Party.

Questions

1 What problems are connected with trying to establish how far the middle class are unionised?

2 What reasons does May give for not seeing the rise of middle class unionism as evidence of proletarianisation?

3 What characteristics of middle class unionism *would* suggest that they were increasingly indicative of the proletarianisation of the middle class?

4 If the growth of middle class unionism is not evidence that the middle class are becoming increasingly like the working class in terms of attitudes, work situation, and so on, what other types of evidence could be put forward in defence of this idea?

R. Crompton and G. Jones
White Collar Proletariat, 1984, pp. 125–6, 128

Summary and conclusions

At the aggregate level, the mobility experience of the men in our population repeats the trends already described in large-scale, random survey studies. We have shown that most men who have pursued white-collar careers will have been promoted by the age of 35 and that, as a consequence, the age distribution of male clerks is markedly skewed towards the youngest age ranges, with a second minor peak in the age curve which is largely explained by the presence of 'late entrants' into clerical work from diverse occupational backgrounds. . . .

This kind of evidence has been used to refute the thesis of clerical 'proletarianisation'. For reasons that we have already detailed at some length, we would not accept that such evidence entirely refutes the 'proletarianisation' thesis. In addition, our empirical material has enabled us to explore the processes of male mobility in some detail, and the conclusions we draw in relation to both present and future patterns of male mobility are rather different from those of previous authors.

First, we would dispute whether mobility from routine clerical grades to the lower levels of non-manual supervision and administration should be regarded as a 'class move'. In the previous chapter we have demonstrated that the *work* of the majority of men on these grades is best described as that of a 'leading operator' or as 'skilled clerical'; in this chapter we have shown that many clerks apparently never proceed beyond these grades or those just above. On the reasonable assumption that eventual mobility to 'management' proper *does* constitute a 'class move', then only a minority (rather than the majority as is implied by previous studies) of men who start their working lives as clerks will eventually make an unambiguous 'class move'. However (and this might be regarded as evidence against our interpretation), promotion itself, even if only to a relatively low level, clearly affects the attitudes of the men concerned. Men who have been promoted are more likely to indicate that they intend to pursue an organisational career, and express a greater degree of job interest and satisfaction with their work. Thus we can see that the workings of the internal labour market will modify the impact of technological and other forms of 'deskilling' —a point that has already been emphasised by 'radical' labour-market theorists.

Previous research has suggested that patterns of

male mobility in non–manual work are to be viewed as stable 'processes of reproduction'. ... On our evidence, however, these apparently stable processes look rather fragile. They are essentially *contingent* on (i) the continuing presence of women on lower clerical grades; (ii) substantial wastage—particularly among women, but of men as well—among young clerks, and (iii) the reproduction of higher–level positions to be promoted to. ... Recent evidence suggests that women are increasingly acquiring qualifications and delaying the age of child–bearing. If, as a consequence, only a minority of women presently employed as clerks achieve promotion, this will constitute a serious threat to the established pattern of male non–manual careers.

If reported intentions are any guide to the future (and, of course, they may not be), then continuing wastage among the younger men cannot be assured, as the vast majority indicated that they hoped to pursue 'organisational careers' through promotion within their own organisation. In any case, the present economic recession has reduced the range of opportunities available, even if occupational mobility were to be 'forced' or contemplated.

In two of the three organisations we studied (Lifeco and Cohall), the more senior positions that young clerks might hope to be promoted to were, as a consequence of economic difficulties and technological change, actually being reduced in number.

Therefore, although (for men at any rate), the presence of internal labour markets has ameliorated the impact of the deskilling and routinisation of work in the past, it is likely that if these structures fail to provide the same protection in the future, resistance and hostility will be directed towards the employers and their representatives. In short, if changes in the nature of white–collar work are eventually complemented by changes in white–collar work histories, the impact on attitudes and values could be considerable.

Glossary

Aggregate collective.
Skewed twisted, or biased towards something.
Class move a move from one social class to another.
Deskilling removing the skill from a job so that it becomes routine.
Lifeco the fictional name of a real life assurance company.
Cohall the fictional name of a real county hall.
Ameliorated made better.

Questions

1 'This kind of evidence has been used to refute the thesis of clerical proletarianisation'. What kind of evidence, and how can it be used to do this?

2 Why don't Crompton and Jones think that 'this kind of evidence' *does* refute the idea of male proletarianisation?

3 In what way does the presence of women in clerical occupations affect the validity of the proletarianisation thesis, according to Crompton and Jones?

4 What social changes will make male proletarianisation more likely in the future, according to the authors?

5 What other white–collar occupations, besides clerical ones, might Crompton and Jones' argument be relevant to?

6 The authors are suggesting that the presence of women in white–collar work has insulated men from the worst effects of proletarianisation. What criticisms have you got of this thesis?

J. Goldthorpe and D. Lockwood,

The Affluent Worker in the Class Structure, 1969, pp. 153, 158–9, 162–4

Broadly speaking, our findings show that in the case of the workers we studied there remain important areas of common social experience which are still fairly distinctively working–class; that specifically middle–class social norms are not widely followed nor middle–class life–styles consciously emulated; and that assimilation into middle–class society is neither in process nor, in the main, a desired objective. . . .

The findings discussed in Chapter 3 underline the argument that increases in earnings, improvements in working conditions, more enlightened and liberal employment policies and so on do not in themselves basically alter the class situation of the industrial worker in present–day society. Despite these changes, he remains a man who gains his livelihood through placing his labour at the disposal of an employer in return for wages, usually paid by the piece, hour or day. Advances in industrial technology and management may in some cases result in work–tasks and –roles becoming more inherently rewarding or at any rate less stressful; but it is by no means clear that any overall tendency in this direction is established. Certainly, new forms of industrial organisation also give rise to new forms of strain or deprivation in work—as, for example, those associated with the imperatives of scale, with multiple–shift working or with the blocking of promotion opportunities for men on the shop floor. Moreover for many industrial workers, and especially for those who do not possess scarce skills, obtaining earnings sufficient to support a middle–class standard of living may well mean taking on work of a particularly unrewarding or unpleasant kind—work, that is, which can be experienced only as labour. And indeed for men in most manual grades the achievement of affluence is likely to require some substantial amount of overtime working on top of a regular working week which is already longer than that of white–collar employees. Finally, it is evident that many types of industrial work, and often those that afford high earnings, exert a seriously restrictive effect upon out–of–work life; in this respect again shifts and overtime are major factors, and the impact of the former at least will become more rather than less widely felt. . . .

The styles of life of those relatively affluent manual workers and their families who live in new housing areas undoubtedly tend to differ, in various well–documented ways, from those typical of more traditional working–class communities. But the results of our study reviewed in Chapter 4 bring out the point that such changes need not betoken the adoption of specifically middle–class models of sociability; and indeed the life–styles that we recorded would seem better interpreted in terms of the adaptation of old norms to new exigencies and opportunities than in terms of any basic normative reorientation. What is clearer still is that affluence, and even residence in localities of a 'middle–class' character, do not lead on, in any automatic way, to the integration of manual workers and their families into middle–class society. As is shown by the couples we studied, remarkably few 'social' relationships with white–collar persons may in fact be formed; and, so far as we could tell in our case, not primarily because of white–collar exclusiveness but rather because our affluent workers and their wives had no particular desire to develop such relationships and in general tended to follow a family–centred and relatively privatised pattern of social life. . . .

Among the couples in our sample, as was seen in Chapter 5, powerful motivations to gain higher material standards of living did not in the main appear to be accompanied by status striving. Rather, what was notable was the degree to which, despite their considerable gains as consumers, our respondents' orientations to the future were still conditioned by their unchanged class situation as producers; and further, the fact that while their social horizons were largely free from traditionalistic limitations, this did not result in the acceptance of distinctly middle–class social perspectives. In this as in other respects, one very obvious but often disregarded observation may be made; namely, that a break with working–class traditionalism need not take the form of a shift in the direction of 'middle–classness', and that evidence of the former chance cannot therefore be taken as evidence of the latter. . . .

A factory worker can double his living standards and still remain a man who sells his labour to an employer in return for wages; he can work at a control panel rather than on an assembly line without changing his subordinate position in the organisation of production: he can live in his own house in a 'middle–class' estate or suburb and still remain little involved in white–collar social worlds.

In short, class and status relationships do not change entirely *pari passu* with changes in the economic, technological and ecological infrastructure of social life: they have rather an important degree of autonomy, and can thus accommodate considerable change in this infrastructure without themselves changing in any fundamental way. . . .

On the contrary, our own research indicates clearly enough how increasing affluence and its correlates can have many far-reaching consequences—both in undermining the viability or desirability of established life-styles and in encouraging or requiring the development of new patterns of attitudes, behaviour and relationships.

In this connection we may usefully return to the notion of 'normative convergence' between certain manual and non-manual groups which we initially suggested as a more plausible interpretation than that of *embourgeoisement* of ongoing changes on the boundaries of the working and middle classes. It will be recalled that this process was seen as chiefly involving in the case of white-collar workers a shift away from their traditional individualism towards greater reliance on collective means of pursuing their economic objectives; and in the case of manual workers, a shift away from a community-oriented form of social life towards recognition of the conjugal family and its fortunes as concerns of overriding importance. So far as the latter aspect is concerned, our findings clearly show how a family-centred and privatised style of life was indeed the norm among the manual workers we studied, and how the economic advancement of their families was a matter of paramount importance to them. . . .

More unexpectedly, an absence of solidaristic orientations was revealed among our Luton workers not only in their pattern of out-of-work sociability but in their working lives as well, and in fact in the general way in which they interpreted the social order. As we have earlier described, the meaning that they gave to the activities and relationships of work was a predominantly instrumental one; work was defined and experienced essentially as a means to the pursuit of ends outside of work and usually ones relating to standards of domestic living. At the same time, class consciousness was even less in evidence than status consciousness; and in so far as coherent images of the class structure were to be found, these most often approximated 'money' models in which extrinsic differences in consumption standards, rather than relationships expressing differences in power or prestige, were represented as the main basis of stratification.

Thus, while the results produced by our critical case can lend little support to the idea of the 'middle-class' worker, they do on the other hand provide ample material to characterise at least one manifestation of that hitherto somewhat shadowy figure, the 'new' worker. . . .

Glossary

Norms customary patterns of behaviour.

Emulate copy.

Imperatives necessities.

Betoken indicate.

Exigencies urgent needs or demands.

Normative reorientation change in norms.

Status striving attempting to gain more status.

Traditionalistic limitations (here) old-fashioned attitudes.

Pari passu at the same pace, simultaneously.

Infrastructure base, foundation.

Autonomy independence of action.

Correlates things that accompany something else, are found with it.

Normative convergence the increasing similarity of the norms of two social groups.

Individualism emphasis on oneself.

Conjugal family (here) the nuclear as opposed to the extended family.

Privatised centred on the home, not in the public domain.

Paramount supreme.

Solidaristic orientations group-centred, as opposed to individual-centred feelings. Examples in the workplace: feeling part of a team or a union.

Instrumental concerned with another goal; (here) making money.
Coherent clear, well-defined.
Extrinsic lying outside something, not being part of it.

Questions

1 Give examples of the following: 'middle class social norms', 'liberal employment policies', 'imperatives of scale'.
2 What reasons do Goldthorpe and Lockwood give for their findings that:
   (a) the affluent workers are not becoming like the middle class?
   (b) the affluent workers still retain the class situation of the working class?
3 What evidence do the authors cite for the normative convergence of the middle class and the working class? What other evidence could you use to support this idea?
4 Goldthorpe and Lockwood conducted their study in the 1960s. What changes since then may call into question the relevance of their results for modern Britain? What, in your opinion, has happened to the class position of the working class since then?

R. L. Davis and J. Cousins
'The "New Working Class" and the Old', in M. Blumer (ed.),
Working Class Images of Society, 1975, pp. 202–03

There are several historical parallels ... that have implications which Goldthorpe and Lockwood only finally, and rather begrudgingly, acknowledge. First, 'Affluence' can be reified into a state of near permanence; as we have been recently reminded once again, such permanence cannot be assumed (Glyn and Sutcliffe, 1972).[1] The possibilities of class action once this is clear (coupled with the exposure of the 'cash-nexus') are a reality. (Recent strikes might well be instanced as demonstrating this— e.g. those of the miners and the dockers.) Second, the 'new' industries and associated communities do provide arenas in which class conflict can arise since they are not 'encumbered' with those community structures which inhibit the development of con- sciousness. However, that they might become 'encumbered' is a possibility too. As Westergaard says, referring to Luton:

'if conditions "favourable" to the simple "embour- geoisement" thesis were deliberately chosen, in order the more firmly to refute that thesis if it should fail to hold water, just the same conditions happen also to be "favourable" to the "privatisa- tion" hypothesis which the authors put in its place' (Westergaard, 1970, p. 119).[2]

The evidence in south–east Northumberland points to a lag in the development of community institu- tions and structures; as does evidence from the Yorkshire coalfield, where 'only since 1870 has an identifiable mining community come into existence in Yorkshire' and the distinctive community took until the First World War to emerge there—i.e. a thirty-year lapse between settlement and identity (Storm Clark, 1971).[3]

The linkage of prosperity and affluence; labour mobility and economic growth with aggressive wage bargaining and political radicalism is not a new departure in the analysis of the British working class. The 'new' worker is nothing new. In the early 1700s commentators were pointing out the con- nection between the availability of smart-looking cotton dresses and the impudence of maidservants. The real argument against the embourgeoisement thesis is not to posit a 'new' working class. The so- called 'old' working class areas have in the past been boom areas like Luton and have shown much the same kind of characteristics. Not only this, but they too were regarded as locations of a new working class in their day. The argument against the embourgeoisement thesis is a theoretical one. To be a proletarian is not to be pauperised but to be a commodity. The so-called 'new' working classes by their very privatisation and instrumentality have been some of the most proletarian sections of the British working class; and possessing, because they were affluent, much more confidence and capability in its organisation. Militancy in pre-war Britain was found on building sites and in aircraft factories, not in mines and shipyards. The so-called traditional community should be associated not with class consciousness and militancy but with political isolation and defeat. Those very aspects which Lockwood saw as accompanying the new worker and affecting an ever larger part of the working class, were in fact threatening the differen-tiation of the working class, the sectionalism of its organisation and the sectoralism of its experience. These are the true supports of working class conservatism and, in the traditional working class community, find, certainly not their only, but perhaps one of their chief, expressions.

We contend, finally, that the contrasts between 'new' and 'old' that have been drawn both in the past and contemporaneously have obscured rather more than they have made clear. Since, in the most recent case, the contrast has been drawn with the use of an ideal-typificatory method, one must subject such a method to intense scrutiny. To avoid the misleading effects of that method, one solution might be sought in making the resultant typology ever more sophisticated—to include newly dis-covered factors and dimensions, or ones which ought to have been included in the first place. Our own conclusion, however, is that to veer away from such intellectual jig-saw puzzling is necessary, and that a greater concern with what people are (were) actually doing and the situational and his-torical circumstances they are (were) doing it in is the proper concern of sociology. Should such a concern be 'prejudicial to the scientific status of the discipline', then indeed 'so much the worse for that'.

---

¹⁻³See Bibliography

Glossary

Reified literally made like a god, generally used to mean giving something more importance than it deserves.

Cash-nexus the world of money. The phrase implies an interconnected network of demands and necessities which can control the lives of the people within it.

Refute disprove.

Proletarian a worker without property, one who is forced to sell his/her labour in order to live.

Pauperised made poor.

Differentiation distinctions between things.

Sectionalism occurs where something is divided up into distinguishable parts. Used here it implies a lack of common interest or action.

Sectoralism occurs where something is divided into discrete components.

Ideal-typificatory an 'ideal type' is a sociological device first described by Max Weber. It is a methodological tool to make the study of society easier and involves the exaggeration of the most important aspects of the subjects of study while simultaneously ignoring their less important features. This makes it easier to see the distinctive effects they have in society. Weber used ideal types of Protestantism and of capitalism to see how the first helped create the second. Goldthorpe and Lockwood have used an 'ideal-typificatory method' in that they have chosen a group of the working class which exaggerates those features which are most like the middle class (affluent, removed from traditional working class communities, home owners, etc.). They did this in order to test the embourgeoisement thesis. Their argument was that if embourgeoisement was not occurring in these circumstances then it would not be found anywhere amongst the working class.

Typology a system of classification.

Questions
1 Put into your own words the reasons the authors of this passage give for rejecting Goldthorpe and Lockwood's claim to have discovered a 'new class' with distinctive norms and values, different from those of the working class and the middle class.
2 As Davis and Cousins criticise Goldthorpe and Lockwood's study, which was aimed at refuting the embourgeoisement thesis, does this mean that they, Davis and Cousins, subscribe to that thesis?
3 Imagine that you worked on the Goldthorpe and Lockwood study of the affluent workers of Luton. Prepare a defence of your study against the criticisms raised by Davis and Cousins.
4 In your view, are the arguments that Davis and Cousins put forward against the Goldthorpe and Lockwood study justified? Give evidence to support your answer.

Question on May, Crompton and Jones, Goldthorpe and Lockwood, and Davis and Cousins extract

'While the theory of embourgeoisement was effectively discredited many years ago, the proletarianisation thesis has only recently been shown to be empirically inaccurate.' Discuss.

A. Heath
Social Mobility, 1981, pp. 75–7, 105–6, 135–6

Britain is not a society in which individual position in the class structure is fixed at birth. The sons of foremen and technicians (Class V), for example, are spread out across the class structure in an apparently random manner. Fluidity rather than occupational inheritance seems a better characterisation of this intermediate area of the British class structure. Occupational inheritance, however, is more in evidence when we look at the extremes. Almost half the sons from Class I homes followed in their fathers' footsteps into Class I jobs; well over half the sons from working–class homes likewise followed in their father's footsteps. But this still means that there were many men from these classes who experienced upward or downward intergenerational mobility. One in seven men from Class I homes were downwardly mobile into blue–collar jobs; one in five men whose fathers held semi– or unskilled manual jobs were upwardly mobile into white-collar work.

The upwardly mobile greatly outnumbered the downwardly mobile. The reason is simple. There was increasing 'room at the top'. In 1972 twice as many sons held Class I jobs as their fathers had done, and this meant there was plenty of room for newcomers to these elite occupations. Indeed, the newcomers outnumbered the 'second generation' by three to one. But the obverse of expansion at the top was contraction at the bottom. And the obverse of the heterogeneity of Class I is the homogeneity of the working class. Here it is the 'second generation' who outnumber the new recruits by three to one.

The routes which people followed into Class I were most often (but far from exclusively) educational ones. The man who went to a secondary modern school and left at the minimum leaving age with no qualifications was far more likely than his better educated peer to end up in a working–class job; the secondary modern school was a great leveller. And the most frequented route for upward mobility went via the grammar school. But the role of education in mobility can be (and often has been) greatly exaggerated. It was harder, but not impossible, for men to gain access to the established professions without formal educational qualifications, but many more men with little formal schooling climbed the promotion ladder to the higher levels of industrial management.

While many 'new men' climbed the educational and promotional ladders into the elite occupations that make up Class I, progress into the very highest echelons of society—the governing elite—was harder. The bureaucracies of government and industry were the most open channels of upward mobility, and the boardrooms of the City were perhaps the most closed. The *carrière ouverte aux talents* that the modern bureaucracy purports to give is neither wholly myth nor wholly fact: 11 per cent of the top civil servants whose names appear in *Who's Who* are the second generation of their families to appear in that elite publication—seventy-five times the 'chance' number; but 31 per cent were the sons of routine clerical or manual workers. These figures document one of the fundamental features of mobility in modern Britain: children from privileged backgrounds have substantial, indeed grotesque, advantages in the competition for elite positions, but when they take their place in the elite they may find that they are outnumbered by men from humbler origins.

These data also reveal that the greater inequalities of opportunity are not those between children from white-collar and blue-collar homes but between the elite and non-elite. The figures cannot be estimated accurately, but the rough orders of magnitude would probably be correct if we were to say that a man from a working-class home has about one chance in fifteen hundred of getting into *Who's Who*; the man from a white-collar background has perhaps one chance in five hundred; the man from the higher professional and managerial home has one chance in two hundred; but the man from the elite home has a one-in-five chance. Silver spoons continue to be distributed.

Trends

There is little support here for any simple thesis. The memorable slogans of 'trendless fluctuation' and 'expanding universalism' offer us half-truths at best. Certainly we have seen fluctuations in mass mobility during the twentieth century, the depression years bringing greater immobility and the expanding opportunities of the post-war years reversing the trend. But these were almost certainly fluctuations around a long-run rising tendency. The sheer arithmetic of the occupational structure means that if we go back to, say, the seventeenth century, when manual workers and farm labourers came to far more than 50 per cent of the population and the urban middle class to less than 10 per cent, total mobility rates across the manual/non-manual line must necessarily have been far lower than they are today.

If we turn to elite mobility we find some support for the rival thesis of expanding universalism. The reforms of the civil service and the military were the embodiment of a shift from ascription to achievement. Open competitive entry instead of patronage and purchase gave new opportunities to the educated offspring of the upper middle classes and there can be little doubt that the nineteenth century saw greater access to these particular elite occupations.

But the City, on the other hand, was not reformed (and still has not been), nor is it obvious that expanding universalism is the best characterisation of the changes in the higher echelons of industry. The spread of bureaucracy has seen the rise of the salaried employee to the boardroom, but the group which has lost out is that of the independent entrepreneur. It is not the victory of achievement over ascription but of one kind of achievement over another—that of the salaried bureaucrat over the self-made man.

Further back in time we lose sight of the underlying trends in a mist of patchy data and shifting definitions. Each historian seems to think that his own particular time or group were unusually open, and perhaps they were. The same story of expanding opportunities that explains the increase in mass mobility in the mid-twentieth century may also account for the accessibility of the gentry in the seventeenth, as land flooded on to the market, and of management and capitalism in the eighteenth as the industrial revolution got under way. Fluctuations there may well have been as new opportunities arose, were filled, and closed.

But our one long-run time-series of any credibility, the marriage records of the peerage, shows a continuous if uneven move to greater openness. This has little to do with universalism and achievement and does not mean that social barriers between the different strata of society have crumbled. Rather, it suggests that the exclusivity of the hereditary peerage has declined as the aristocracy has gradually merged with an only slightly broader grouping—the landed gentry, the military and the financial elite. The English elite has never been completely impermeable, and has become slightly less so over time, but its different sectors have not all opened their doors equally wide and they are not equally happy about whom they will let in.

The mobility of women

The general tendency of women's mobility patterns is to increase the openness of the class structure. Through marriage women experience slightly more mobility than men do through the labour market; their husband's class position is less closely linked to their father's than to their father-in-laws'. And this means that there is, in a sense, greater equality between women in their prospects of advantageous life–chances than among men.

Women's occupational mobility shows a much more radical departure from the male patterns, with the enormous concentration of women in lower white–collar employment. Again, womanhood is a leveller. The restrictions on women's job prospects means that they are much less divided by their social origins than are men. Class discrimination divides men, but sexual discrimination brings women together. Doubtless, if sexual discrimination and segregation within the labour market vanished, class divisions might reassert themselves more strongly; but at present women's chances of occupational mobility are relatively poor and relatively equal.

The chances of *single* women, however, provides an interesting contrast with those that face the majority of employed (often part–time) women workers. They are more likely to be upwardly mobile and less likely to be downwardly mobile than single men, and middle–class single women are particularly good at avoiding the drop into manual work. But whether this means that the opportunities are there for women if they choose to take advantage of them is uncertain (if not improbable): single women are a distinctive group who may well have had to make a definite choice between work and family; they may be more committed to their work than the typical man; and they are only a small minority—if the majority of women followed their example, sexual discrimination in the labour market might well result in chances for women, on average, being distinctly worse. The few good 'women's jobs' would simply not go round as far.

The overall consequence of women's mobility patterns is to increase the number of families with cross–class affiliations and thus to increase the proportion of the population experiencing cross-pressure. The outcomes for class solidarity and class conflict have yet to be studied but it may well have the effect of increasing the size of the 'middle mass' with no strong class allegiance and a more calculative orientation to employers, unions and parties. It may well increase the instability and unpredictability of class action and political preference.

Glossary

Intergenerational mobility social mobility which occurs between the generations, i.e. sons and daughters move to a different class position than that held by their parents.

Obverse the opposite of something.

Heterogeneity composed of diverse elements.

Homogeneity composed of identical elements.

Echelons (here) strata.

Carrière ouverte aux talents literally 'career open to those with talent', i.e. an occupation based upon meritocratic principles.

Purports pretends.

Orders of magnitude estimates which give an idea of the size of something without being very precise (due to lack of information).

Trendless fluctuation change in rate with no overall trends over time.

Expanding universalism the idea of a society increasingly open to social mobility and meritocratic.

Ascription social position based upon inherited or socially given characteristics (as occurs with, for example, the Royal Family).

Achievement social position earned (e.g. through educational qualifications).

Impermeable cannot be penetrated.

Cross–class affiliations having connections with two or more social classes.

Calculative orientation considering only the financial return that can be gained from something.

Questions

1 From which section of the class structure is movement most likely?

2 (a) What was the most common method by which social mobility was achieved?

   (b) What other methods of social mobility are there?

3 Distinguish between male and female patterns of social mobility.
4 What are the advantages which children from privileged backgrounds have in the competition for elite positions?
5 What reasons can you suggest for the fact that the opportunities for upward mobility, at least in some occupations, increased after the Second World War?
6 What special methodological problems does the study of social mobility present to the sociologist who wishes to establish its nature and extent?
7 Why have studies of social mobility such as the Nuffield Mobility Study generated so much heated debate amongst sociologists?

A. Gorz
Farewell to the Working Class, 1982, pp. 67–73, 87

For over a century the idea of the proletariat has succeeded in masking its own unreality. This idea is now as obsolete as the proletariat itself, since in place of the productive collective worker of old, a non-class of non-workers is coming into being, prefiguring a non-society within existing society in which classes will be abolished along with work itself and all forms of domination. . . .

This non-class encompasses all those who have been expelled from production by the abolition of work, or whose capacities are under-employed as a result of the industrialisation (in this case, the automation and computerisation) of intellectual work. It includes all the supernumeraries of present-day social production, who are potentially or actually unemployed, whether permanently or temporarily, partially or completely. . . .

That traditional working class is now no more than a privileged minority. The majority of the population now belong to the post-industrial neo-proletariat which, with no job security or definite class identity, fills the area of probationary, contracted, casual, temporary and part-time employment. In the not too distant future, jobs such as these will be largely eliminated by automation. Even now, their specifications are continually changing with the rapid development of technology, and their requirements bear little relation to the knowledge and skills offered by schools and universities. The neo-proletariat is generally over-qualified for the jobs it finds. It is generally condemned to under-use of its capacities when it is in work, and to unemployment itself in the longer term. Any employment seems to be accidental and provisional, every type of work purely contingent. It cannot feel any involvement with

'its' work or identification with 'its' job. Work no longer signifies an activity or even a major occupation; it is merely a blank interval on the margins of life, to be endured in order to earn a little money. . . .

Learning trades they will never regularly practise, following courses without outlets or practical utility, giving them up or failing them because 'after all, what does it matter', they go on to work in the post office during the summer, to pick grapes in the autumn, to join a department-store for Christmas, and to work as a labourer in the spring. . . .

The only certainty, as far as they are concerned, is that they do not feel they belong to the working class, *or to any other class*. They do not recognise themselves in the term 'worker' or in its symmetrical opposite, 'unemployed'. . . .

Instead of being the worker's mode of insertion into a system of universal cooperation, work is now the mode of subordination to the machinery of universal domination. Instead of generating workers able to transcend their finite particularity and define themselves directly as social producers in general, work has come to be perceived by individuals as the contingent form of social oppression in general. . . .

Whatever the number of jobs remaining in industry and the service sector once automation has been fully achieved, they will be incapable of providing identity, meaning and power for those who fill them. For there is a rapid decline in the amount of labour-time necessary to reproduce not *this* society and its mechanisms of domination and command, but a viable society endowed with everything useful and necessary to life. The requirement could be a mere two hours a day, or ten hours a week, or fifteen weeks a year, or ten years in a lifetime.

The substantially longer period of social labour maintained in contemporary society has accelerated rather than slowed down the devaluation, in the ethical sense, of all forms of work. The amount of time spent working and the relatively high level of employment have been artificially maintained because of the inextricable confusion which exists between the production of the necessary and the superfluous, the useful and the useless, waste and wealth, pleasures and nuisances, destruction and repair. Whole areas of economic life now have the sole function of 'providing work', or of producing for the sake of keeping people working. . . .

Since it (the non–class) plays no part in the production of society, it envisages society's development as something external, akin to a spectacle or a show. It sees no point in taking over the machine–like structure which, as it sees it, defines contemporary society, nor of placing anything whatsoever under its control. What matters instead is to appropriate areas of autonomy outside of, and in opposition to, the logic of society, so as to allow the unobstructed realisation of individual development *alongside* and *over* that machine–like structure. . . .

The priority task of a post–industrial left must therefore be to extend self–motivated, self–rewarding activity within, and above all, outside the family, and to limit as much as possible all waged or market–based activity carried out on behalf of third parties (even the state). A reduction in work time is a necessary but not a sufficient condition. For it will not help to enlarge the sphere of individual autonomy if the resulting free time remains empty 'leisure time', filled for better or worse by the programmed distractions of the mass media and the oblivion merchants, and if everyone is thereby driven back into the solitude of their private sphere.

More than upon free time, the expansion of the sphere of autonomy depends upon a freely available supply of convivial tools[1] that allow individuals to do or make anything whose aesthetic or use–value is enhanced by doing it oneself. Repair and do–it–yourself workshops in blocks of flats, neighbourhood centres or rural communities should enable everyone to make or invent things as they wish. Similarly, libraries, places to make music or movies, 'free' radio and television stations, open spaces for communication, circulation and exchange, and so on, need to be accessible to everyone.

---

[1] See Bibliography

Glossary

Supernumeraries the number of people above those required to complete a task.

Neo–proletariat literally, 'new proletariat'. Gorz means by this those members of the working class who are now without a stable job.

Probationary the period before being accepted as a member of the workforce. One's performance is assessed during this period.

Contingent uncertain.

Transcend go beyond.

Envisages perceives.

Autonomy freedom from constraints.

Oblivion merchants those institutions in society which seek to make us forget ourselves, our situation and our problems (hence keeping the situation stable).

Questions

1 What is the nature of the 'non–class' which has replaced the working class, according to Gorz?

2 What social and economic changes have led to the creation of the non–class?

3 Gorz's comments do not seem to be founded upon empirical research. What evidence would you seek to collect in order to test his ideas?

4 Write a short description of what you imagine a 'convivial society' to be like.

Bibliography

Source of extracts

T. May, *Middle Class Unionism*, in R. King and N. Nugent, *Respectable Rebels: Middle Class Campaigns in Britain in the 1970s*, Hodder & Stoughton, London, 1979

R. Crompton and G. Jones, *White Collar Proletariat*, Macmillan, London, 1984

J. Goldthorpe and D. Lockwood, *The Affluent Worker in the Class Structure*, Cambridge University Press, Cambridge, 1969

R. L. Davis and J. Cousins, *The 'New Working Class' and the Old* in M. Blumer (ed.), *Working Class Images of Society*, Routledge & Kegan Paul, London, 1975

A. Heath, *Social Mobility*, Fontana, Glasgow, 1981

A. Gorz, *Farewell to the Working Class*, Pluto Press, London, 1982

Reference in the Introduction

D. Lockwood, *The Blackcoated Worker*, Unwin University Books, London, 1958

References in Davis and Cousins extract

1 A. Glyn and B. Sutcliffe, *British Capitalism, Workers and the Profit Squeeze*, Penguin, Harmondsworth, 1972

2 J. Westergaard, *Sociology: the myth of classlessness* in R. Blackburn, *Ideology in Social Science*, Fontana, Glasgow 1972

3 C. Storm Clark, *The Miners 1870–1970*, Victorian Studies 15, 1971

Reference in Gorz extract

1 Tools that 'enhance the ability of people to pursue their own goals in their unique way', Ivan Illich, *Tools for Conviviality*, Calder and Boyars, London, 1973

Further reading

Diamond Commission, *Royal Commission on the Distribution of Income and Wealth*, HMSO, 1979

A. Giddens, *The Class Structure of the Advanced Societies*, Hutchinson, London, 1973

J. Goldthorpe *et al.*, *Social Mobility and Class Structure in Modern Britain*, Oxford University Press, Oxford, 1980

P. Martin, *Social Stratification*, in R. J. Anderson and W. W. Sharrock (eds), *Applied Sociological Perspectives*, Allen & Unwin, London, 1984

T. Noble, *Structure and Change in Modern Britain*, Batsford, London, 1981

F. Parkin, *Marxism and Class Theory: a Bourgeois Critique*, Tavistock, London, 1979

I. Reid, *Social Class Differences in Britain*, Grant McIntyre, London, 1981

J. Scott, *The Upper Class — Property and Privilege in Britain*, Macmillan, London, 1982

J. Westergaard and H. Resler, *Class in a Capitalist Society*, Penguin, Harmondsworth, 1970

◪ The Sociology of Gender

Introduction　This chapter is divided into three sections, each dealing with one of the many issues relating to women's position in society. The first concerns the nature and types of feminism. The second contains extracts about the position of women in the economy. The last section, containing just one reading, is about females in the education system.

The first selection, from D. Bouchier's *The Feminist Challenge*, describes three varieties of modern feminism: liberal, socialist and radical. Liberal feminists believe in progressive reform to bring about equality for women. They advocate local campaigns on issues such as equal pay, educational and job opportunities, abolition of stereotypes in the media, and so on. They involve themselves in the community and in established institutions by setting up advice centres on problems which are particularly relevant to women, such as contraception and abortion. They work in political parties and publish journals oriented to feminism.

Socialist feminism derives from Marxist thought, particularly Engels' *The Origin of the Family, Private Property and the State*, and holds that a separate struggle for the liberation of women from men is necessary in addition to the general struggle against capital because of the deeper exploitation of women in capitalism. Committed socialist feminists often work within the labour movement, publish books and journals and form revolutionary organisations in order to further the struggle for a feminist socialism. The more moderate socialist feminists are quite close to liberal feminists in their activities and aims.

Radical feminism is similar to socialist feminism in its philosophy but is a more recent phenomenon. The main difference between the two is that the radical feminists do not link the oppression of women to the capitalist system but to men in general. Radical feminists work alongside the first two and in addition tend to build alternative social structures to the established ones in society. These include communes or, at a less-organised level, small group counter–cultures. They aim to raise the consciousness of women and one of the ways they do this is by developing the discipline of women's history. In this they aim to document the achievements of women and the historical exploitation and suppression of women by men.

The second extract in this section, from S. L. Bartky's *Toward a Phenomenology of Feminist Consciousness* is an investigation of the effect of feminism on a woman's consciousness. Bartky adopts a phenomenological approach, one designed to give the reader an empathetic understanding of what feminist consciousness is about. We are led to understand how such a consciousness affects one's everyday life and actions, or at least this is the author's aim.

The second section concerns the position of women in the economy. The first extract, from functionalist Talcott Parsons, acknowledges that women occupy a subordinate place in terms of economic activity. He implies, however, that this is a natural state of affairs and will not change, nor should it. This is because, he argues, women are best at expressive or affective (emotional) roles while men are best at instrumental roles (bread–winning). Parsons' position on this mirrors that of Murdock, discussed in the introduction to the family chapter.

The second extract, from the Fawcett Society's booklet *The Class of '84* discusses the sex discrimination that girls are subjected to on Youth Training Schemes. Such discrimination is an alternative explanation for women's subordinate position in the economy to that put forward by Parsons. The authors of this extract conducted a survey of 175 young people drawn from all nine Manpower Services Commission regions in Great Britain. 139 girls and twenty-two boys were interviewed, together with fourteen girls who had not joined the Youth Training Scheme. This last group was used for comparative purposes. The overall aim of the study was to examine the position of girls in this increasingly important form of training for future careers. The authors believe that:

> Open equally to boys and girls, the Youth Training Scheme is potentially a means by which traditional attitudes limiting job choice may be changed, a very necessary policy in a time when the economic structure is changing, and should provide the means to end sex discrimination in training.

However, their general conclusion is that in many cases 'girls had not had equal access with boys to good quality skills training'.

The booklet ends with a series of recommendations, including a series of positive discrimination measures, in favour of girls on the Youth Training Scheme.

The third extract is from socialist feminist I. Bruegel's article 'Women as a Reserve Army of Labour'. While Parsons' extract is written from a functionalist position and the Fawcett Society's is a small–scale empirical study, this one seeks to situate the facts about women's employment in Britain within a Marxist understanding of the working of the British economy. Bruegel sees women as an ideal (from the capitalists' point of view) reserve army of labour. This Marxist term refers to a group of people whose labour can be made use of at times when demand and profitability are high but dispensed with in times of recession. Bruegel identifies significant changes in the place women occupy in the economy—changes that have only occurred in recent years—and argues that important consequences will result from these changes.

The final extract documents the underachievement of girls relative to boys in the British education system. From I. Reid and E. Wormald's *Sex Differences in Britain*, this selection examines relative performance of boys and girls at 'A', 'O' and CSE level as well as the types of further and higher education to which the sexes have tended to progress.

D. Bouchier

The Feminist Challenge, 1983, pp. 65–71, 75, 78

Liberal feminism

... the closest thing to formal theory which we find in liberal feminist thought is a view of social processes derived directly from the social sciences.

This view suggests that individuals are trained—by social institutions like the family, the education system and the mass media—into patterns of behaviour or roles which are performed unconsciously and become an integral part of a person's identity. Thus boys learn to be competitive, unemotional and outward-looking, while girls learn to be submissive, to express their feelings and to look for their satisfactions in personal and family affairs. These socially constructed male/female roles then become the basis of a status system which places women in an inferior position. In de Beauvoir's phrase, 'One is not born, but rather becomes a woman.'

For liberal feminists, there are no real villains in this process, nor is it the inevitable product of biological differences or of any particular social or economic system. Sexual roles have been built up over a long period of historical time and have become embedded in our culture. But, since they were constructed by human beings, they can be dismantled by human beings. This must be done by changing the social training which men and women receive from childhood onwards, and by challenging the role stereotypes which continue to discriminate against women. The outcome of this process, say the liberals, would be a convergence of male/female roles from which both women and men would benefit.

The goal of liberal feminism is therefore a redistribution of existing social and economic rewards (status and power) along more egalitarian lines. For the most part, women who follow the liberal tradition do not shrink from the fact that the world is a competitive place, with winners and losers, and it is consistent with this attitude that most of them also reject unfair advantages for women in the form of positive discrimination in education, hiring and promotion. Like the blacks of the early civil rights movement, they ask only for a fair chance.

Liberal feminism embraces a wide range of political commitments, from single-issue campaigns (women in politics, education, media, equal pay) to more comprehensive demands for the equalisation of sex roles. It is worth noting that although liberal feminists are frequently criticised by those of more radical persuasion, even the *minimal* liberal demands, if conceded, would have profound social effects, and that resistance to them outside the movement remains strong. . . .

Socialist feminism

The main pillars of the socialist feminist analysis may be summed up under three headings: wage labour, the family and ideology.

Wage labour

Socialists hold that the root cause of all oppression is economic, though feminists know from the example of the state socialist societies and from their own experiences that powerful cultural mechanisms also work to perpetuate women's inequality. Like any oppressed group, women provide a pool of labour for low-paid and unpleasant work. In addition, they are considered politically docile, seeing their work as secondary to their families, and therefore more easily hired and fired according to economic circumstances. While the unionisation of women has made some progress since 1968, they remain a very exploitable and exploited section of the work-force. . . .

Socialist feminists vary considerably in the degree to which they are committed to the classic Marxist class analysis. Since women span the whole range of wealth and poverty, and their interests are by no means obviously the same, crude class analysis is not found in modern feminism. The emphasis is rather on how capitalism gains from the exploitation of working-class women at work and in the home. This exploitation is seen to differ from men's in at least three ways: women form a reserve army of productive labour, with low wages, no prospects and a total lack of security; they perform unpaid work in the family; and they are super-exploited by capitalism as consumers and sex objects.

The family

As indicated above, the critique of the traditional family has a long history in socialist thought. Marx and Engels called for its abolition and, although not all socialists have followed this revolutionary line, modern socialist feminists continue to argue that the family is at least in need of profound transformation.

For example, much of their recent analysis has focused on an aspect of the family all but ignored by earlier economic theorists—its function as a *private* domain of work. In the home, women are privatised, isolated. Their work at home, whether or not it is done in addition to an outside job, is the most isolated form of labour. Moreover, the fact that it is *unpaid* labour emphasises its mean status. Housework, as Lenin wrote, 'chains the woman to the kitchen and nursery, and she wastes her labour on barbarously unproductive, petty, nerve-racking, stultifying and crushing drudgery'. . . .

Cooking, shopping, cleaning and the upbringing of children are not recognised as commodities which can be sold or exchanged. The labour which they represent is not considered by society as real work, worthy of payment. Yet a simple calculation will show what an enormous amount of labour housework represents. It has been suggested that the wage value for a woman with two young children is £10,000 per year. Women's housework thus contributes vastly to the capitalist economy. . . .

. . . All feminists place great emphasis on the sexual and personal stresses produced by the restrictive patterns of family life and the dependency which is enforced on women by its economic structure. Juliet Mitchell suggested that oppression within the family created in women 'a tendency to small-mindedness, petty jealousy, irrational emotionality and random violence, dependency, competitiveness, selfishness and possessiveness, passivity, a lack of vision and conservatism'. These qualities, she emphasised, were not false stereotypes created by male chauvinism but real, the inescapable result of the woman's powerless condition within the family.

Ideology

. . . Marxist feminists have been particularly keen to develop the theory of ideology, since economic exploitation at work and in the family do not by themselves seem wholly to explain the long subordination of women. The feminine mystique is deeply embedded in the consciousness of women and men, yet is also a social convention which can be exposed as artificial. The task of the Marxist theorist is not simply to strip away such façades, but to show how, by whom and for whose benefit they have been constructed and maintained. This analysis has led towards a gradual convergence of socialist and radical feminist perspectives. . . .

Radical feminism

Patriarchy

. . . patriarchy identifies men as the enemy. Men benefit from their power over women in every way: from ego–satisfaction, to economic and domestic exploitation, sexual domination and political power. In the last analysis patriarchy is maintained by violence. One male act which came to symbolise this power was rape. Whether or not an individual woman has experienced rape, she has certainly experienced the fear. That fear became a potent consciousness–raising device, an unambiguous proof that something was seriously wrong with the male/female relationship. More generally, all violence towards women was taken to be evidence of the intention of men to retain their power.

In its strongest form, sometimes called the 'pro-woman line', the theory of patriarchy labelled *all*

women as victims and *all* men as oppressors. Gender alone defined the conflict. Socialists, by contrast, have argued that patriarchy was a particular case of capitalist class relations (following Engels) and therefore secondary to class. As the theories have developed, there has been a tendency for these two views to converge towards a model of capitalist patriarchy in which sexual and class oppressions are interwoven and inseparable. . . .

Marriage and the family

Marriage was for radicals what capitalism was for socialists, the real institutional source of exploitation. It destroyed the individuality of women and perverted the minds of children, while sustaining the patriarchal power of men.

There were many alternative visions of what might replace the traditional family. Most of them stressed communality and the benefits to be gained by collective child–rearing; all of them assumed the absence or the minimal presence of men. For some groups this was seen as an interim measure, allowing women to take control of their own lives before readmitting men on a new basis. For others it was the vision of the future, without possibility of compromise.

In the latter part of the 1970s a new attitude towards motherhood began to be apparent in the writings of the movement. This was that maternity can be a joy and a benefit to women if it is undertaken as a *freely chosen experience*, and not within the confines of the nuclear family. Both lesbians and single, heterosexual women argued that their rejection of traditional family life should not entail the rejection of pregnancy, birth and motherhood as uniquely female experiences. . . .

Sexuality

It follows from their critique of patriarchy and the monogamous family that radical feminists seek the transformation of sexuality. With its attendant myths of love and romance, sexuality provides the biological link between women and men which makes their antagonism unique. Man is the 'intimate enemy', not a distant symbol like the capitalist, but a very real body in the bed.

The minimal demand of radical feminists was that women should have control over their own sexuality. As long as sex was used by men to dominate women or by women to manipulate men, it would be alienating and unsatisfying. This meant an end to the double standard, an end to monogamy in marriage and an end to compulsory sex in marriage, goals shared by many liberal and socialist feminists.

But the presence of large numbers of lesbian women in the movement quickly produced a more radical argument, based on a now-famous article by Anne Koedt, 'The Myth of the Vaginal Orgasm'. The Freudian root of this myth was that the clitoral orgasm represented immature sexuality while only the vaginal orgasm (which required a man) signalled a full and mature sexual experience. The physiological basis for this distinction had been eliminated once and for all by Masters and Johnson in 1966, but it was the political implications which concerned radical feminists. Koedt exposed how the myth helped sustain the definition of women as passive rather than active sexual subjects, and how it reinforced the false belief that men were essential to the full sexual satisfaction of women.

Once the myth of the vaginal orgasm was out of the way, it became possible to conceive a complete sexual revolution which would enable women to escape the sexual domination of men. If women did not *need* men, and could make an unrestricted choice of heterosexual, bisexual, lesbian or celibate life-styles, the resulting liberation of sexual behaviour would break the hold of the monogamous family, the source of patriarchal power. . . .

Glossary

Egalitarian holding the principle of equal rights.

Positive discrimination giving preference to certain groups in recognition of their disadvantaged position in society.

Chauvinism dogmatic support for a cause-male chauvinism referring to the insistence that women are inferior to men.

Patriarchy male dominance in the family and in society.

Monogamous family one in which there is only one husband and one wife, only one sexual partner.

Questions

1 Summarise in your own words the views about the family held by each of the following: liberal, socialist and radical feminists.

2 What is the 'feminine mystique' (p. 69, line 26) which the author believes is deeply embedded in the consciousness of women and men?

3 Differentiate between the views of liberal feminism, socialist feminism and radical feminism.

4 Are your views on the subject close to any of these perspectives? Present a reasoned criticism of those types of feminism with which you disagree.

S. L. Bartky

'Toward a Phenomenology of Feminist Consciousness' in M. Vetterling-Braggin *et al.* (eds), *Feminism and Philosophy*, 1977, pp. 26–31, 33

Feminist consciousness is consciousness of *victimisation*. To apprehend oneself as victim is to be aware of an alien and hostile force which is responsible for the blatantly unjust treatment of women and for a stifling and oppressive system of sex roles; it is to be aware, too, that this victimisation, in no way earned or deserved, is an *offence*. For some feminists, this hostile power is 'society' or 'the system'; for others, it is, simply, men. Victimisation is impartial, even though its damage is done to each of us personally. One is victimised as a woman, as one among many, and in the realisation that others are made to suffer in the same way that I am made to suffer lies the beginning of a sense of solidarity with other victims. To come to see oneself as victim is not to see things in the same old way while merely judging them differently or to superimpose new attitudes on things like frosting on a cake: the consciousness of victimisation is immediate and revelatory; it allows us to discover what social reality really *is*.

The consciousness of victimisation is a divided consciousness. To see myself as victim is to know that I have already sustained injury, that I live exposed to injury, that I have been at worst mutilated, at best diminished, in my being. But at the same time, feminist consciousness is a joyous consciousness of one's own power, of the possibility of unprecedented personal growth and of the release of energy long suppressed. Thus, feminist consciousness is consciousness both of weakness and of strength. . . .

To apprehend myself as victim in a sexist society is to know that there are few places where I can hide, that I can be attacked anywhere, at any time, by virtually anyone. Innocent chatter—the currency of ordinary social life—or a compliment ('You don't think like a woman'), the well-intentioned advice of psychologists, the news item, the joke, the cosmetics advertisement—none of these is what it is or what it was. Each is revealed (depending on the circumstances in which it appears) as a threat, an insult, an affront—as a reminder, however subtle, that I belong to an inferior caste—in short, as an instrument of oppression or as the articulation of a sexist institution. Since many things are not what they seem to be, and since many apparently harmless sorts of things can suddenly exhibit a sinister dimension, social reality is revealed as *deceptive*. . . .

Feminist consciousness is often afflicted with category confusion—an inability to know how to classify things. The timidity I display at departmental meetings, for instance—is it nothing more than a personal shortcoming, or is it a typically female trait, a shared inability to display aggression, even verbal aggression? And why is the suggestion I make ignored? Is it <u>intrinsically</u> unintelligent or is it because I am a woman and therefore not to be taken seriously? The persistent need I have to make myself 'attractive', to fix my hair and put on lipstick—is it the false need of a <u>chauvinised</u> woman, encouraged since infancy to identify her value as a person with her attractiveness in the eyes of men? Or does it express a wholesome need to express love for one's own body by adoring it, a behaviour common in primitive societies, allowed us but denied to men in our own still-<u>puritan</u> culture? . . .

Feminist consciousness is something like <u>paranoia</u>, especially when the feminist first begins to apprehend the full extent of sex discrimination and the subtle and various ways in which it is enforced. The System and its agents are everywhere, even inside her own mind, since she can fall prey to self-doubt or to a temptation to compliance. In response to this, the feminist becomes vigilant and suspicious: her apprehension of things, especially of direct or indirect communication with other people, is characterised by what I shall call 'wariness'. Wariness is

anticipation of the possibility of attack, of a front or insult, of disparagement, ridicule, or the hurting blindness of others; it is a mode of experience which anticipates experience in a certain way. While it is primarily the established order of things of which the feminist is wary, she is wary of herself, too. She must be always on the alert lest her pervasive sense of injury provoke in her without warning some public display of emotion, such as violent weeping. Many feminists are perpetually wary lest their own anger be transformed explosively into behaviour too hostile to be prudently or safely displayed. . . .

The revelation of the deceptive character of social reality brings with it another transformation in the way the social milieu is present in feminist experience. Just as so many apparently innocent things are really devices to enforce compliance, so are many 'ordinary' sorts of situations transformed into opportunities or *occasions* for struggle against the system. In a light-hearted mood, I embark upon a Christmas-shopping expedition, only to have it turn, as if independent of my will, into an occasion for striking a blow against sexism. On holiday from political struggle, I have abandoned myself to the richly sensuous atmosphere of Marshall Field's. I have been wandering about the toy department, looking at chemistry sets and miniature ironing boards. Then, unbidden, the following thought flashes into my head: what if, just this once, I send a doll to my nephew and an erector set to my niece? Will this confirm the growing suspicion in my family that I am a crank? What if the children themselves misunderstand my gesture and covet one another's gifts? Worse, what if the boy believes that I have somehow insulted him? The shopping trip turned occasion for resistance now becomes a *test*. I will have to answer for this, once it becomes clear that Marshall Field's has not unwittingly switched the labels. My husband will be embarrassed. A <u>didactic</u> role will be thrust upon me, even though I have determined earlier that the situation was not ripe for consciousness-raising. The special ridicule reserved for movement women will be heaped upon me at the next family party—all in good fun, of course. . . .

But this picture is not as bleak as it appears; indeed, its 'bleakness' would be seen in proper perspective had I described what things were like *before*. Coming to have a feminist consciousness is the experience of coming to know the truth about oneself and one's society. This experience, the acquiring of a 'raised' consciousness, is an immeasurable advance over that false consciousness which it replaces. The scales fall from our eyes.

Glossary

Revelatory revealing knowledge.

Intrinsically belonging to the essential nature of something.

Chauvinised (here) meaning a woman who has been taught sexist attitudes.

Puritan practising strictness in behaviour, particularly avoiding pleasure for its own sake.

Paranoia mental illness involving the tendency to suspect others of plotting against you.

Didactic related to the science of teaching. Didactic role = role as a teacher.

Questions

1 Summarise the author's view of the world.

2 Putting yourself in her place, would you have sent a doll to her nephew and an erector set to her niece? Explain why/why not?

3 What is your opinion of the author's feelings about women's position in The United States and Britain?

4 This passage might be considered a purely personal, subjective account on the part of this author with no general validity. Do you consider that such a 'phenomenology of feminist consciousness' is valuable?

T. Parsons and R. F. Bales

Family, Socialisation and Interaction Process, 1956, pp. 189–92

Functionalism, women and work

The membership of large numbers of women in the American labour force must not be overlooked. Nevertheless there can be no question of symmetry between the sexes in this respect, and, we argue, there is no serious tendency in this direction. In the first place a large proportion of gainfully employed women are single, widowed or divorced, and thus cannot be said to be either taking the place of a husband as breadwinner of the family, or competing with him. A second large contingent are women who either do not yet have children (some of course never will) or whose children are grown up and independent. The number in the labour force who have small children is still quite small and has not shown a marked tendency to increase. The role of housewife is still the overwhelmingly predominant one for the married woman with small children.

But even where this type does have a job, as is also true of those who are married but do not have dependent children, above the lowest occupational levels it is quite clear that in general the woman's job tends to be of a qualitatively different type and not of a status which seriously competes with that of her husband as the primary status-giver or income-earner.

It seems quite safe in general to say that the adult feminine role has not ceased to be anchored primarily in the internal affairs of the family, as wife, mother and manager of the household, while the role of the adult male is primarily anchored in the occupational world, in his job and through it by his status–giving and income–earning functions for the family. Even if, as seems possible, it should come about that the average married woman had some kind of job, it seems most unlikely that this relative balance would be upset; that either the roles would be reversed, or their qualitative differentiation in these respects completely erased.

The distribution of women in the labour force clearly confirms this general view of the balance of the sex roles. Thus, on higher levels typical feminine occupations are those of teacher, social worker, nurse, private secretary and entertainer. Such roles tend to have a prominent expressive component, and often to be 'supportive' to masculine roles. Within the occupational organisation they are analogous to the wife–mother role in the family. It is much less common to find women in the 'top executive' roles and the more specialised and 'impersonal' technical roles. Even within professions we find comparable differentiations, e.g. in medicine women are heavily concentrated in the two branches of pediatrics and psychiatry, while there are few women surgeons.

Glossary

<u>Qualitative differentiation</u> making distinctions between things on the basis of real differences in their nature, rather than their size or number (quantitative differentiation).

<u>Expressive</u> (here) emotional.

<u>Analogous</u> similar to something.

<u>Pediatrics</u> relating to children and their diseases.

Questions

1 In one or two sentences, express the point that Parsons is trying to make.

2 What evidence would you need to gather in order to establish whether Parsons' argument is valid in the British case?

3 What alternative explanations are there for the distinctive position which women occupy in the economy, described in the last paragraph? If you have read the first extract in this chapter consider how the three different types of feminists would answer this question.

The Fawcett Society
The Class of '84, 1985, pp. 15–18, 42

Sex discrimination

Overwhelmingly, girls who were training in non–traditional work had male supervisors and those in traditional work had female supervisors. The position regarding the sex distribution of teachers and tutors in off–the–job training was not so clear cut, but where girls who were taking technical or other non–traditional off–the–job training said they had both men and women teachers, the latter often covered communication and social skills classes only.

Most of the girls, when asked if there was any difference in how girls and boys were treated in their scheme, said there was not, but since most of them were training in traditional women's work in which few boys took part, this is not surprising. Of the 29 girls who said that they had experienced sex-discrimination, half were in non–traditional skills training. A few mentioned actual sexual harassment. Furthermore, it was clear from what the girls themselves said that those who were following a non–traditional training course where they were inevitably in a small minority among 'a load of boys' suffered at least initially from stress and pressures not faced by the boys.

Two girls on <u>Mode B2 schemes</u> said, 'The boys were always bossy and always claiming to be better than the girls. They got on my nerves'; 'The boys were male chauvinist pigs'; 'You have to be hard and give them as good as they give you'. One of these girls had left her engineering course because of the unpleasant attentions of the boys and transferred to another scheme in electronics

where she experienced less harassment. Some girls noticed that although the young people were treated alike in the workshop, sometimes 'the College was a bit hard on the boys', they were 'told off' more.

For the girls doing craft and technician training in well–established training schemes in larger firms where women were already employed in the technical field, there was no experience of adverse discrimination. These companies were short of qualified technicians and were campaigning to recruit more girls. The girls trained alongside the boys and felt they were enjoying equal opportunity.

They were encouraged to think for themselves and make their own decisions. In one company, the girls were warned that when they left the training department to go into the works, they must beware of too much paternalism or they would not learn to do things themselves. In another company a girl said she got more help from the instructor than the boys did and the boys got 'told off' more.

The girls in non–traditional work on the whole found more discrimination among the boys of their own age at college than among the men at the place of work. Comments were: 'At first the boys didn't like speaking to me, but when I had shown them that my wiring was as good as theirs, they began to accept me'. In fact, this girl felt she had to perform better than the boys to be accepted. Another girl said the boys were jealous because the teacher encouraged her more. She worked hard and they did not, and she was doing better. She commented that, 'Some boys are not grown up but I ignore them'. A girl in a group of 17 boys at college, said it was strange at first being the only girl. 'You are a novelty, but the novelty wears off and you soon get used to it.' Several mentioned that the boys often teased for a joke but it was all very friendly—and 'sometimes a boy will let a girl go first in the tea queue'. Girls also mentioned being helped with heavy lifting.

Two girls, both training in agriculture, complained of open sex discrimination and sexual harassment. One said she was not taken seriously and not allowed to do some of the things the boys did (e.g. change a tyre on a tractor). It was upsetting to have to 'kick up a row' to be allowed to do things and show she was capable. She didn't know if she would stay in farming because 'employers find it difficult to believe that a girl can be interested in agriculture'. The other girl said one of her college instructors was 'a real lecher' and just stood and laughed at anything she did. The boys made her stand back while they did the welding saying, 'You're a girl. What are you doing here? You should be in an office.' But she found 'the boys are OK when you get to know them' and then they helped her. She had learnt to be tough and stand up for herself.

Three girls on the same course in 'sport & community leadership' (Mode B2) felt at the beginning that they had been 'let off more lightly' than the boys, but they had protested and now felt they had insisted successfully on equality of treatment from the staff. The evidence suggested that only girls who persisted and learned to cope with such pressures were likely to complete the course.

· More serious from a training and career point of view were the inequalities in the training content and work experience itself. One girl on a Mode B2 office work course contrasted the equal treatment in college with what she saw as less advantageous work experience placements for the girls. She had gone with a boy trainee to the same company but reckoned he had received a much wider work experience than she had. A girl in the electronics industry who had ambitions of becoming an electronics engineer was channelled into operating computers while the boys were studying electronics, and she had been offered a non-technical job in the computer department. A girl on a bricklaying course was told she must not go up the scaffolding. A girl in motor mechanics had been put in the parts department where she was learning to sort the parts and supply them to customers, and she hopes to be employed in this department as she saw no prospect of being accepted in the workshop. A girl in a department with only male staff had to overcome their 'hesitation' in treating her equally as far as the heavier jobs were concerned. An apprentice joiner complained that she was being kept in the joiners' shop instead of going out on jobs and wondered whether this was because management could not cope with providing the 'special facilities' (i.e. toilets) on site. A girl doing a catering course said that the boys were given more instruction. Another girl said that the boys on her B1 scheme got a choice while the girls were 'pushed into' traditional areas. On the induction course at the building site she had been told not to join in.

'Traditional women's work'

Traditional women's work is concentrated in only *three* of the nine *industrial categories*.

These are:

Community, social and personal services	(41% of all gainfully employed women)	
Wholesale & retail trade & hotels and restaurants	(21% of all gainfully employed women)	Total = 87%
Manufacturing	(25% of all gainfully employed women)	

The greatest disproportion between men and women is seen in:
  (a) the construction industry
  (b) transportation and communications industry.

There has been no significant change in industrial segregation over the past decade (1965–1975). If anything, women are becoming even more concentrated, particularly in the traditional female areas such as the services, retail trade and finance and insurance (where there is a substantial need for clerical occupations).

Segregation of occupations by sex is even more pronounced. Most women are concentrated in a small range of traditionally female occupations, in which they constitute almost the entire labour force. Typical female occupations are those of clerks, typists and secretaries, nurses and other health care workers, teachers and other child–care workers, social workers, cleaning and household service workers, sales clerks, and in the manufacturing field, garment and textile workers.

Glossary

Mode B2 schemes Mode B schemes are community-based YTS schemes in which trainees are placed with training workshops, local authorities or voluntary organisations, often gaining work experience in addition. B2 schemes specifically place the trainee in a college of further education.

Mode B1 schemes training in establishments other than further education. Mode A schemes are employer based.

Questions

1 What is meant by 'sexual harassment' and in what circumstances were girls on YTS schemes most likely to encounter it?

2 Why do you think some girls found more discrimination among boys of their own age at college than among men in their work placement?

3 Consider the argument that because of the discrimination girls experience in non-traditional occupations (like that described by the girl who left the engineering course) training schemes should be set up that are 'girls only' in these areas.

4 Bearing in mind that the authors of this passage are best described as 'liberal feminists' (see the extract by Bouchier), suggest the reasons they would put forward to explain the facts about 'traditional women's work'. Are the reasons *you* would give different for these?

5 Having established reasons for the distinctive nature of women's occupations, suggest policies which would improve the situation.

I. Bruegel

Women as a Reserve Army of Labour: a Note on Recent British Experience, in E. Whitelegg *et al.* (eds), *The Changing Experience of Women*, 1982, pp. 114–15

Over the last few years there have been two conflicting processes at work affecting women's employment. On the one hand, within any given industry or job, women, particularly part-time women workers, have suffered from greater rates of job loss than men. This has come about partly, no doubt, through explicit or barely-veiled discriminatory policies, but more important, probably, has been the exploitation of the weaknesses of married women's labour market position, weaknesses which derive in one way or another from a primary definition of women as housewives and mothers. On the other hand, the continued expansion of parts of the service sector on the basis of the availability of cheap female labour has mitigated the effects of the crisis on women's employment opportunities. It is important to recognise that the protection that women's jobs have had through the expansion of the service sector is a protection based on the cheapness of female labour. The low pay offered to women in the expanding service sectors virtually precludes any wholesale takeover by men, even when unemployment is high. Given

certain technological constraints which have until now made the service sectors highly labour intensive, the service sector did require a reserve 'army' of cheap labour to draw on to expand its output. As a result, in virtually all capitalist countries the expansion of service industry went hand in hand with the expansion of women's paid employment in the post-war years. Since services were less vulnerable to recession than other sectors of employment, they have afforded women a certain protection from unemployment in times of recession. However, with the development of microprocessors this 'protection' is likely to wear thin, since the advantages women offer to capital— cheap and relatively docile labour—become less and less relevant.

Moreover, the type of work women do—low level, repetitive and boring—is probably more susceptible to rationalisation, whether it is manufacturing or service work, than ever before. In Germany, where rationalisation of office work has gone further than in Britain, service work no longer protects women's employment as a whole from the impact of crisis, the degree of protection in the United States is also significantly less than in Britain. Thus the analysis in this note must be seen in its historical perspective.

While it is probably true for all periods that the marginal position of married women in the labour force has made them, individual for individual, more vulnerable to redundancy than male workers, the particular form of capitalist expansion and restructuring over the last thirty years — the expansion of labour-intensive public and private services and administrative occupations — greatly extended the employment opportunities of women. The result was that women's employment continued to expand even when men's jobs were being cut back fast.

The long-term shift towards women in the work-force cushioned women's employment against the shorter-term (cyclical) recessions. The signs are that this particular phase of capital restructuring may be over; that one of the bases of the long-term expansion of female employment — the cheapness of female employment — may be declining in relative significance, given new technological developments. Hence many groups of women who have traditionally regarded their jobs as secure will find themselves threatened with rationalisation on a scale comparable to the wholesale elimination of jobs in the traditional male strongholds — mining, railways, docks. The implications of this analysis are not that the solution lies in attempting to equalize the incidence of increasing unemployment between men and women. Rather, it is that the fight for jobs will increasingly be a fight for women's jobs. Thus if the labour movement is to be able effectively to resist unemployment, now more than ever before it urgently needs to devise more effective strategies of defending women's jobs and the right of women to work.

Glossary

Restructuring (here) meaning changes in the nature of the industrial structure — away from heavy industry and towards the service sector of the economy.

Cyclical recessions Marxist economic theory holds that capitalist economies periodically go through periods where consumption declines and production of goods has to be cut back. This is due to the contradiction between the capitalist's search for profit, achieved partly by keeping wages low, and the need to sell the goods produced. With low wages, workers cannot afford to buy the goods, they remain unsold for lack of a market and a recession begins.

Questions

1 Why does Bruegel describe women as a 'reserve army of labour'
2 What does the future hold for women in employment, according to Bruegel, and what is the basis for this argument?
3 What evidence would you need to collect in order to support the argument that Bruegel is putting forward here?
4 What criticisms could be made of this Marxist–feminist approach to women's position in the economy?

Questions on Parsons and Bales, The Fawcett Society and Bruegel extracts

The authors of all three passages in this section agree that there are persistent inequalities by sex in the occupational structure of advanced industrial societies such as Britain and America. Complete the following table which refers to their views on this issue:

	Parsons and Bales	The Fawcett Society	Bruegel
Cause of inequality			
Is inequality a good or a bad thing? Why?			
What is the best strategy to put the situation right (if a strategy is needed)?			

I. Reid and E. Wormald
Sex Differences in Britain, 1982, pp. 88–91

Attainment in older children

By the time pupils sit their first public examinations, the specific subject specialisation hinted at in the primary school has become firmly established. Table 5.1 shows the attainment by subject of girls and boys at higher-grade Certificate of Secondary Education and General Certificate of O-level (that is, CSE grade 1 and GCE grades A, B and C), during the academic year 1977–8. More girls than boys were successful in English (42 compared with 32 per cent). In mathematics the position was reversed: girls 21 and boys 29 per cent. Boys were likely to gain more passes in the sciences and girls in the arts.

In examinations at 16, girls did well overall; table 5.2 indicates that they were more likely to gain CSE and GCE O-level passes. Fewer girls (only 12 per cent) than boys (14 per cent) attempted no public examination at this level, or attempted but did not pass. At this stage, by these measures girls are rather more successful than boys, though the inter-

Table 5.1
Percentage of school leavers obtaining higher-grade* GCE O-level or CSE, by sex and subject, England and Wales, 1977–1978

	Girls	Boys	All
English	42	32	37
French	17	11	14
Music/drama/visual arts	15	10	13
Mathematics	21	29	25
Physics	6	18	12
Chemistry	6	13	10
Biology	18	12	15
Any subject	54	49	51

*Grades A—C in GCE and grade 1 in CSE
(Derived from table iii, *Statistics of Education 1978*, 1981, vol. 2)

ests of both sexes lie within specific subject ranges. This pattern represents what might be expected as a development of the situation found in primary school, where girls generally showed a more positive attitude than boys towards school and a tendency towards competence in language, though limited skill in mathematics.

There is little difference in the proportion of the sexes staying on at school for either one year (girls 28 per cent, boys 27 per cent) or two years (girls 18 per cent, boys 19 per cent) beyond the minimum school-leaving age (*Social Trends No. 11*, 1981), but it is at A-level that boys begin to outperform girls. Although boys are only marginally more likely to enter for A-levels (girls 17 per cent, boys 18 per cent)—as table 5.2 shows—and, although an approximately equivalent percentage of boys and girls obtain one or two A-level passes, a higher overall percentage of boys gain A-levels because

Table 5.2

Percentage of school leavers with qualifications, by sex, England and Wales, 1977–1978

	Girls	Boys	All
A-level GCE passes			
3 or more subjects	7	10	9
2 subjects	4	4	4
1 subject	3	3	3
Any subject	14	17	16
Higher-grade* GCE O-level or CSE passes			
5 or more subjects	10	8	9
1—4 subjects	29	24	27
Any subject	39	32	36
Lower-grade† GCE O-level or CSE passes	33	36	34
School leavers sitting			
CSE examinations	74	71	73
GCE O-level examinations	57	54	55
GCE A-level examinations	17	18	18
No examinations	12	14	13
Examinations but with no passes	1	1	1

*Grades A–C in GCE and grade 1 in CSE
†All grades other than those specified as higher*
(Derived from table D, *Statistics of Education 1978*, 1981, vol. 2)

Table 5.3

The destinations of school leavers in England and Wales, 1977–1978, by sex (percentages)

	Girls	Boys	All
Degree courses	5.7	8.8	7.3
Teacher-training courses	0.9	0.2	0.5
GCE A- and O-level courses	4.1	3.4	3.7
Secretarial courses	5.2	*	2.5
Nursing courses	1.4	*	0.7
Other courses†	8.4	5.4	6.9
Employment	65.3	73.8	69.7
Unknown	9.0	8.4	8.7

*Extremely small numbers, around 100
†Includes catering courses, which girls are twice as likely to enter as boys
(Derived from table ii, *Statistics of Education 1978*, 1981, vol. 2)

they are more successful at the three-or-more pass level. There is, then, a reversal of the situation at the O-level stage, when more girls gained passes. At A-level too differences in subject choice by the sexes are very pronounced. On the basis of their O-level qualifications, it might be expected that a higher proportion of girls than boys would enter for A-level examinations. However, they participate less—a tendency also evident at entry into higher education. Recently, qualified women's participation in higher education has decreased more rapidly than that of men; 'out of those qualified to enter higher education, currently around one in nine men and one in four women ... do not take up that option' (Roweth, 1981).

Just over 3 per cent more men than women enter degree courses at universities, polytechnics or other establishments (table 5.3). In universities, the percentage of female undergraduates has increased over the past decade (from 32 to 37 per cent) but still represents only just over a third of the total undergraduate population. ... The percentage of women reading science degrees (which has always been lower than that of men) shows a slight decrease of 2 per cent, while male decrease is 4 per cent, suggesting a reaction to social or cultural pressures or influences of a general nature, probably unrelated to the sex of the student. ... Once at university, however, women progress very similarly to men, though they gain proportionately fewer first-class honours degrees.

[1]See Bibliography

Questions

1 At what point in their school careers do girls underachieve in terms of qualifications obtained relative to boys?

2 Suggest some reasons for this.

Questions on all the extracts

Complete the following table, considering the final extract in relation to the others:

	Liberal feminism (The Fawcett Society)	*Socialist feminism* (Bruegel)	*Radical feminism*	*Functionalism* (Parsons)
Reason for educational inequality				
Best strategy in order to correct matters				
General aim of the proposed reforms				

Bibliography

Source of extracts

D. Bouchier, *The Feminist Challenge*, Macmillan, London, 1983

S. L. Bartky, 'Toward a Phenomenology of Feminist Consciousness', in M. Vetterling–Braggin *et al.* (eds), *Feminism and Philosophy*, Littlefield, Adams and Co., Totowa, New Jersey, 1977

T. Parsons from T. Parsons and R. F. Bales, *Family, Socialisation and Interaction Process*, Routledge & Kegan Paul, London, 1956, in M. Anderson (ed.) *Sociology of the Family*, 2nd edition, Penguin, Harmondsworth, 1980

The Fawcett Society, *The Class of '84*, The Fawcett Society, London, 1985

I. Bruegel, *Women as a Reserve Army of Labour: a Note on Recent British Experience*, in E. Whitelegg *et al.* (eds), *The Changing Experience of Women*, Martin Robertson, Oxford, in association with the Open University, Milton Keynes, 1982

I. Reid and E. Wormald, *Sex Differences in Britain*, Grant McIntyre, London, 1982

Reference in the Introduction

F. Engels, *The Origin of the Family, Private Property and the State*, Lawrence and Wishart, London, 1972

Reference in Reid and Wormald extract

B. Roweth, 'Enigma APR = QLR × QPR', *The Guardian*, 9 January 1981

Further reading

J. Archer and B. Lloyd, *Sex and Gender*, Penguin, Harmondsworth, 1982

D. L. Barker and S. Allen (eds), *Sexual Divisions in Society*, Tavistock, London, 1976

A. Coote and B. Campbell, *Sweet Freedom; the Struggle for Women's Liberation*, Picador, London, 1982

M. Daly, *Gyn/Ecology*, Women's Press, London, 1978

L. Dominelli and E. McLeod, *Feminism and Welfare*, Macmillan, London, 1985

S. Firestone, *The Dialectic of Sex*, Paladin, St Albans, 1970

F. Heidensohn, *Women and Crime*, Macmillan, London, 1985

P. Hunt, *Gender and Class Consciousness*, Macmillan, London, 1980

A. Oakley, *Sex Gender and Society*, Temple Smith, London, 1982

A. Pollert, *Girls, Wives, Factory Lives*, Macmillan, London, 1981

S. Rowbotham, *Hidden From History*, Pluto Press, London, 1974

J. Siltanen and M. Stanworth (eds), *Women and the Public Sphere*, Hutchinson, London, 1984

B. and C. Smart (eds), *Women, Sexuality and Social Control*, Routledge & Kegan Paul, London, 1978

D. Spender, *Women of Ideas*, Routledge & Kegan Paul, London, 1982

⚎ Methodological Techniques

The methods available to the sociologist can be placed under the following categories: asking questions, conducting experiments, observing behaviour and using official statistics and other secondary data. Within each of these categories there is a wide variety of alternative techniques. The choice between them is conditioned, among other things, by the nature of the subject of study and the perspective of the sociologist conducting it.

Within the category 'asking questions' might be included such quantitative techniques as structured interviews and closed-ended questionnaires. These are preferred by sociologists of a 'scientific' inclination (i.e. positivists) and are often used where large samples are required as they can be administered in large numbers, being quick and cheap, and the results they provide are easily collated. On the other hand the more phenomenologically-inclined sociologist would prefer to conduct unstructured interviews and administer open-ended questionnaires in order to get a deeper understanding of the views and attitudes of respondents. Such techniques usually mean it is necessary to forgo quantitative data and large sample sizes.

The category of 'experiments' includes controlled and uncontrolled experiments. The former seek to emulate natural scientific techniques by keeping variables constant and comparing an experimental group with a control group in order to measure the effect of changes introduced in the former. This is the type preferred by positivists in circumstances where this approach is possible. Uncontrolled experiments do not seek to be so precise in measuring cause and effect, they are conducted in order to throw up results which may be interesting or illuminating rather than 'proving' anything. These are preferred by phenomenologists who are seeking insights into the behaviour of individuals and groups.

Under the heading of 'observation' are included non-participant observation, in which the researcher is apart (even hidden) from the subjects he/she is observing, and participant observation in which the researcher becomes involved in the activities of the subjects he/she is studying. The latter technique is believed to provide a deeper understanding of the motives and meanings of the subjects of the study, although it is criticised for allowing too much subjectivity into the study. In some circumstances, of course, participant observation is not possible or advisable, for example where the study concerns only females when the researcher is male, or where participation would involve the researcher in dangerous or illegal activity.

Finally the category of 'official records' and other secondary data includes the use of quantified official statistics (preferred by positivists) or, for the phenomenologist concerned more with understanding attitudes and gaining insights into behaviour, studying diaries, letters, personal accounts of events and any other non–quantified source.

Each of the four extracts in the chapter concerns one of these four categories: questioning, experiments, observation and the use of secondary data. The first selection, from the Glasgow University Media Group's *War and Peace News*, discusses opinion polling. This is a technique which is used predominantly by professional organisations rather than sociologists but which utilises the sociological technique of structured interviews. In this piece the Media Group discuss the problems associated both with structured interviews in general and opinion polls in particular. They did not use this method themselves in their studies of news production. Instead their technique is the analysis of video tape–recorded news broadcasts. This involves the quantitative measurement of the content of the broadcasts in order to establish the presence of bias in news output. Their interest in opinion polling relates to the way in which the results of the polls themselves become part of the 'reality' which they are intended to measure and define.

The second extract provides an example of a controlled experiment in sociology. It was conducted by R. Rosenthal and L. Jacobson in 'Oak School' in the USA. The hypothesis being put to the test was that teachers' labelling of some pupils as being potentially gifted academically could act to create an increase in academic performance in those pupils. This concept is known as the self–fulfilling prophecy. The extract gives details of how a control and experimental group were selected, how the experiment was conducted and what its results were. Rosenthal and Jacobson's is one of the few examples of a systematic attempt to emulate the laboratory method of natural science to test a sociological hypothesis. How far it succeeded is open to discussion and the questions following the extract invite the student to consider the issues involved.

The third extract is from Ken Pryce's *Endless Pressure*, a study of the West Indian community of St Paul's in Bristol. Here he describes his participant observation methodology and the reasons why he preferred it as the main method of research. While he did supplement this technique with methods of a more quantitative nature, which he also describes in this extract, these are subsidiary to participant observation. He defends his choice of the qualitative, even impressionistic, participant observation approach in some detail.

In the extract from *Suicide*, Durkheim explains why he chose to study such an apparently personal and individual act as suicide through the use of quantitative official statistics. Clearly these do not give any insight into the motives of the particular people concerned, but for Durkheim this is unnecessary, for reasons he makes clear. Not included here is an account of the way in which he used suicide statistics in the study, so a brief summary would be useful. His method is the search for concomitant variations, which refers to the identification of a correlation between two factors, A and B. In this case A is the suicide rate and B is the hypothesised 'cause' of suicide. First he examines the hypothesis that suicide may be explained by reference to the physical or psychological make up of individuals or by the nature of their physical environment. Each of these is taken in turn as 'factor B'. He finds no correlation here. Then he goes on to look for correlations between the suicide rate in different areas and a number of other factors: alcoholism, racial type, height, age, climate and so on. Again, he finds no correlation. However he *can* demonstrate positive correlations between the number of Protestants in a region and the suicide rate there. Conversely the more Catholics there are the lower the suicide rate. Similarly there are positive correlations between a high suicide rate and being unmarried and living in urban areas. The common factor linking Protestants, unmarried people and those in cities is their lack of social integration. Protestantism is a faith which leaves the individual alone before God; there is little in the way of support or mediation by the Church through rituals, confession and mass. Protestants are said to have weaker bonds between them than those between Catholics. Similarly unmarried people and city dwellers have few social bonds, argues Durkheim. Durkheim's overall conclusion is that, 'Suicide varies inversely with the degree of integration of the social groups of which the individual forms a part.'

This 'law' has been established by Durkheim without reference to the individual motivations of people who have committed suicide. It has been established purely through the logical use of quantitative data.

Glasgow University Media Group
War and Peace News, 1985, pp. 305–06, 308

The relationship between public opinion, public opinion polls and the reporting of polls is not straightforward. The issues we point to here are, by and large, well known to most social scientists but we think they are worth noting because of the role which opinion polls have come to play in our society.

The information conveyed by opinion polls is usually the product either of face–to–face or telephone interviewing. The kind of knowledge this gives us can be problematical. The interviewer–interviewee encounter is itself a social relationship and interviewers are trained to try to establish a 'successful' relationship so that they can sustain communication and accomplish the basic objectives of the interview. From an examination of the literature on interviewing, Cicourel concluded:

'The nature of responses generally depends on the trust developed early in the relationship, status differences, differential perception and interpretation placed on questions and responses, the control exercised by the interviewer, and so forth. The validity of the schedule

becomes a variable condition within and between interviews.'
Aaron V. Cicourel, *Method and Measurement in Sociology*, Free Press, 1964, p. 99

Cicourel's statement embraces more than problems about the wording of questions, but even that should give pause for reflection. Forty years ago, Hadley Cantril delineated eleven types of 'poor' questions. These referred to questions too vague to permit precise answers; obscure in meaning; misunderstood because they contain technical or unfamiliar words; not adequately circumscribed, not providing exhaustive alternatives; containing too many possibilities of choice; carrying unforeseen implications; giving only surface references; containing stereotypes; likely to elicit stereotyped answers; and referring to matters which mean nothing to some of the sample (Hadley Cantril *et al., Changing Public Opinion*, Princeton University Press, 1944). Cantril's list has its own built–in problems, but for the most part we have to take on trust that these criteria are met by opinion pollsters.

The interview itself is an unusual social situation. Catherine Marsh has pointed out that the notion of an opinion is a very individualistic one:

'... any of the usual activities undertaken in arriving at a view on an issue, such as discussing it with others, are forbidden in the interview situation, as the interviewer is supposed to elicit those views that the respondent holds as an individual. Fundamental to this approach is the idea that everybody holds an opinion about everything. Further, it is held that these opinions are fixed and latent, with the potential to cause actions and verbal behaviour; responses to questionnaire items can therefore be treated as indicators of underlying attitudes. But this is a perversion of the way in which people have ideas, interact with one another and change their views.'

Catherine Marsh, 'Opinion polls—social science or political manoeuvre?', in John Irvine, Ian Miles and Jeff Evans (eds), *Demystifying Social Statistics*.

The opinion pollsters can reasonably remind us that they have a good record on predicting General Elections. We should remember, however, that we are relating a clearly understood intention—that of voting or not for a particular party—which refers to a specific event in the near future and which involves the respondent in a direct way. There is a close relationship between attitudes and behaviour. Yet this cannot be treated as a paradigm case for all attitude studies—where the relationship between feelings, beliefs, intentions and behaviour may be much more problematical and uncertain. In such cases it is not clear what the variously tabulated results signify. In practice we are offered interpretations as to the significance of poll findings: these are speculative inferences rather than logical deductions based on validated axioms.

An instructive example of what happens when pollsters comment on their own work is provided by Robert Worcester and Simon Jenkins's article in *Public Opinion*, June/July 1982, 'Britain rallies round the Prime Minister'. This was a commentary on a series of surveys carried out by MORI for various clients—the *Daily Star*, *Sunday Times*, *Economist* and BBC's *Panorama*—in relation to the Falklands conflict. These were a mixture of telephone and face-to-face interviews. No distinction is made in the discussion of the findings. The samples were quota not random samples and included re-interviewing from a panel in some instances. Again there is no discussion of the methodological significance of this or any caveats made. As Marsh points out:

'Quota samples have the advantage of speed, but the error margins around the results are known to be a lot wider than with random sampling designs. It is good practice to report the error margins with all results, but this is done infrequently ...' p. 276 (Marsh, op. cit.)

The opinion poll is a social invention which has its roots in market research and election studies. It has typically operated in the context of doing work for client organisations such as political parties, businesses, the press and broadcasting. When the polls are made public the reporting-back process through the media can be subject to various filters. From the original findings (with all their methodological problems that are usually left unremarked) more selection, simplification, compression and re-emphasis can take place. In this way we learn what 'the public', in which we are included, are supposed to think about this or that. It thereby plays a part in the social process, which it purports to describe and define; it becomes part of the social milieu within which issues are discussed and evaluated.

Glossary   Problematical giving rise to a problem or problems.

Schedule (here) referring to interviewing schedule, i.e. the list of questions to be asked.

Delineated outlined.

Elicit encourage a response.

Paradigm case (here) meaning a perfect example or pattern which is followed elsewhere.

Speculative inferences guesses (speculations) based on conclusions suggested by the evidence (inferences).

Logical deductions rational conclusions arrived at by examining firm evidence.

Validated axioms ideas considered self–evident or obvious (axioms)
which have been proven to be true (validated).

MORI the name of a commercial opinion polling organisation.

Quota sample a method of choosing a sample to interview based
upon the process of identifying the type of person who should be
questioned and then asking interviewers to go out and find those
sorts of people. Statisticians consider quota sampling to be
unreliable because there is an element of choice on the part of the
interviewer. This can affect the reliability of the results to a
considerable degree, increasing the margin of error.

Random sample a method of choosing a sample to be interviewed
which is free of error resulting from selectivity by researcher or
interviewer. Names or addresses are simply chosen at random from
a list of the total population to be studied.

Panel a group of people who are asked questions at regular intervals
to establish changes in their attitudes.

Caveats provisos or qualification of previous statements.

Error margins the degree to which the results of a survey are in error.
They are expressed in terms of plus or minus a certain figure,
e.g. + or − 5%, to indicate that results are accurate to within those
limits.

Questions

1 Give an example of one question to illustrate each of Hadley
Cantril's eleven types of 'poor' questions. Provide a corrected
version in each case.

2 Put the first quote from C. Marsh into your own words.

3 In some countries it is illegal to publish results of opinion polls
shortly before a general election. Why is this and do you consider
the introduction of such a law in the United Kingdom would be an
advisable step?

4 Outline two topics which would be suitable for research using
structured questionnaires and two which would not be suitable. In
each case explain why you consider this method suitable or
unsuitable.

R. Rosenthal and L. Jacobson

Pygmalion in the Classroom, 1968, pp. 174–7, 180

Oak School is a public elementary school in a lower–class community of a medium–size city. The school has a minority group of Mexican children who comprise about one–sixth of the school's population. Every year about 200 of its 650 children leave Oak School, and every year about 200 new children are enrolled.

Oak School follows an ability–tracking plan whereby each of the six grades is divided into one fast, one medium, and one slow classroom. Reading ability is the primary basis for assignment to track.

The Mexican children are heavily over-represented in the slow track.

On theoretical grounds it would have been desirable to learn whether teachers' favourable or unfavourable expectations could result in a corresponding increase or decrease in pupils' intellectual competence. On ethical grounds, however, it was decided to test only the proposition that favourable expectations by teachers could lead to an increase in intellectual competence.

All of the children of Oak School were pre-tested with a standard nonverbal test of intelligence. This test was represented to the teachers as one that would predict intellectual 'blooming' or 'spurting'. The IQ test employed yielded three IQ scores: total IQ, verbal IQ, and reasoning IQ. The 'verbal' items required the child to match pictured items with verbal descriptions given by the teacher. The reasoning items required the child to indicate which of five designs differed from the remaining four. Total IQ was based on the sum of verbal and reasoning items.

At the very beginning of the school year following the schoolwide pretesting, each of the eighteen teachers of grades one through six was given the names of those children in her classroom who, in the academic year ahead, would show dramatic intellectual growth. These predictions were allegedly made on the basis of these special children's scores on the test of academic blooming. About 20 per cent of Oak School's children were alleged to be potential spurters. For each classroom the names of the special children had actually been chosen by means of a table of random numbers. The difference between the special children and the ordinary children, then, was only in the mind of the teacher.

All the children of Oak School were retested with the same IQ test after one semester, after a full academic year, and after two full academic years. For the first two retests, children were in the classroom of the teacher who had been given favourable expectations for the intellectual growth of some of her pupils. For the final retesting all children had been promoted to the classes of teachers who had not been given any special expectations for the intellectual growth of any of the children. That follow-up testing had been included so that we could learn whether any expectancy advantages that might be found would be dependent on a continuing contact with the teacher who held the especially favourable expectation.

For the children of the experimental group and for the children of the control group, gains in IQ from pretest to retest were computed. Expectancy advantage was defined by the degree to which IQ gains by the 'special' children exceeded gains by the control-group children. After the first year of the experiment a significant expectancy advantage was found, and it was especially great among children of the first and second grades. The advantage of having been expected to bloom was evident for these younger children in total IQ, verbal IQ, and reasoning IQ. The control-group children of these grades gained well in IQ, 19 per cent of them gaining twenty or more total IQ points. The 'special' children, however, showed 47 per cent of their number gaining twenty or more total IQ points.

During the subsequent follow-up year the younger children of the first two years lost their expectancy advantage. The children of the upper grades, however, showed an increasing expectancy advantage during the follow-up year. The younger children who seemed easier to influence may have required more continued contact with their influencer in order to maintain their behaviour change. The older children, who were harder to influence initially, may have been better able to maintain their behaviour change autonomously once it had occurred.

Differences between boys and girls in the extent to which they were helped by favourable expectations were not dramatic when gains in total IQ were considered. After one year, and after two years as well, boys who were expected to bloom intellectually bloomed more in verbal IQ; girls who were expected to bloom intellectually bloomed more in reasoning IQ. Favourable teacher expectations seemed to help each sex more in that sphere of intellectual functioning in which they had excelled on the pretest. At Oak School boys normally show the higher verbal IQ while girls show the higher reasoning IQ.

It will be recalled that Oak School was organised into a fast, a medium, and a slow track system. We had thought that favourable expectations on the part of teachers would be of greatest benefit to the children of the slow track. That was not the case. After one year, it was the children of the medium track who showed the greatest expectancy advantage, though children of the other tracks were close behind. After two years, however, the children of the medium track very clearly showed the greatest benefits from having had favourable expectations held of their intellectual performance. It seems surprising that it should be the more average child of a lower-class school who stands to benefit more from his teacher's improved expectation.

After the first year of the experiment and also after the second year, the Mexican children showed greater expectancy advantages than did the non-Mexican children, though the difference was not significant statistically. One interesting minority-group effect did reach significance, however, even with just a small sample size. For each of the Mexican children, magnitude of expectancy advantage was computed by subtracting from his or her gain in IQ from pretest to retest, the IQ gain made by the children of the control group in his or her classroom. These magnitudes of expectancy advantage were then correlated with the 'Mexican–ness' of the children's faces. After one year, and after two years, those boys who looked more Mexican benefited more from their teachers' positive prophecies. Teachers' pre–experimental expectancies for these boys' intellectual performance were probably lowest of all. Their turning up on a list of probable bloomers must have surprised their teachers. Interest may have followed surprise and, in some way, increased watching for signs of increased brightness may have led to increased brightness . . .

On the basis of other experiments on interpersonal self-fulfilling prophecies, we can only speculate as to how teachers brought about intellectual competence simply by expecting it. Teachers may have treated their children in a more pleasant, friendly, and encouraging fashion when they expected greater intellectual gains of them. Such behaviour has been shown to improve intellectual performance, probably by its favourable effect on pupil motivation.

Teachers probably watched their special children more closely, and this greater attentiveness may have led to more rapid reinforcement of correct responses with a consequent increase in pupils' learning. Teachers may also have become more reflective in their evaluation of the special children's intellectual performance. Such an increase in teachers' reflectiveness may have led to an increase in their special pupils' reflectiveness, and such a change in cognitive style would be helpful to the performance of the nonverbal skills required by the IQ test employed.

To summarise our speculations, we may say that by what she said, by how and when she said it, by her facial expressions, postures, and perhaps by her touch, the teacher may have communicated to the children of the experimental group that she expected improved intellectual performance. Such communications together with possible changes in teaching techniques may have helped the child learn by changing his self concept, his expectations of his own behaviour, and his motivation, as well as his cognitive style and skills.

Glossary

IQ intelligence quotient; a numerical measure of intelligence established by testing. The average IQ is 100.

Semester the American equivalent of our school term.

Experimental group the group which had been the subject of one introduced change in order to assess its effect (in this case the suggestion to the teacher that they would spurt or bloom academically in the near future).

Control group a group used to compare with the experimental group, hopefully identical with it in all but one respect—the change introduced by the researchers into the experimental group. Comparison allows the effect of this change to be measured.

Expectancy advantages advantages gained from the teacher's expectation of an improvement in academic attainment.

Autonomously with independence or freedom.

Speculations theorising about a subject.

Cognitive style pattern of thinking.

Questions

1 What was the point of lying to the teachers about the nature of the test which was given to the children at the beginning of the study?

2 What happened to the intellectual performance of the younger members of the experimental group and why?

3 How do Rosenthal and Jacobson explain their findings? Can you see any problems with this explanation or the way they arrived at it?

4 Problems with this type of 'laboratory study' in sociology could be summarised under the following headings. Show how these problems might have affected the Oak School study in particular and add any other criticisms you may have of it or problems that you can identify.
(a) ethical problems (i.e. the manipulation of people by researchers).
(b) problems connected with trying to identify the causes or results of the experiment.
(c) problems with trying to ensure that the experimental group and control group are identical in all respects except the one change introduced into the experimental group by researchers.
(d) problems connected with showing that the results are not chance or 'one–off' results.
(e) problems connected with the fact that the researchers have to be present to conduct the study and therefore might themselves influence its results, the so–called 'Hawthorne effect'.

5 'Despite its obvious advantages, the laboratory method is hardly ever used in sociology'. Explain and discuss.

K. Pryce
Endless Pressure, 1979, pp. 279, 294–7

The main method adopted for the research on which this study is based was participant observation. Participant observation, because it deposits one inside the culture of the group studied and forces on one the role of involved actor and participant, affords the academic researcher a unique opportunity of getting the right leads and following through situations whereby he can replace superficial impressions with more accurate insights. By combining his outsider's perception with an insider's view of the way of life under consideration, the researcher can thus get behind the statistical shapes and patterns and explore at first hand the wide variety of adaptive responses he encounters, studying them from the value position of the people themselves, in their own terms and on their own ground. All the time he does this through prolonged, intensive direct exposure to actual life–conditions over a relatively long period of time. Not only can the findings of this intensive approach supplement and add significance to data gathered by more quantitative techniques, they can generate fruitful hypotheses which quantitative research can later refine and test . . .

Although participant observation was my main method of approach in this study, other data–gathering techniques were used to supplement and reinforce it. For instance, a very limited use was made of data published in books, of parliamentary papers and monographs, to orient the study historically and in particular to demonstrate that West Indians face a double problem of poverty and identity–confusion due to imperialism, and that their slave heritage was of paramount importance in determining the variations in their reactions to discrimination in Britain.

In addition, quite a lot of factual information was gleaned from back–dated copies of the *Bristol Evening Post* and offical documents published by the Bristol city corporation, which were useful in providing a demographic backdrop to the local situation. Articles published in the *Evening Post* also yielded valuable information on the Bristol omnibus dispute of 1963.

To fill in gaps in the data gathered through pure observation, as well as to augment the biographical details of some of my informants—especially teenyboppers—it was necessary also to pay several visits to the offices of local probation officers, who allowed me unrestricted access to their files.

I also used a tape–recorder to good effect. Formally and informally I interviewed a wide range of people. . . .

During the field–work one of my informants . . .

was an inmate of Horfield prison. . . . I listened to his case in court, and also visited him at Horfield . . . during his term of imprisonment.

Understanding of local problems was greatly increased by participation in many social and political organisations in the St Paul's area, as well as by sitting on official committees set up by liberal welfare agencies functioning on a community level. Several happy weekends were also spent at week–end camps with mixed groups of youngsters from the St Paul's area, and while studying the church I paid several visits to more than one white Pentecostalist church in the St Paul's district.

A word about note–taking. As stated already, a vast amount of the data used in the study was obtained through the use of a tape–recorder. However, for most of the documentary and descriptive material, including verbatim remarks and speeches made by people in different situations, I had to rely heavily on memory. My method was to write down these observations as soon as possible after hearing or observing them. The rule of thumb I constantly exercised was to record them while they were still fresh in my mind, generally the same day. It was my practice never to record anything, especially conversations, after three days. I believe most of the information I recorded in this way was fairly accurate, if not accurate word for word, accurate in tone, flavour and in the emotions expressed. In the technique of writing down conversations and descriptions of scenes afterwards, it is surprising how efficient one's memory can become with practice. . . .

In sum, this thesis can be regarded as an ethnography of the variable pattern of working–class responses that typify a black West Indian community reacting to its disadvantaged position in a white capitalist society, with some attempt to give a structural analysis and an interpretation based on the motives, emotions and understandings of the actors involved. . . .

A study such as this one has its drawbacks from the point of view of hard science. To name some: the selection of the hypotheses explored was guided by my own biases; I freely use quasi–statistical terms such as 'most', 'many', 'the majority of', when in fact the actual number of people on which these generalisations are based is a mere fraction compared with the total number[1] making up the community; and the evidence presented is plausible and illustrative rather than documentary or systematic.

A further problem arising out of the built-in limitations of the participant observation technique is that as a male researcher I had only limited access to the women in the West Indian community for research purposes. This is a problem that should be easily appreciated. Moreover, as in any working–class community there is a tendency for males and females in all age groups to associate in single–sex peer groups. . . .

To correct the masculine bias of the research, then, what is needed is a female researcher investigating issues that involve the West Indian female population *per se*.

To these deficiencies in the work I readily admit. Yet I would still stand firmly behind the method and the main findings. Limitations they are, but such limitations are unavoidable in any qualitative study using the participant observation method. Participant observation permits the researcher to understand the problems of a group in a way that no other method will.

As far as the validity of the findings is concerned, any misgivings should be allayed by the fact that the study in its present form is no more than a very general and exploratory analysis, providing a view of broad patterns of behaviour not hitherto touched on in race relations studies in Britain. What I think I have achieved is a preliminary study of low–level empirical generalisations which, because they are framed analytically in ideal–typical terms, can be subjected to verification or proof by more rigorous methods of analysis and which provide a foundation for more systematic theorising on race relations.

[1] See Bibliography

Glossary

Quantitative techniques methods which give results which are expressed in numerical terms; for example in closed–ended questionnaires where x% of respondents answer 'yes', y% answer 'no' and z% answer 'don't know'.

Hypotheses suggested reasons to explain some phenomenon.

Monograph essay on a single subject or class of subjects.

Identity–confusion not knowing who you are (e.g. a West Indian's background is a mixture of African slave, native of the West Indies and white).

Paramount supreme.

Demographic concerning population.

Verbatim literal record of what was said.

Ethnography a description of a culture or subculture.

Structural analysis an explanation which seeks to explain phenomena in terms of the surrounding environment; e.g. technology, class structure, housing characteristics, etc.

Quasi–statistical almost, but not quite, numerical.

Per se for itself, in itself.

Qualitative study one which gives results which are not numerical in form but are judgemental and subjective; for example, the description of a subculture resulting from a detailed participant observation study of it.

Low–level empirical generalisations general statements which have only local or limited applicability; e.g. only to one geographical area, social group or point in time.

Ideal–typical based on an ideal type; see glossary on page 59.

Verification proving that something is true.

Questions

1 Why did Pryce choose to use participant observation as his main research method and how does he view the role of 'more quantitative techniques'?

2 What problems might result from 'relying heavily on memory' other than the obvious one of forgetfulness?

3 Generally, what disadvantages are there to participant observation as a research method?

4 Which sociological perspective would you say Pryce subscribes to? What evidence from the passage made you come to this conclusion?

5 Imagine that you are a female researcher interested in correcting Pryce's self-confessed 'masculine bias' in the study of Bristol's West Indian community. Outline the research procedures that you would adopt and justify them.

E. Durkheim

Suicide: A Study in Sociology, 1979, pp. 47–8, 51–2

Since suicide is an individual action affecting the individual only, it must seemingly depend exclusively on individual factors, thus belonging to psychology alone. Is not the suicide's resolve usually explained by his temperament, character, antecedents and private history?

The degree and conditions under which suicides may be legitimately studied in this way need not now be considered, but that they may be viewed in an entirely different light is certain. If, instead of seeing in them only separate occurrences, unrelated and to be separately studied, the suicides committed in a given society during a given period of time are taken as a whole, it appears that this total is not simply a sum of independent units, a collective total, but is itself a new fact *sui generis*, with its own unity, individuality and consequently its own nature—a nature, furthermore, dominantly social. Indeed, provided too long a period is not considered, the statistics for one and the same society are almost invariable.

This is because the environmental circumstances attending the life of peoples remain relatively unchanged from year to year. To be sure, more considerable variations occasionally occur; but they are quite exceptional. They are also clearly always contemporaneous with some passing crisis affecting the social state. Thus, in 1848 there occurred an abrupt decline in all European states.

If a longer period of time is considered, more serious changes are observed. Then, however, they become chronic; they only prove that the structural characteristics of society have simultaneously suffered profound changes. It is interesting to note that they do not take place with the extreme slowness that quite a large number of observers has attributed to them, but are both abrupt and progressive. After a series of years, during which these figures have varied within very narrow limits, a rise suddenly appears which, after repeated vacillation is confirmed, grows and is at last fixed. This is because every breach of social equilibrium, though sudden in its appearance, takes time to produce all its consequences. Thus, the evolution of suicide is composed of undulating movements, distinct and successive, which occur spasmodically, develop for a time, and then stop only to begin again. . . .

At each moment of its history, therefore, each society has a definite aptitude for suicide. . . .

Not only is this rate constant for long periods, but its invariability is even greater than that of leading demographic data. General mortality, especially, varies much more often from year to year and the variations it undergoes are far greater. . . .

The suicide–rate is therefore a factual order, unified and definite, as is shown by both its permanence and its variability. For this permanence would be inexplicable if it were not the result of a group of distinct characteristics, solidary one with another, and simultaneously effective in spite of different attendant circumstances; and this variability proves the concrete and individual quality of these same characteristics, since they vary with the individual character of society itself. In short, these statistical data express the suicidal tendency with which each society is collectively afflicted. We need not state the actual nature of this tendency, whether it is a state *sui generis* of the collective mind, with its own reality, or represents merely a sum of individual states. Although the preceding considerations are hard to reconcile with the second hypothesis, we reserve this problem for treatment in the course of this work. Whatever one's opinion on this subject, such a tendency certainly exists under one heading or another. Each society is predisposed to contribute a definite quota of voluntary deaths. This predisposition may therefore be the subject of a special study belonging to sociology. This is the study we are going to undertake.

We do not accordingly intend to make as nearly complete an inventory as possible of all the conditions affecting the origin of individual suicides, but merely to examine those on which the definite fact that we have called the social suicide–rate depends. The two questions are obviously quite distinct, whatever relation may nevertheless exist between them. Certainly many of the individual conditions are not general enough to affect the relation between the total number of voluntary deaths and the population. They may perhaps cause this or that separate individual to kill himself, but not give society as a whole a greater or lesser tendency to suicide. As they do not depend on a certain state of social organisation, they have no social repercussions. Thus they concern the psychologist, not the sociologist. The latter studies the causes capable of affecting not separate individuals but the group. Therefore among the factors of suicide the only ones which concern him are those whose actions are felt by society as a whole. The suicide–rate is the product of these factors. This is why we must limit our attention to them.

Glossary   Antecedents things which came before.

Sui generis of its own kind, peculiar or unique.

Vacillation move from side to side, to change one's mind frequently.

Social equilibrium the stability of society.

Undulating moving up and down.

Spasmodically at intermittent intervals.

Demographic relating to population.

Mortality death; mortality rate = death rate, usually measured in
   number of deaths per 1,000 people in a given area in a given year.

Solidary being of a united, coherent nature.

Questions

1 According to Durkheim, why is the suicide rate relatively static in
   any one society from year to year?
2 Why is the study of suicide a suitable subject of study for the
   sociologist and what is the difference between a sociological and a
   psychological study of the subject in Durkheim's opinion?
3 What problems are associated with the use of statistics in the study
   of suicide?
4 What technique would *you* use in the study of suicide?

**Questions on
Rosenthal and
Jacobson, Pryce
and Durkheim
extracts**

1 Complete the following table; according to the views represented:

	Rosenthal and Jacobson	Pryce	Durkheim
Sociological research should try to . . .			
Main problems with this method are . . .			
Relationship of sociology and natural science is . . .			
Sociological perspective subscribed to is . . .			
Study could be improved by . . .			

2 Examine the relationship between a researcher's personal and
   theoretical biases and the method which she or he adopts in
   sociological research.
3 'Questions of practicality often guide a researcher's choice of
   method more than any other single consideration.' Explain and
   discuss this statement.

Bibliography

Source of extracts

Glasgow University Media Group, *War and Peace News*, Open
   University Press, Milton Keynes, 1985

R. Rosenthal and L. Jacobson, *Pygmalion in the Classroom*, Holt,
   Rinehart and Winston, New York, 1968

K. Pryce, *Endless Pressure*, Penguin, Harmondsworth, 1979

E. Durkheim, *Suicide: A Study in Sociology*, Routledge & Kegan Paul, London, 1979, first published in England 1952

Reference in the Introduction

C. Marsh, 'Opinion polls—social science or political manoeuvre?', in John Irvine, Ian Miles and Jeff Evans (eds), *Demystifying Social Statistics*, Pluto Press, 1981, p. 270.

Reference in Pryce extract

1 The West Indian population of Bristol was estimated at 8,000 in 1963. See John Morgan, 'Colour bar, Bristol fashion', *New Statesman*, 10 May 1963

Further reading

A. F. Chalmers, *What is This Thing Called Science?*, Open University Press, Milton Keynes, 1978

E. E. Cuff and G. C. F. Payne (eds), *Perspectives in Sociology*, Allen & Unwin, London, 1981

E. Durkheim, *The Rules of Sociological Method*, Collier Macmillan, Toronto, 1964

B. J. Franklin and H. W. Osborne (eds), *Research Methods*, Wadsworth Publishing, Belmont, 1971

A. Giddens, *New Rules of Sociological Method*, Hutchinson, London, 1976

P. Jones, *Theory and Method in Sociology*, Bell & Hyman, London, 1985

E. Kane, *Doing Your Own Research*, Marion Boyars, London, 1984

R. Keat and J. Urry, *Social Theory as Science*, Routledge & Kegan Paul, London, 1975

P. McNeill, *Research Methods*, Tavistock, London, 1985

◩ The Sociology of Development

Introduction The five extracts in this chapter are each designed to illustrate one perspective on the nature of social change; particularly the movement to industrialism and why this does, or in many cases does not, occur.

The first reading, from W. W. Rostow's *The Stages of Economic Growth*, illustrates a determinist and materialist viewpoint. It is determinist because Rostow believes societies evolve through a pre-determined series of stages, which he describes in this piece. His theory is materialist because, for Rostow, the economic (or 'material') base of society is its most important dimension. Changes in the economic structure of society necessitate parallel changes in other dimensions; for example in its culture, family structure, and so on. An instance of this is the abundance of consumer goods made available by high technology and mature industrialism in Rostow's 'age of high mass consumption' which gives rise to a democratic, stable and largely middle class form of society. Rostow's rosy vision of the future contrasts sharply with Marx's view of advanced capitalism, which will bring with it poverty, misery, unemployment and alienation. This contrast is made explicit by Rostow, who subtitles his book 'a non-communist manifesto'. Apart from this crucial difference, however, Marx and Rostow have much in common. Marx, too, is a determinist and materialist, although the extent of his determinism and materialism have been hotly debated by sociologists. Like Rostow he sees society as moving through five stages: primitive communism, ancient society, feudal society, capitalism and, finally, communism. This, too, is a largely pre-determined evolution but there is the possibility of taking U-turns or coming to a sudden halt, and changes such as this. The fundamental difference between each stage is, for Marx, the level of production technology which has been developed. His materialism is evident from the belief that the nature of the production technology (the 'means of production') gives rise to particular class structures (the 'relations of production') and other social characteristics.

The second extract, from Max Weber's *The Protestant Ethic and the Spirit of Capitalism* illustrates a very different perspective. Weber is answering Marx's materialist philosophy and trying to show how ideas, rather than just technology, can influence the course of social development. Weber does not see people as the puppets of greater economic forces which push society along evolutionary paths but believes that we are in charge of our own fates. In *The Protestant Ethic and the Spirit of Capitalism*, Weber shows how ideas, notably religious beliefs, can have an important influence on the direction society takes. He is, therefore, both an idealist—someone who believes in the power of ideas to shape the structure of society—and a voluntarist— believing social change is in the hands of men and women, not pre-determined in direction and shape. In this passage, Weber traces the way the 'Protestant Ethic' (hard work, abstinence from pleasure, and the avoidance of waste) gave rise to attitudes of rationality, dedication to one's occupation, and so on which were essential to the development and continued existence of capitalism. According to Weber, this 'Spirit of Capitalism', the stress on work for its own sake and a suspicion of pleasure, is absent in more relaxed, hedonistic cultures. It gave rise to the accumulation of wealth, because money was not squandered in the pursuit of pleasure. This wealth would be invested in industry (there being little else to do with it) which then created yet more capital. Among the workforce, the spread of the Spirit of Capitalism led to hard and efficient work and a dedication to the job, which also gave impetus to the accumulation of wealth for the capitalist.

Although a very early theory of development, Weber's approach is popular among sociologists of development and others today. The need for 'correct' attitudes, especially among entrepreneurs, is stressed by many writers. Walter Elkan in *Introduction to Development Economics* says, 'Development depends on having people who are enterprising'. David McLelland in *The Achieving Society* suggests that a certain level of ambitiousness is essential if a society is to develop. He calls this the need for achievement, in short, 'nAch'. This should be spread through-out the population but its presence is most crucial among entrepreneurs who can lead society into development. A recent study by M. Morishima called *Why Has Japan 'Succeeded'?* uses a similar perspective to explain the industrial success of Japan and the relative failure of China. The Japanese version of Confucianism, stressing obedience to one's superiors, was more appropriate to economic development than the Chinese version, which stressed obedience to one's own conscience.

The third extract, from W. E Moore's *Social Change*, gives a critical appraisal of theories like those of Rostow and Marx which suggest that there is a single cause of social change. He calls these 'monistic' theories of determinism, because they see social change as determined by one (mono) factor, rather than being multi-causal in nature. Moore also suggests that Weber's Protestant Ethic, or some equivalent of it, while useful in social development, is not essential. He is also critical of theories which suggest that the nature of industrialism imposes certain social and cultural characteristics on the industrialising society regardless of previous history and culture. The most well-known example of this type of theory is *Industrialism and Industrial Man* by C. Kerr *et al*. Kerr argues that the 'logic of industrialism' means that industrial society must always be large scale, state managed, urban, that it will allow social and geographical mobility and have a population who are highly skilled, educated and contented. The similarities between Kerr's and Rostow's approaches are clear. In this passage, though, Moore lists the sources of difference between industrialised nations. He also states what he considers to be the essential conditions for industrialisation. His own perspective is close to what has been called 'modernisation theory'. This largely rejects the materialist/idealist divide and argues that a variety of factors are necessary for modernisation to occur. The factors include an appropriate family structure (nuclear, for greater mobility and capacity to accumulate wealth), appropriate values and religion (along Protestant lines), a written language, a developed education system, and appropriate technology with sufficient capital to improve it. Given these pre-requisites the social and economic structure will be in a suitable position to move towards 'modernity'. Aid and development projects funded by the First World (the capitalist economies) will help the underdeveloped countries to acquire these features. Writers in the 'modernisation school' of the sociology of development include N. J. Smelser, S. N. Eisenstadt, E. E. Hagen and T. Parsons.

The approach adopted by writers in the modernisation school is totally rejected by the sociologists of development who are usually categorised as 'dependency theorists'. The fourth extract comes from a book by one of their number, A. Gorz's *Paths to Paradise*. Dependency theory sees the underdevelopment of the Third World as being a result of its dependent relationship with the First World. The wealth of the latter is gained at the expense of the poverty and starvation in the former, this argument runs. For example, multinational companies operating in Third World countries pay low wages to native employees, exploit domestic markets, make competition virtually impossible for domestic entrepreneurs and, to cap it all, expatriate the profits they make in this venture back to the developed world. The disruption caused in Third World economies by the interference of multinational companies means that instead of being simply 'not developed' they are actually a unique form of economic structure. In this extract, Gorz discusses how the agricultural infrastructure in poor countries is distorted in the interests of the rich ones. Third World populations are left without work and food while crops which are either inedible (rubber or jute, for example) or too expensive for Third World inhabitants are sold abroad for a profit. Other writers in the school of dependency theory are: Paul Baran, André Gunder Frank, and Theresa Hayter.

The final extract, from B. Warren's *Imperialism: the Pioneer of Capitalism*, gives an account of development and underdevelopment from a straightforwardly Marxist perspective. Marx's view of imperialism by capitalist countries was that it would generally have beneficial effects for the Third World. Factories would be built, railway tracks laid, ports constructed and so on. The infrastructural base for the future development of capitalism (and then communism) would thus be prepared, albeit unwittingly, by such imperialistic countries as Britain and Spain. While many, but by no means all, dependency theorists regard themselves as neo-Marxists, this is one area of Marx's thought with which they strongly disagree. For them imperialist penetration of India not only laid the basis for the exploitation of its wealth in the age of imperialism and colonialism but also prepared the ground for the more subtle forms of exploitation in the neo-colonial period (i.e. when formal independence had been granted but economic dependence remained). In this extract, however, Warren supports Marx's view and rejects the arguments of the dependency theorists. For him, as for Marx, imperialism is the 'pioneer' of capitalism in the underdeveloped world. Progress to communism, after capitalism has run its course, will be attained in the Third World through the development of the productive capacity of its countries and the growth of its working class as a revolutionary force.

> Whatever the new world being created in Latin America, Asia and Africa is to be, nothing can be gained from a refusal to recognise the existence of the developing capitalist societies there.

W. W. Rostow
The Stages of Economic Growth, 1971, pp. 4–10, 158–9

It is possible to identify all societies, in their economic dimensions, as lying within one of five categories: the traditional society, the preconditions for take–off, the drive to maturity, and the age of high mass–consumption.

The traditional society
... the central fact about the traditional society was that a ceiling existed on the level of attainable output per head. This ceiling resulted from the fact that the potentialities which flow from modern science and technology were either not available or not regularly and systematically applied. ...

Population—and, within limits, the level of life—rose and fell not only with the sequence of the harvests, but with the incidence of war and of plague. Varying degrees of manufacture developed; but, as in agriculture, the level of productivity was limited by the inaccessibility of modern science, its applications, and its frame of mind. ...

Family and clan connexions played a large role in social organisation. The value system of these societies was generally geared to what might be called a long–run fatalism; that is, the assumption that the range of possibilities open to one's grandchildren would be just about what it had been for one's grandparents. ...

Although central political rule—in one form or another—often existed in traditional societies, transcending the relatively self-sufficient regions, the centre of gravity of political power generally lay in the regions, in the hands of those who owned or controlled the land. ...

The <u>preconditions</u> for take–off
The preconditions for take–off were initially developed, in a clearly marked way, in Western Europe of the late seventeenth and early eighteenth centuries as the insights of modern science began to be translated into new production functions in both agriculture and industry, in a setting given dynamism by the lateral expansion of world markets and the international competition for them. ... Among the Western European states, Britain, favoured by geography, natural resources, trading possibilities, social and political structure, was the first to develop fully the preconditions for take–off. ...

The idea spreads not merely that economic progress is possible, but that economic progress is a necessary condition for some other purpose, judged to be good: be it national dignity, private profit, the general welfare, or a better life for the children. Education, for some at least, broadens and changes to suit the needs of modern economic activity. New types of enterprising men come forward—in the private economy, in government, or both—willing to mobilise savings and to take risks in pursuit of profit or modernisation. Banks and other institutions for mobilising capital appear. Investment increases, notably in transport, communications, and in raw materials in which other nations may have an economic interest. The scope of commerce, internal and external, widens. ...

The take–off
We come now to the great watershed in the life of modern societies: the third stage in this sequence, the take–off. The take–off is the interval when the old blocks and resistances to steady growth are finally overcome. The forces making for economic progress, which yielded limited bursts and enclaves of modern activity, expand and come to dominate the society. Growth becomes its normal condition. Compound interest becomes built, as it were, into its habits and institutional structure.

In Britain and the well-endowed parts of the world populated substantially from Britain (the

United States, Canada etc.) the proximate stimulus for take-off was mainly (but not wholly) technological. ...

During the take-off new industries expand rapidly, yielding profits a large proportion of which are reinvested in new plant; and these new industries, in turn, stimulate, through their rapidly expanding requirement for factory workers, the services to support them, and for other manufactured goods, a further expansion in urban areas and in other modern industrial plants. ...

New techniques spread in agriculture as well as industry, as agriculture is commercialised, and increasing numbers of farmers are prepared to accept the new methods and the deep changes they bring to ways of life. ...

The drive to maturity
After take-off there follows a long interval of sustained if fluctuating progress, as the now regularly growing economy drives to extend modern technology over the whole front of its economic activity. ...

The make-up of the economy changes unceasingly as technique improves, new industries accelerate, older industries level off. The economy finds its place in the international economy: goods formerly imported are produced at home; new important requirements develop, and new export commodities to match them. ...

Formally, we can define maturity as the stage in which an economy demonstrates the capacity to move beyond the original industries which powered its take-off and to absorb and to apply efficiently over a very wide range of its resources—if not the whole range—the most advanced fruits of (then) modern technology. ...

The age of high mass–consumption
As societies achieved maturity in the twentieth century two things happened: real income per head rose to a point where a large number of persons gained a command over consumption which transcended basic food, shelter, and clothing; and the structure of the working force changed in ways which increased not only the proportion of urban to total population, but also the proportion of the population working in offices or in skilled factory jobs—aware of and anxious to acquire the consumption fruits of a mature economy. ...

One failure of Marx's system began to be revealed before he died; and he did not know how to cope with it. Some believe that his inner recognition of this failure is responsible for the fact that *Das Kapital* is an unfinished book. The failure took the form of the rise in industrial real wages in Western Europe and the perfectly apparent fact that the British and Western European working classes were inclined to accept ameliorative improvements; accept the terms of democratic capitalism rather than concentrate their efforts on the ultimate bloody show–down, the seizure of property and its turn–over to a State which somehow, in Marx's view, the workers might then control. The First International which he formed and led disintegrated in the early 1870's, the union leaders turning their backs on Marx and seeking gradual reform within their own societies.

And so Marx—and Engels too—ended with a somewhat disabused view of the industrial worker on whom they counted so much to make their dialectic come true: the worker was content with a bit of fairly regular progress; a sense that things were getting better for himself and his children; a sense that, by and large, he was getting a fair share from the lay-out of society as a whole; a willingness to fight for what he wanted within the rules of political democracy, under a regime of private property ownership; a tendency to identify himself with his national society rather than with the abstract world of allegedly down-trodden industrial workers everywhere; a willingness, despite conflict and inequity, to live with his fellow-men rather than to conspire to kill them. ...

Glossary   Preconditions things which are necessary before something else can happen.

Fluctuating progress uneven development towards modernism.

Transcended went beyond.

Ameliorative making things better.

Disabused revealed to someone that something is an illusion.

Dialectic clash of opposites which results in the creation of a synthesis of them. Marx and Engels considered that the dialectical clash between the poverty–stricken proletariat and the wealthy bourgeoisie would lead to a new, classless society.

Questions

1 Summarise the characteristics of each of Rostow's five stages in your own words.
2 By which dates, approximately, did Britain attain: (a) take–off; (b) the drive to maturity; (c) the age of high mass consumption?
3 Elaborate on why Britain was able to achieve take–off. On the basis of this analysis what policies would you recommend to help underdeveloped countries to achieve take off?
4 Why could Rostow's theory be described as a determinist one?
5 Critically assess Rostow's conception of the 'age of high mass–consumption'.

M. Weber

The Protestant Ethic and the Spirit of Capitalism, 1968, pp. 155–59, 180–81, 183

In order to understand the connection between the fundamental religious ideas of ascetic Protestantism and its maxims for everyday economic conduct, it is necessary to examine with especial care such writings as have evidently been derived from ministerial practice. For in a time in which the beyond meant everything, when the social position of the Christian depended upon his admission to the communion, the clergyman, through his ministry, Church discipline, and preaching, exercised an influence ... which we modern men are entirely unable to picture. In such a time the religious forces which express themselves through such channels are the decisive influences in the formation of national character.

For the purposes of this chapter, though by no means for all purposes, we can treat ascetic Protestantism as a single whole. But since that side of English Puritanism which was derived from Calvinism gives the most consistent religious basis for the idea of the calling, we shall, following our previous method, place one of its representatives at the centre of the discussion. Richard Baxter stands out above many other writers on Puritan ethics, both because of his eminently practical and realistic attitude, and, at the same time, because of the universal recognition accorded to his works, which have gone through many new editions and translations. ...

Now, in glancing at Baxter's *Saints' Everlasting Rest*, or his *Christian Directory*, or similar works of others, one is struck at first glance by the emphasis placed, in the discussion of wealth and its acquisition, on the ebionitic elements of the New Testament. Wealth as such is a great danger; its temptations never end, and its pursuit is not only senseless as compared with the dominating importance of the Kingdom of God, but it is morally suspect. Here asceticism seems to have turned much more sharply against the acquisition of earthly goods than it did in Calvin, who saw no hindrance to the effectiveness of the clergy in their wealth, but rather a thoroughly desirable enhancement of their prestige. ... The real moral objection is to relaxation in the security of possession, the enjoyment of wealth with the consequence of idleness and the temptations of the flesh, above all of distraction from the pursuit of a righteous life. In fact, it is only because possession involves this danger of relaxation that it is objectionable at all. For the saints' everlasting rest is in the next world; on earth man must, to be certain of his state of grace, 'do the works of him who sent him, as long as it is yet day'. Not leisure and enjoyment, but only activity serves to increase the glory of God, according to the definite manifestations of His will.

Waste of time is thus the first and in principle the deadliest of sins. The span of human life is infinitely short and precious to make sure of one's own election. Loss of time through sociability, idle talk, luxury, even more sleep than is necessary for health, six to at most eight hours, is worthy of absolute moral condemnation. ...

Thus inactive contemplation is also valueless, or even directly reprehensible if it is at the expense of one's daily work. For it is less pleasing to God than the active performance of His will in a calling. Besides, Sunday is provided for that, and, according to Baxter, it is always those who are not diligent in their callings who have no time for God when the occasion demands it.

Accordingly, Baxter's principal work is dominated by the continually repeated, often almost passionate preaching of hard, continuous bodily or mental labour. The sexual asceticism of Puritanism differs only in degree, not in fundamental principle, from that of monasticism; and on account of the Puritan conception of marriage, its practical influence is more far-reaching than that of the latter. For sexual intercourse is permitted, even within marriage, only as the means willed by God for the increase of His glory according to the commandment, 'Be fruitful and multiply'. Along with a moderate vegetable diet and cold baths, the same prescription is given for all sexual temptations as is used against religious doubts and a sense of moral unworthiness: 'Work hard in your calling'. But the most important thing was that even beyond that labour came to be considered in itself the end of life, ordained as such by God. St Paul's, 'He who will not work shall not eat' holds unconditionally for everyone. Unwillingness to work is symptomatic of the lack of grace. . . .

One of the fundamental elements of the spirit of modern capitalism, and not only of that but of all modern culture: rational conduct on the basis of the idea of the calling, was born—that is what this discussion has sought to demonstrate—from the spirit of Christian asceticism. . . .

The Puritan wanted to work in a calling; we are forced to do so. For when asceticism was carried out of monastic cells into everyday life, and began to dominate worldly morality, it did its part in building the tremendous cosmos of the modern economic order. This order is now bound to the technical and economic conditions of machine production which today determine the lives of all the individuals who are born into this mechanism, not only those directly concerned with economic acquisition, with irresistible force. . . .

Here we have only attempted to trace the fact and the direction of its influence to their motives in one, though a very important, point. But it would also further be necessary to investigate how Protestant Asceticism was in turn influenced in its development and its character by the totality of social conditions, especially economic. The modern man is in general, even with the best will, unable to give religious ideas a significance for culture and national character which they deserve. But it is, of course, not my aim to substitute for a one-sided materialistic an equally one-sided spiritualistic causal interpretation of culture and of history. Each is equally possible, but each, if it does not serve as the preparation, but as the conclusion of an investigation, accomplishes equally little in the interest of historical truth.

Glossary

Ascetic Protestantism Christian denominations stemming from Luther and Calvin's rejection of Catholicism. They stress the austere avoidance of pleasure and worldly things.

Maxims principles or guiding rules.

Communion religious rite symbolising becoming one with Christ and the Church.

Puritanism a branch of Protestantism, one which practised extreme strictness of religion and morals.

Calvinism Protestant doctrine derived from the preaching of John Calvin (1509–1564).

Calling one's role in life or vocation, ordained by God.

Richard Baxter an early Calvinist.

Ebionitic pertaining to the doctrine of the Ebionites who were a first century Christian group believing that Jesus was merely a real man and that Mosaic law was binding upon Christians.

State of grace being one of those chosen by God to enjoy everlasting life.

Reprehensible arousing disapproval.

<u>Monasticism</u> living in a monastery under religious vows.
<u>Symptomatic</u> being a symptom of something, suggesting its presence.
<u>Materialistic</u> stressing the power of material things (the economy and technology, primarily) to bring about change.
<u>Spiritualistic</u> stressing the power of beliefs and ideas to bring about change, 'idealistic' is a synonym.

Questions

1 What was the central characteristic of Baxter's work according to Weber?
2 Why did ascetic Protestantism stress the avoidance of pleasure and the need to work hard in this life?
3 What is the relationship between ascetic Protestantism and the rise of capitalism according to Weber?
4 Why were Britain, America and Germany the most successful countries economically in the early stages of the industrial revolution, according to Weber's perspective? On the basis of this analysis what policies would you recommend to help underdeveloped countries to achieve development?

W. E. Moore
Social Change, 1974, pp. 24–25, 98–102, 117–18

The myth of a singular theory of change
The widely voiced complaint, or admission, that 'we have no theory of social change' rests on a <u>misapprehension</u> of the nature of social systems and the <u>ubiquity</u> of change within them. Of course, were there some single and invariable 'prime mover' that would account for each and every change in the characteristics of patterned action, the social analyst's tasks would be greatly simplified. Any such change could be casually catalogued as another manifestation of the uniform and universal law. The analyst could then turn his attention to other and still questionable regularities in social phenomena. This appeal has characterised the various 'monistic' theories or varieties of <u>determinism</u>, from biological evolution to the alleged primacy of technological innovation. None of these determinisms has survived the combined onslaught of logical analysis and opposing facts, and the quest was in any event based on <u>false premises</u> and analogies. . . .

Industrialisation: conditions

Values
Values provide the rationale for particular norms, or rules of organisation and conduct. The value of economic growth requires, for example, a fairly high degree of individual mobility and a <u>placement system</u> grounded on merit in performance, and that requirement is likely to come into conflict with a number of strongly supported values relating to the primacy of kinship position and obligations as a moral virtue. In this sense extensive value changes are the most fundamental condition for economic transformation. . . .

There is another value, however, that is likely to be of <u>temporal</u> as well as logical significance. That is a high degree of national integration or in short, *nationalism*. . . .

Institutions
The institution of *property* provides a normative definition of rights in scarce values. The essential condition for industrialisation is that such rights be transferable, for new uses of land and other resources, raw materials and semi-finished products, and financial capital are entailed in mobilising the 'factors of production'. . . .

Labour, too, must be mobile. Labour mobility entails not only the likelihood of geographical relocation but also, and more significantly, social relocation. . . .

In particular, for the complex array of tasks entailed in an industrial system, labour recruitment must be strongly based on performance qualifications without primary regard to prior social position.

An industrial order also requires a commercialised system of *exchange*. Even socialist states have not been able to avoid placing monetary values on resources and goods as they move through the productive system, and financial payments to all economic participants form the essential link between specialised producers and generalised consumers.

Most financial transactions must operate on credit. Thus agreements or contracts must be dependable, and if necessary enforceable. All this assumes *political stability* extensive in space and time. ...

A problem–solving orientation and dedication to deliberate change are rather general characteristics in fully industrial societies, but some degree of such orientation among governors and administrators is a condition for even getting started.

Organisation

This means concretely that some approximation to the model of the specialised and hierarchically governed *bureaucracy* or 'administrative organisation' is essential. ...

An appropriate *fiscal organisation of the state*, at least as banker and tax collector, is also necessary. ...

Motivation

Although Weber's emphasis on the importance of the 'Protestant Ethic' as precedent to the emergence of capitalism is clearly not a necessary precondition of industrialisation in the contemporary world, some degree of 'achievement orientation', of ambition for personal betterment and the acquisition of the education and skills to further that ambition, must exist in some groups and spread rather widely, if sustained growth is to be accomplished. ...

Convergence and divergence among industrial societies

Let us go back to the industrialisation process to find the principal, enduring sources of difference:

The common structural requirements of industrialism mean that some antecedent structures cannot persist, and until they are changed they constitute barriers or impediments. But they are quite unlikely to be destroyed totally and without trace. In particular, the manner of their removal, the way the problem was solved, will almost certainly have enduring consequences.

Various aspects of what may be called the 'trajectory' of change also produce differences in enduring social tensions. These include differences in sequence and timing of structural changes, in the rate of industrialisation, in the historical era in which 'modernisation' begins.

Although the older industrial economies by no means developed completely independently, contemporary developing areas can in a sense avail themselves of combinations of technology and social forms from a single world system, politically disordered though that system is.

With regard to societies now industrialising, the notion of convergence derives in part from the fundamental theoretical error that assumes industrialism to be a stable destination. Although developing areas are changing, so are 'developed' ones.

With regard to societies now characterised as advanced or developed, there remain marked differences in political regimes, and there is no basis for assuming that the future will bring greater similarity, except possibly, and paradoxically, in details.

It is one thing to say that industrial societies share a range of principal structural features, and quite another, and a grossly improper thing, to say that the relative importance of those structures in society as a whole is the same or that the kinds of strain and linkage among them are the same. It is all very well to note that the Soviet factory manager resembles his American counterpart, but it does not follow that the structure of power and responsibility and the political environment of decision are similar. They are not, and no strong or even vagrant breeze now blowing is likely to make them so.

Glossary
Misapprehension misunderstanding.
Ubiquity being everywhere at the same time.
Monistic theories founded on the idea that there is only one important driving force of social change.

Determinism the doctrine that social change must occur in a certain predetermined pattern.

False premises incorrect assumptions used as the foundation of an argument.

Analogies comparable cases or situations (false analogies meaning here that the cases thought to be comparable were, in fact, of different sorts and therefore not really comparable).

Placement system method of allocating people into occupations and social roles.

Temporal to do with the time taken for social change.

Factors of production those things necessary to produce goods.

Fiscal relating to public revenue; taxes.

Antecedent; coming before something else.

Paradoxically absurd or self–contradictory.

Questions

1 Construct a list of the things necessary, according to Moore, for industrialisation to occur.

2 Why does Moore think that industrialised countries will continue to be different from each other in at least some respects (i.e. why does he reject the strong form, at least, of the convergence thesis)?

3 On the basis of this analysis what policies would you recommend to help underdeveloped countries to achieve development?

A. Gorz
Paths to Paradise, 1985, pp. 92–4, 96, 98

Their famine, our food

... The diversion of the world's nutritional resources is organised by major industries, by international brokers, by oil companies and banks who have never asked for our opinion or waited for our consent. But the fact remains that we profit from this diversion; it is reflected in our eating habits. We consume far more than our share of the world's nutritional resources.

Just look at the figures. According to nutritionists, we require a daily intake of 2,400 calories (plus vitamins, proteins and mineral salts) to lead a normal active life. For 13 per cent of Latin Americans, 25 per cent of Africans and 28 per cent of Asians, the daily intake is fewer than 2,200 calories. For 59 per cent of Bengalis, it is fewer than 1,800. For Europeans, it is 3,000. ...

But of course we are not stealing ... directly from the poor nations ... or so it might seem at first glance. For the industrialised countries themselves are among the biggest producers and exporters of grain. North America, Argentina, Australia and France produce the bulk of world exports. But anyone who tells us that this grain

surplus is the result of our more effective techniques is lying. In reality, the surplus hides a huge shortage of other food supplies. The industrialised world has a grain surplus because it makes Third World labourers produce a vast quantity of food for its own exclusive use. Overall, the rich countries monopolise 25 per cent of the poor countries' land in order to meet their own nutritional requirements.

What is grown on this land? Pineapples, bananas, avocados and strawberries from Africa or Central America are only the latest developments. The bulk of the land we have grabbed is given over to huge plantations of coffee and cocoa; of soya, groundnuts and other oil–yielding crops; of sugar cane and, more recently, cassava.

In Ghana, for example, cocoa takes up no less than 56 per cent of all cultivated land. Groundnuts, in Senegal, take up 52 per cent. Caribbean countries export sugar and fruit in quantities which represent 2,550 calories per inhabitant per day, while their children suffer from malnutrition. The eight sub–Saharan countries, at the height of the catastrophic drought of 1971–73, continued to export two to five times as much protein as they imported in cereal form. In Brazil well over 12 million acres, or a fifth of all cultivated land, is used to grow soya for Western Europe.

Everywhere these cash crops are cultivated, food crops and the population's nutritional standards suffer. Because we take its land for groundnuts, Senegal must import half its rice and all its wheat. Throughout East Africa, food crops of millet, sweet potatoes, etc., are sacrificed to cash crops for which the industrialised world pays, partly at least, in cereals, of which African imports have trebled in 10 years.

The spread of soya plantations in Brazil has forced a reduction in the cultivation of black beans—the main protein source for the poor—to such an extent that the Brazilians' own protein *supplies* have dropped by 6 per cent while *production* of protein has risen by 68 per cent. The situation is the same in Thailand: this country, which not long ago had a substantial rice surplus, today can provide only 1,900 calories per person per day. But it exports six to eight million tons of cassava per year to Europe. The German–Dutch company organising this export hopes to raise the figure to 20 million tons by 1985.

Now cassava which, just like soya, Europe feeds to cattle, can be and has been till now, food for humans. Why is it sold to us as fodder? Why do countries like Brazil, Zaire, Nigeria, Sudan and India, where a large proportion of the population is under-nourished, choose to sell their agricultural produce to rich countries instead of using it to feed themselves? It is certainly not because the peasants benefit from it: their food crops would give them two or three time as much nutrition as the price they get for their cash crops allows them to buy. No, the answer really lies in this blunt statement from Frères des Hommes: 'a Normandy pig or cow, or a Parisian cat or dog,

greater purchasing power than landless peasants in the Third World.'

This is what we have to understand—growing soya for our cows is more profitable for the big landowners in Brazil than growing black beans for the Brazilian masses. Because our cows' purchasing power has risen above that of the Brazilian poor, soya itself has got so expensive in Brazil that a third of the population can no longer afford to buy either its beans or its oil. . . .

Because it takes between four and 20 kilos of cereals and pulses to obtain one kilo of animal proteins, meat, till the middle of this century, was considered a luxury, and one which people could easily do without. Factory farming has changed all that. Thanks to the protein-rich crops and to cassava, fish meal and so on, bought cheaply in the Third World, agribusiness multinationals have been able to introduce 'indoor' stock farming. They supply prepared animal feed, precise instructions, shed designs, chicks, piglets, calves and lambs to the 'farmers', from whom they repurchase the animals when they have reached a standard weight and condition. . . .

But surely the consumers, at least, are benefiting? Yes, insofar as they have cheap, plentiful food. No, because the standard of their nutrition is falling, their food is unhealthy. Daily per capita consumption is currently 300 grams of meat, 100 grams of sugar and 200 grams of cereal. We eat 330 per cent of the average amount of sugar needed for a healthy diet, 200–300 per cent of the fat, 160–200 per cent of the protein; our calorie intake is 50 per cent too high. On the other hand, our diet is seriously lacking in calcium and fibre, and often in vitamins. Dental caries, cardio-vascular disease, kidney- and gallstones, varicose veins, haemorrhoids, stomach cancer, etc., are the results, and lead to massive consumption of drugs and medication.

Glossary　　　Cassava tropical plant with edible roots.
Agribusiness agricultural production based on capitalist tenets.
Per capita per head of the population.
Dental caries decay of teeth.
Cardio–vascular disease disease affecting the heart and the vessels
　　　which transmit blood to it.
Haemorrhoids piles—swollen venous tissue near the anus.

Questions　　　1 What is the cause of famine in the Third World, according to this extract?

2 Why is it that farmers in the Third World grow cash crops rather than food crops?

3 Contrast Gorz's explanation of Third World famine with generally accepted 'common–sense' explanations.

4 What policies would you recommend should be implemented in order to tackle famine in the Third World if you were Gorz?

B. Warren

Imperialism: The Pioneer of Capitalism, 1980, pp. 7–10

Schematic outline of the arguments

The argument that follows is divided into two parts. The first sketches the development of Marxist theory on imperialism, analysing the intellectual and social–historical dimensions of the reversal of Marx's own view of the progressive character of imperialism. Some of my major contentions may be summarised as follows:

1 The unique achievements of capitalism, both cultural and material, must not be overlooked, particularly the fact that capitalism released individual creativity and organised co–operation in production. . . .

2 There is an important connection between capitalism and parliamentary (bourgeois) democracy; the latter provides the best political environment for the socialist movement and creates conditions that favour a genuine learning process by the working class. In fact, the view that capitalism serves as a bridge to socialism must be upheld. The fact that the first successful socialist revolution took place in a country at the early stages of capitalist industrialisation is by no means as destructive of the traditional Marxist view as is frequently maintained. Lenin's . . . understanding and development of the concept of the *progressiveness* of capitalism, were central to the elaboration of a successful revolutionary strategy.

3 But it was Lenin himself, in his *Imperialism: The Highest Stage of Capitalism*, who initiated the ideological process through which the view that capitalism could be an instrument of social advance in pre–capitalist societies was erased from Marxism. . . .

   I . . . argue that Lenin was wrong about the alleged economically retrogressive effect in the industrialised countries of monopolisation between 1870 and 1914 (or between 1900 and 1914). Indeed, this period was marked by rising overall growth rates, significant agricultural advances, higher living standards, and the emergence of a new phase of technological progress.

4 The Marxist analysis of imperialism was sacrificed to the requirements of bourgeois anti-imperialist propaganda and, indirectly, to what were thought to be the security requirements of the encircled Soviet state. . . .

5 The more recent theories of 'underdevelopment' are best regarded as postwar versions of Lenin's *Imperialism*, the theory of 'neo-colonialism' having provided a vehicle for the wholesale transfer of Lenin's theory into the period of independence. Powerful new social and political forces may be identified—principally burgeoning Third World nationalism after the Second World War—that provide a reasonable explanation for the ideological dominance of the underdevelopment fiction, since the Leninist theory of imperialism, with its emphasis on parasitism and the pillage of the Third World, was perfectly suited to the psychological needs and political requirements of Third World nationalists.

The second part of the book is devoted to a polemic against widely accepted views that imperialism (and subsequently neo–colonialism) is and has been a socially retrogressive force preventing or distorting economic development and thereby creating relationships of mounting subordination and dependence between rich and poor countries. The major theses of this section may be schematised as follows.

1 Contrary to current Marxist views, empirical evidence suggests that the prospects for successful capitalist development in many underdeveloped countries are quite favourable. This implies both substantial industrialisation and the capitalist transformation of traditional agriculture.

2 Empirical evidence further shows that substantial advances along these lines have

already been achieved, especially in industria-lisation, while capitalist agriculture is develop-ing more slowly (although here too there has been significant progress). More specifically, the period since the end of the Second World War has witnessed a major surge in capitalist social relations and productive forces in the Third World.

3 Direct colonialism, far from having retarded or distorted <u>indigenous</u> capitalist develop-ment that might otherwise have occurred, acted as a powerful engine of progressive social change, advancing capitalist develop-ment far more rapidly than was conceivable in any other way, both by its destructive effects on pre-capitalist social systems and by its implantation of elements of capitalism. In-deed, although introduced into the Third World externally, capitalism has struck deep roots there and developed its own increas-ingly vigorous internal dynamic.

4 Insofar as there are obstacles to this develop-ment, they originate not in current relation-ships between imperialism and the Third World, but in the internal contradictions of the Third World itself.

5 The overall, net effect of the policy of 'imper-ialist' countries and the general economic relationships of these countries with the underdeveloped countries actually favours the industrialisation and general development of the latter.

6 Within a context of growing economic inter-dependence, the ties of *'dependence'* (or subor-dination) binding the Third World and the imperialist world have been and are being markedly loosened with the rise of indigenous capitalisms; the distribution of political-economic power within the capitalist world is thereby growing less uneven. Consequently, although one dimension of imperialism is the domination and exploitation of the non-communist world by a handful of major ad-vanced capitalist countries (the United States, West Germany, Britain, France, Japan, etc.), we are nevertheless in an era of declining imperialism and advancing capitalism.

Glossary

<u>Imperialism</u> one country's forced rule over another country.

<u>Progressive</u> (here) meaning contributing to economic development in the subordinate countries in an imperialist relationship.

<u>Monopolisation</u> the situation in which there are fewer and fewer companies competing in a particular sector of the economy, eventually leaving only one.

<u>Neo-colonialism</u> colonialism is the situation in which one country sets up a government in another and controls it through that government. Neo-colonialsim is a situation said to occur after the formal independence of the ruled country has been granted. It is politically independent but economically still controlled by its former master.

<u>Burgeoning</u> beginning to grow rapidly.

<u>Underdevelopment fiction</u> (here) meaning the incorrect ideas of dependency theory. He particularly rejects dependency theory's view that the rich countries actively 'underdevelop' the poor ones, destroying their domestic economies and preventing independent growth.

<u>Polemic</u> controversial discussion.

<u>Retrogressive</u> having a negative effect, giving rise to a backward move.

<u>Empirical</u> based on observation or experiment, not theory.

<u>Indigenous</u> produced in a region, belonging to it.

Questions

1 Briefly summarise the points that Warren is making here.

2 How is it that a Marxist like Warren can speak approvingly of the cultural and material achievements of capitalism?

3 From the evidence presented here, does Warren favour revolutionary socialism or its achievement through parliamentary procedures?

4 What reasons are there for the development of the (erroneous) 'dependency theory' of authors like Baran, Frank and Gorz?

5 How could one test the six points Warren makes against the view that contact with the rich capitalist world has been detrimental to the development of the Third World?

Questions on all the extracts

1 Assess the contribution made by either Karl Marx or Max Weber to our understanding of social change.

2 Examine the causes of poverty and famine in the Third World.

3 Examine the differences between 'the sociology of development' and 'the sociology of underdevelopment'.

4 Complete the following table, according to the views represented:

	Rostow	*Weber*	*Moore*	*Gorz*	*Warren*
Reasons for on-development in the Third World . . .					
Prospects for the future development of Third World countries					
Influence of the First and Second Worlds on the Third					
Best development strategy for Third World governments					
Rich countries can assist development in poor ones by					

Bibliography

Source of extracts

W. W. Rostow, *The Stages of Economic Growth*, Cambridge University Press, Cambridge, 1971

M. Weber, *The Protestant Ethic and the Spirit of Capitalism*, Unwin University Books, London 1968, first published in Britain 1930

W. E. Moore, *Social Change*, Prentice Hall, Englewood Cliffs, 1974, first published 1963

A. Gorz, *Paths to Paradise*, Pluto Press, London, 1985

B. Warren, *Imperialism: The Pioneer of Capitalism*, New Left Books, London, 1980

References in the Introduction

W. Elkan, *Introduction to Development Economics*, Penguin, Harmondsworth, 1973

D. McLelland, *The Achieving Society*, Van Nostrand Reinhold, Toronto, 1961

M. Morishima, *Why Has Japan 'Succeeded'?* Cambridge University Press, Cambridge, 1982

C. Kerr *et al.*, *Industrialism and Industrial Man*, Penguin, Harmondsworth, 1973

N. J. Smelser, *Towards a Theory of Modernisation*, in A. and E. Etzioni, *Social Change*, Basic Books, New York, 1964

S. N. Eisenstadt, *Readings in Social Evolution and Development*, Pergamon Press, London 1970

E. E. Hagen, *On The Theory of Social Change*, Dorsey, Homewood, Illinois, 1962

T. Parsons, *Societies: Evolutionary and Comparative Perspectives*, 1966, and *The System of Modern Societies*, 1971, both Prentice Hall, New Jersey

T. Hayter, *The Creation of World Poverty*, Pluto Press, London, 1981

P. Baran, *The Political Economy of Growth* (Fourth Edition), Monthly Review Press, New York, 1967

A. G. Frank, *Sociology of Development and the Underdevelopment of Sociology*, Pluto Press, London, 1971

Further reading

W. Brandt, *North and South*, Pan, London, 1980

W. Brandt, *Common Crisis*, Pan, London, 1983

A. G. Frank, *Crisis in the World Economy*, Heinemann, London, 1980

S. George, *How the Other Half Dies*, Penguin, Harmondsworth, 1977

J. Goldthorpe, *Sociology of the Third World*, Cambridge University Press, Cambridge, 1975

T. Hayter, *Aid as Imperialism*, Penguin, Harmondsworth, 1974

A. Hoogvelt, *The Sociology of Developing Societies*, Macmillan, London, 1976

M. Kidron and R. Segal, *The State of the World Atlas*, Pan, London, 1981

The Sociology of the Family

Introduction This chapter is orientated around two arguments; that 'the family' is found in some form in every society and that its presence is beneficial both to the society as a whole and to the individuals who compose it. The first section contains five extracts which all concern the question of the universality of the nuclear family. In many ways they are a 'reply' to the functionalist view of the family which was dominant in the discipline during the 1940s, 50s and 60s. Functionalist sociologists such as G. P. Murdock believe that the family is a universal institution. In *Social Structure*, Murdock defined the family as:

> A social group characterised by common residence, economic cooperation and reproduction ... [it includes] adults of both sexes, at least two of whom maintain a socially approved sexual relationship, and one or more children, own or adopted ...

Murdock conducted a survey of 250 societies and found that the institution of the family existed in all of them. It was in one of three forms: nuclear, polygamous or extended. The reason for its universal presence lies, according to Murdock, in the functions it fulfils both for the individual and for the collectivity. Firstly sex binds the married parents together into a close grouping. Secondly as a cooperating economic unit the family is particularly efficient:

> Man, with his superior physical strength, can undertake the more strenuous tasks, such as lumbering, mining, quarrying, land clearance and housebuilding. Not handicapped, as is woman, by the physiological burdens of pregnancy and nursing, he can range further afield to hunt, to fish, to herd and to trade. Woman is at no disadvantage, however, in lighter tasks which can be performed in or near the home. ... All known human societies have developed specialisation and cooperation between the sexes roughly along this biologically determined line of cleavage.

A further function of the family, argues Murdock, is to efficiently care for and socialise children, hence reproducing the society containing the family unit. Murdock concludes that:

> In the nuclear family or its constituent relationships, we thus see assembled four functions fundamental to human social life—the sexual, the economic, the reproductive and the educational. Without provision for the first and third, society would become extinct; for the second, life itself would cease; for the fourth, culture would come to an end. The immense social utility of the nuclear family and the basic reason for its universality thus begin to emerge in strong relief.

The evidence presented in the first five extracts suggests that Murdock's conclusion might be based more on his own preconceptions than on firm theoretical or empirical foundations. The piece from D. Gittins demonstrates the cultural variability of child–rearing practices and of attitudes towards 'the family'. She suggests that because of this variability we might conclude that the 'notion of there being such a thing as "the family" is . . . highly controversial'.   The extract from Marxist–feminist M. Barrett's book, *Women's Oppression Today*, criticises other feminists, particularly S. Firestone, for 'falling for' ideological notions about the universality of the family. Barrett agrees with Murdock on one thing; that the family performs functions in society. However, for Barrett it is only functional for the capitalist system, not for society as a whole. It is, in fact, extremely harmful to individual members of the proletariat, particularly the women. Moreover it is not a universal or necessary institution, she suggests. In a socio–economic system other than capitalism as it is currently organised it would not exist, nor would it need to. L. Segal, the author of the third extract, is in accord with this approach and suggests that the ideological notion of 'the family', a stereotypical image, is found less and less often in reality. The evidence from *Social Trends* and *The General Household Survey* in the fourth selection provides material for the student to examine this proposition.

The fifth and final extract in this section comes from *Black and White Britain* by C. Brown of the Policy Studies Institute (PSI) and provides evidence about differences in family type in black and white households in Britain. The PSI interviewed 5,001 black adults in 3,083 households and, for comparison, a further 2,305 whites. Cluster sampling was used with a bias towards areas of high black residency. Questionnaires were also used to support the interviews. As well as information on family types, data was collected on housing and employment, area of residence, education, support and care, racial attacks and views on race relations. Where possible comparison was made with data from similar surveys conducted in 1966 and 1974 by the Political and Economic Planning Group.

The second section of this chapter contains three extracts which focus on the question of the functionality of the nuclear family. The first, from T. Parsons, deals with the changes in the family's function in advanced industrial societies, changes which are both quantitative and qualitative. Murdock identifies numerous functions. According to Parsons, the family now performs only two out of these. These functions are of quite a different nature to the original ones, being concerned more with the personality of the individual than with society as a whole. On a macroscopic level, the family has lost some of its functions, yet it is still most important to, and beneficial for, the individual.

This view of the benificent nature of the family is directly questioned by psychoanalysts Laing and Esterson. The extract from their *Sanity, Madness and the Family* seeks to locate the sources of schizophrenia within the nuclear family. They use the term 'schizophrenic' for a person who has been clinically diagnosed as having schizophrenia, because they question whether it exists at all as an illness independent of others' attribution of its presence. They note that there has been no generally agreed objective clinical criteria for the diagnosis of schizophrenia, no set of symptoms consistent for all 'patients' diagnosed, no abnormal physical changes or irregularities, no generally agreed effective treatment 'except perhaps sustained careful interpersonal relations and tranquillisation'. Schizophrenia runs in families but obeys no clear genetic laws. The authors believe that insights into schizophrenia can be gained by studying the family nexus and the influences people have on each other in face to face interaction. However, Laing and Esterson do not present a full–blown theory of the familial 'causes' of schizophrenia:

> Our findings are presented with very few interpretations. ... The psycho–analyst frequently makes attributions about the analysand's motives, experiences, actions, intentions, that the analysand himself disavows or is unaware of. The reader will see that we have been very sparing about making attributions of this kind in respect to the members of these families.

This, however, can make the book rather frustrating as it gives the reader clues, but the authors provide no further enlightenment. This extract consists of Laing's notes on one case study he investigated.

It is an interesting and suggestive fact that the rate of mental illness is higher among females than males, indeed the cases cited by Laing and Esterson in *Sanity, Madness and the Family* exclusively concern female patients. Feminists such as Jessie Bernard suggest that the occupation of housewife and the female role in our society in general are damaging for women, especially in producing mental and 'nervous' disorders:

> It is wives who are driven mad, not by men but by the anachronistic way in which marriage is structured today–or, rather, the life style which accom–panies marriage today and which demands that all wives be housewives. In truth, being a housewife makes women sick.

The final extract in this chapter comes from Jessie Bernard's *The Wife's Marriage* and it presents some evidence on this point.

M. Barrett

Women's Oppression Today: Problems in Marxist Feminist Analysis, 1980, pp. 195–7, 211–12

The arguments to which I am referring have been discussed in earlier chapters and I shall merely recapitulate the main points here. Perhaps the clearest example of this tendency would be those radical feminist analyses which locate patriarchy as the outcome of divisions between men and women in 'the family'. Shulamith Firestone, for instance, argues that the nuclear family is merely one development from a basic 'biological family' which 'has existed everywhere throughout time'. 'Natural' patterns can be transcended by 'human' agency in Firestone's view, but she dismisses the 'anthropological sophistries' of the '"cultural relativity" line'. She characterises the biological family as the reproductive unit and asserts that it

rests on the 'facts' that 1. women are at the mercy of their reproductive biology and are therefore dependent upon men for survival; 2. human infants are dependent upon adults for a long period; 3. a basic mother/child interdependency is universal; and 4. the natural reproductive division between the sexes is the origin of all divisions of labour, economic and cultural classes, and possibly of castes.

These 'facts', then, are the intractable and universal material to which human arrangements must adapt—the procrustean bed of repro–ductive biology. Because of women's depen–dence on men, the 'biological family is an inher–ently unequal power distribution'[1]. It is interesting to consider the extent to which, although Firestone puts forward a feminist polemic and is concerned to show how advances in reproductive technology could liberate women, her analysis incorporates popular assumptions about the family. The 'facts' of which she speaks are culturally and historically variable. Childbirth, for instance, is considerably more disruptive to women's lives in some societies than in others. The dependence of children upon adults has varied widely at different points in time, with contemporary capitalism reaching the apogee of decades of financial and emotional dependence. As Ariès has convincingly demonstrated, the concept of 'childhood' itself is an historically specific one[2]. The universality of mother/child interdependence has been challenged by anthropological evidence of different cultural childrearing practices[3]. These first three 'facts' are all no more than a description of beliefs about the family in contemporary capitalism that Firestone has generalised into universal biological imperatives. The fourth 'fact' is a theoretical assertion bearing no obvious relationship to the premises it is supposed to follow. We can conclude nothing more from all this than that the ideology of the family has succeeded, with this writer at least, in presenting historically variable structures and meanings as 'natural' and therefore inevitable. . . .

The family–household system of contemporary capitalism constitutes not only the central site of the oppression of women but an important organising principle of the relations of production of the social formation as a whole. This, as I have suggested before, is not necessarily inevitable, since the argument that it would not be possible for capitalism's relations of production to be organised in other ways has yet to be proven. Furthermore, it is evident that the contemporary family–household system has incorporated a substantial element from struggles between the interests of men and those of women, by and large in favour of the former. However, it still remains the case that the specific combination of gender and class relations that characterises this system has entrenched gender division in the fabric of capitalist social relations in a particularly effective way.

The family–household constitutes both the ideological ground on which gender difference and women's oppression are constructed, and the material relations in which men and women are differentially engaged in wage labour and the class structure. Women's dependence on men is reproduced ideologically, but also in material relations, and there is a mutually strengthening relationship between them. It is not simply that an ideology of the family causes women to be used as 'reserve army' labourers and as cheap reproducers of labour power; nor is it simply that capitalism creates an ideology of gender difference to legitimate the exploitation of women. The ideological and the material cannot be so neatly separated as either of these formulations would imply.

The family–household system is effective, or has become so, in a number of ways. Not least of these is its role in securing one major division in the working class. The division between the perceived and real interests of men and women in the working class has proved of major importance to capital, and undoubtedly the establishment of women, children and others as dependent upon a male wage has contributed to this. Such a system maximises motivation to work on the part of the wage labourer and reduces the likelihood of militancy that might jeopardise the maintenance of non–labouring household members. The tendency of the family–household system is to encourage conservatism and militate against protest, and the close relationship between the economic aspects of household support and highly intense personal and emotional relationships is an important factor in this. These relationships, between parents and children, husbands and wives and so on apparently constitute what Christopher Lasch has called the 'haven in a heartless world' of capitalism[4]. They are not, of course, any such haven, although they may appear as such experientially. The material site on which they take place is located in the relations of production of capitalism and their private, intensely individual character draws on the ideology secured by the bourgeoisie as well as pre–capitalist notions of gender and sexuality.

The family–household system provides a uniquely effective mechanism for securing continuity over a period of time. It has proved a stable (intractable) system both for the reproduction of labour power, and as an arrangement to contain personal life, in the face of major social upheavals. The family–household system, as Mary McIntosh points out, characterises societies of different kinds where reproduction occurs through a wage system[5], and indeed the similarities between the system in Britain and, say, the Soviet Union are apparent. . . .

[1–5]See Bibliography

Glossary

Patriarchy male domination.

Intractable something which cannot be removed.

Procrustean bed something into which other things must be forced if they do not fit, thus enforcing uniformity. The term comes from a Greek legend.

Polemic controversial argument.

Apogee highest point.

Biological imperatives things rooted in the physical nature of beings which make them act in certain ways.

Relations of production Marxist term referring to the class structure in a particular system of production.

Questions

1 What does the author mean by 'the family–household system'?

2 Explain what the author is referring to when she mentions the 'procrustean bed'.

3 Give an account of:
   (a) Firestone's argument and
   (b) the reasons why Barrett rejects it.

4 What is the relationship between the 'family–household system' and capitalism, according to this extract?

5 How could it be argued that 'The family–household system of contemporary capitalism constitutes ... the central site of the oppression of women ...'?

6 What arguments could be made against the central thesis of this passage?

D. Gittins

The Family in Question, 1985, pp. 64–7, 70, 72

We assume that because we (think we) know who our parents are and how they made us that kinship is therefore a biological fact. Consider, however, stories we have all heard about children who were brought up by parent(s) for perhaps twenty years, who all along believed their parents were their biological parents, but then discovered that they had in fact been adopted. Such people often suffer severe 'identity crises' because they no longer know 'who they are' or who their parents are. Their suffering is caused by the way in which we define kinship in our society, namely, in strictly biological terms, differentiating clearly between a 'biological' and a 'social' parent. The biological parent is always seen by our society as the 'real' parent with whom a child should have the strongest ties and bonds. Knowledge of parenthood through families is the central way in which individuals are 'located' socially and economically in western society. This, however, is a culturally and histori-

cally specific way of defining parenthood and kinship. Other cultures and groups in modern society believe that the person who rears a child is by definition the real parent, regardless of who was involved in the actual reproduction process.

In many poor families in Western Europe and America well into this century it was not uncommon for children to be raised by a grandparent, other kin, or friend, and such children often thought of those who raised them as their parents, even though acknowledging that they also had biological parents who were different. R. T. Smith[1] found such practices common in Guyana and Jamaica, and reports how:

'close and imperishable bonds are formed through the act of "raising" children, irrespective of genetic ties. ... What is erroneously termed "fictive kinship" is a widespread phenomenon ... while a father may be defined minimally as the person whose genetic material mingled with that of the mother in the formation of the child during one act of sexual intercourse the father "role" varies a good deal in any but the most homogeneous societies. . . .'

It is thus essential to get away from the idea that kinship is a synonym for 'blood' relations— *even though it may often be expressed in those terms*—and to think of it as a social construction which is highly variable and flexible. . . .

In the Trobriand Islands . . . it is believed that intercourse is not the cause of conception, semen is not seen as essential for conception . . . (but) from the entry of a spirit child into the womb . . . it is the repeated intercourse of the same partner which "moulds" the child.'

Because fatherhood is always potentially unknown, and always potentially contestable, it is therefore also always a social category. Motherhood, on the other hand, is always known. Yet apart from carrying and giving birth to a child, the biological base of motherhood stops there. The rest is socially constructed, although it may be—and often is—attributed to biology or 'maternal instinct'. Whether or not women breastfeed their children has been historically and culturally variable. Baby bottles are no modern invention, but were used in ancient Egypt and in other cultures since. Historians have noted the number of babies given to 'wet nurses' in earlier times in Europe as a sign of lack of love and care for infants on the part of mothers. But we can never really know the emotions felt by people hundreds of years ago or their motivations for their practices. The most we can do is to note that their customs were different. To use our own ideology of motherhood and love and apply it universally to all cultures is a highly ethnocentric and narrow way of trying to understand other societies.

Notions of motherhood and 'good mothering' are highly variable: in Tahiti young women often have one or two children before they are considered, or consider themselves to be, ready for an approved stable relationship. It is considered perfectly acceptable for the children of this young woman to be given to her parents or other close kin for adoption. . . . The girl can decide what her relationship to the children will be, but there is no sense in which she is forced into 'motherhood' because of having had a baby.

Who cares for children and rears them is also variable, although in most cases it is women who do so rather than men. Often those women who rear children may well claim some kinship tie to the biological mother—for example, grandmother or aunt, but this tie may simply be created as a result of rearing another woman's child. Motherhood, therefore, if taken to mean both bearing and rearing children, is not universal and is not a biological 'fact'.

Nor can it be argued that there is such a thing as maternal 'instinct', although it is commonly believed to exist. Women are capable of conceiving children today from the age of 13 or 14, and can continue to bear children approximately every two years until they are 45 or 50. This could mean producing around eighteen or nineteen children (although fecundity declines as women age), and this, of course, seldom occurs. Few women in western society marry before they are 18 or 19, and few women in contemporary society have more than two or three children. Contraceptives control conception, not instincts, and unless it were argued that women are forced to use contraceptives, there is little scope to argue for such a thing as maternal instinct.

Consider further that women who conceive babies now when they are *not* married are not hailed as true followers of their natural instinct, but are considered as 'immoral', 'loose', 'whores', and so on. As Antonis . . . notes: 'maternal instinct is ascribed to *married women* only.' That women can conceive and bear children is a universal phenomenon; that they do so by instinct is a fallacy. So is the notion that they always raise them. From the moment of birth motherhood is a social construction. . . .

The notion of there being such a thing as 'the family' is thus highly controversial and full of ambiguities and contradictions. Childbearing, childrearing, the construction of gender, allocation of resources, mating and marriage, sexuality and ageing all loosely fit into our idea of family, and yet we have seen how all of them are variable over time, between cultures and between social sectors. The claim that 'the family' is universal has been especially problematic because of the failure by most to differentiate between how small groups of people live and work together, and what the ideology of appropriate behaviour for men, women and children within families has been.

Imbued in western patriarchal ideology, as discussed previously, are a number of important and culturally specific beliefs about sexuality, reproduction, parenting and the power relationships between age groups and between the sexes. The sum total of these beliefs make up a strong symbol-system which is labelled as the family. Now while it can be argued that all societies have beliefs and rules on mating, sexuality, gender and age relations, the content of rules is culturally and historically specific and variable, and in no way universal. Thus to claim that partriarchy is universal is as meaningless as claiming that the family is universal. ... Patriarchal ideology is embedded in our socio–economic and political institutions, indeed, in the very language we use, and as such encourages, cajoles and pressurises people to follow certain paths. Most of these are presented and defined in terms of 'the family', and the family is in turn seen as the bulwark of our culture. The pressures of patriarchal ideology are acted out—and reacted against—in our inter- personal relationships, in marriage and non–marriage, in love and hate, having children and not having children. In short, much of our social behaviour occurs in, and is judged on the basis of, the ideology of 'the family'.

Relationships are universal, so is some form of co–residence, of intimacy, sexuality and emotional bonds. But the *forms* these can take are infinitely variable and can be changed and challenged as well as embraced. By analysing the ways in which culture has prescribed certain, and proscribed other, forms of behaviour, it should be possible to begin to see the historical and cultural specificity of what is really meant when reference is made to 'the family'.

---

[1] See Bibliography.

Glossary

Fictive kinship supposed family relations which are not founded on any blood ties.

Ethnocentric regarding one's own culture as the most important and as having 'correct' norms and values.

Fecundity fertility.

Imbued permeated with.

Symbol–system a set of inter–relating ideas, each of which evokes powerful associations.

Patriarchal ideology the belief in the justness of male superiority in society.

Bulwark something that acts as a defence.

Questions

1 According to the author of this passage what change should we make in the way we think of 'the family'?

2 What are the arguments the author is presenting against the notion that the family is a universal institution?

3 Give some examples to illustrate the case that 'patriarchal ideology is embedded in our socio–economic and political institutions, indeed in the very language we use'.

4 Can you identify any differences between the attitude towards the family held by this author and the previous one?

5 How could one argue that, despite this author's arguments, the family is a universal institution?

L. Segal

What is to be Done about the Family?, 1983, pp. 10–11

So what has happened to the family? Our traditional family model of the married heterosexual couple with children—based on a sexual division of labour where the husband as breadwinner provides economic support for his dependent wife and children, while the wife cares for both husband and children—remains central to all *family ideology*. But it no longer corresponds to the typical *household unit*. It never was a perfect fit. But today it hardly seems to fit at all. (For instance, today 56 per cent of married women work outside the home, whereas in the 1920s it was 20 per cent.) Changes in family ideology do not seem to keep pace with other changes in our lives. Can current family ideology therefore ob-scure the nature of how we live, and the problems we face? In search of an answer, this book will explore changes in the way we live, and their complex relationship to the persistence of traditional family ideology. What is the connection between our actual experience of family life and our image of the family?

Glossary Heterosexual attracted to the opposite sex.

Social Trends 1985, pp. 73 and 38

Table 1 *Households: by type*

	Great Britain						*Percentages and thousands*		
	Percentages						*Thousands*		
	1961	*1971*	*1976*	*1981*	*1982*	*1983*	*1961*	*1971*	*1981*
No family									
One person									
Under retirement age	4	6	6	8	8	8	726	1,122	1,469
Over retirement age	7	12	15	14	15	16	1,193	2,198	2,771
Two or more people									
One or more over retirement age	3	2	2	2	1	1	536	444	387
All under retirement age	2	2	1	3	2	2	268	304	535
One family									
Married couple only	26	27	27	26	27	27	4,147	4,890	4,989
Married couple with 1 or 2 dependent children	30	26	26	25	24	24	4,835	4,723	4,850
Married couple with 3 or more dependent children	8	9	8	6	6	6	1,282	1,582	1,100
Married couple with independent child(ren) only	10	8	7	8	8	8	1,673	1,565	1,586
Lone parent with at least 1 dependent child	2	3	4	5	4	5	367	515	916
Lone parent with independent child(ren) only	4	4	4	4	4	4	721	712	720
Two or more families	3	1	1	1	1	1	439	263	170
Total households	100	100	100	100	100	100	16,189	18,317	19,493

Table 2 *Divorce*

England & Wales, Scotland and Northern Ireland

	1961	1971	1976	1978	1979	1980	1981	1982	1983
Petitions filed (thousands)									
England & Wales									
By husband	14	44	43	47	46	49	47	47	45
By wife	18	67	101	116	118	123	123	128	124
Total	32	111	145	164	164	172	170	174	169
Decrees nisi granted (thousands)									
England & Wales	27	89	132	152	140	151	148	149	150
Decrees absolute granted (thousands)									
England & Wales	25	74	127	144	139	148	146	147	147
Scotland	2	5	9	8	9	11	10	11	13
Northern Ireland	0.1	0.3	0.6	0.6	0.8	0.9	1.2	1.4	1.5
United Kingdom	27	80	136	153	148	160	157	159	162
Persons divorcing per thousand married people									
England & Wales	2.1	6.0	10.1	11.6	11.2	12.0	11.9	12.0	12.2

General Household Survey 1981, pub. 1983, p. 20

Table 3 *Family type, with martial status of lone mothers: 1971 to 1981*
Families with dependent children*. Figures = percentages   *Great Britain*

Family type		1971–73		1973–75		1975–77	1977–79		1979–1981
Married couple†		91.8		90.7		89.8	88.9		88.1
Lone mother		7.1		8.0		8.8	9.7		10.4
single	1.2		1.3		1.5	1.7		2.2	
widowed	1.8		1.9		2.0	1.9		1.7	
divorced	1.9		2.5		3.2	3.8		4.1	
separated	2.1		2.2		2.1	2.3		2.5	
Lone father		1.2		1.3		1.3	1.3		1.5
Base = 100%		14105		13655		13972	13178		12984

*Persons aged under 16, or aged 16–18 and in full–time education, in the family unit and living in the household.
†Including married women whose husbands were not defined as resident in the household.

Questions on the Gittins extract, Social Trends, and General Household Survey

1 Examine Table 1 and then answer the following questions:
(a) What was the total number of one person households in 1961 and 1981?

(b) What percentage did these make up of the total number of households in 1961 and 1981?

(c) Which group accounts for most of the increase?

(d) What reasons might there be for this?

2 Examine Table 2 and then answer the following questions:

(a) Identify trends in the divorce rate between 1961 and 1983?

(b) What reasons might there be for this?

(c) Does this evidence necessarily mean that the family is dying as a social institution? If not, why not? What else would we need to know in order to be able to say this?

3 Examine Table 3 and describe the changes it demonstrates.

4 Does the evidence presented in the tables illustrate the point Segal is making? If not, what other evidence is necessary in order to test her assertion?

5 Sociologists are careful never to accept statistics at face value. What problems or inaccuracies might be associated with these statistics on the family and divorce?

6 'Most people have a stereotypical view of the average British family. This stereotype does not, and perhaps never did, approximate to the reality of the family in Britain'. Explain and discuss the implications of this comment.

C. Brown
Black and White Britain: The Third Policy Studies Institute Survey, 1984, pp. 37–9

Lone–parent households

Compared with white and Asian households, a high percentage of West Indian households consist of a lone parent with children under sixteen. Eighteen per cent of all the West Indian households are of this type, while the figures for Asians and whites are four per cent and three per cent. ... Thirty-one per cent of all West Indian households with any children are headed by a lone parent, compared with five per cent and ten per cent of Asian and white households with children. It should be noted that these are figures for lone parent *households*, as opposed to lone parent *families*: other types of household may have one-parent families within them, and these are not included in these figures.

The relatively large proportion of single–parent households among West Indians and the fact that women outnumber men by a factor of eight to one in this group are indications of patterns of marriage and childbearing that differ from those of whites and Asians. West Indians tend to wait longer in life before setting up married or coha–biting partnerships: this is evidenced by the fact that overall about 40 per cent of West Indian households contain a single adult alone or a lone

parent with children under 16. It is not uncommon for West Indian women to have children in their late teens and twenties and to wait until much later to establish a marital or cohabiting household. It would be wrong, however, to characterise lone parents as predominantly young. Four-fifths of West Indian lone parents are aged 25 or over.

Heads of household

Further illustration of the differences between ethnic groups in terms of their household structure is obtained from the charactieristics of the head of household. In the survey we defined the head of household as the person in whose name the house or flat was held; if the dwelling was held jointly the head of household was taken to be the person who knew most about the housing costs and payments. This definition has been found to be most satisfactory during the pilot research for the project, as has the particular virtue of being independent of the person's sex: often in surveys there is in the head–of–household definition a preference for it to be a man. For instance, if a women wholly owns a house, the General Household Survey will always take her husband as head of household if he lives with her. It was felt that sex should not be a factor in the definition used in this survey, particularly because the implied assumptions about gender roles may be more strained in describing some ethnic groups than in describing others.

A third of West Indian households are headed by women, compared with a quarter of white households and fewer than one in ten Asian households. ... Over half of the white women who are heads of households are widows; further analysis shows that the West Indian women are more often lone parents, single women without children, or women living with their husbands. Only eight per cent of the West Indian female heads of households are widows. It is interesting to compare the extent to which white, West Indian and Asian women who are married or cohabiting are classed as heads of household: this is the case for four per cent of white couples, ten per cent of West Indian couples, and three per cent of Asian couples.

The heads of household age distributions differ radically between whites and blacks: nearly half of the whites are 55 or over, but only 18 per cent and 14 per cent of the West Indians and the Asians respectively are in this age group. The greater incidence of heads of household aged under 45 among Asians when compared with West Indians is because of the later timing of the main period of migration; it is, however, beginning to be balanced by the formation of new 'second generation' West Indian households, and this can be seen in the greater proportion of West Indian heads of households in the very lowest age groups: one in ten of West Indian households is headed by someone aged under 25, more than twice the proportion of white or Asian households.

The differences between ethnic groups in respect of age structure and household structure are reflected in the different marital status figures. Both Asians and West Indians have few widow or widower heads of household because there are so few elderly black people, but in other respects the two groups are as distinct from each other as they are from whites. Ninety per cent of Asian households are headed by a married person, only four per cent by a single person, and only one per cent by a person 'living as married'. By contrast, only 55 per cent of West Indian households are headed by a married man or woman, but 20 per cent are headed by a single person, and seven per cent by someone living as married. The proportion of household heads who are divorced or separated is also very different: 15 per cent for West Indians, and two per cent for Asians. If the age difference is taken into account (that is, if the married and widowed groups are treated as one) the marital status pattern among the whites is rather similar to that of the Asians: despite other differences in household structure, it is clear that the married couple is the basic unit in the vast majority of cases, although marital ties are undoubtedly stronger among the Asians. While over half of the West Indian households are headed by married people, the high proportion headed instead by people with resident partners shows that it is not possible to think in terms of a single dominant household formation pattern as in the case of whites and Asians.

| **Glossary** | Household group of people occupying a residence. |
| | Cohabiting living together (usually meaning as husband and wife). |

Questions

1 Compare and contrast West Indian and Asian households, either in writing or in the form of a table.
2 What reasons might there be for the differences in family structure between the ethnic groups discussed here?
3 How could this evidence be used in a discussion concerning the universality of nuclear family?
4 What further evidence concerning the families of ethnic groups would be useful in such a discussion?

Questions on all five extracts

1 'From the moment of birth motherhood is a social construction'. Discuss.

2 Discuss the view that the nuclear family is always and necessarily found in advanced industrial societies.

3 Is the nuclear family universal?

4 What contributions have feminists made to our understanding of the family?

5 Is it possible to generalise about 'family types' in a given society or ethnic group?

T. Parsons and R. F. Bales

Family, Socialisation and Interaction Process in M. Anderson (ed.), *Sociology of the Family*, 1980, pp. 185, 192, 195–97

Our suggestion is, in this perspective, that what has recently been happening to the American family constitutes part of one of these stages of a process of differentiation. This process has involved a further step in the reduction of the importance in our society of kinship units other than the nuclear family. It has also resulted in the transfer of a variety of functions from the nuclear family to other structures of the society, notably the occupationally organised sectors of it. This means that the family has become a *more specialised agency than before*, probably more specialised than it has been in any previously known society. This represents a decline of *certain* features which traditionally have been associated with families; but whether it represents a 'decline of the family' in a more general sense is another matter; we think not. We think the trend of the evidence points to the beginning of the relative stabilisation of a *new* type of family structure in a new relation to a general social structure, one in which the family is more specialised than before, but not in any general sense less important, because the society is dependent *more* exclusively on it for the performance of *certain* of its vital functions.

The principal functions of the nuclear family

Within this broad setting of the structure of the society, what can we say about the functions of the family, that is, the isolated nuclear family? There are, we think, two main types of considerations. The first is that 'loss of function', both in our own recent history and as seen in broader comparative perspective, means that the family has become, on the 'macroscopic' levels, almost completely functionless. It does not itself, except here and there, engage in much economic pro-

duction; it is not a significant unit in the political power system; it is not a major direct agency of integration of the larger society. Its individual members participate in all these functions, but they do so 'as individuals' not in their roles as family members.

The most important implication of this view is that the functions of the family in a highly differentiated society are not to be interpreted as functions directly on behalf of the society, but on behalf of personality. . . .

A primary function and characteristic of the family is that it should be a social group in which in the earliest stages the child can 'invest' *all* of his emotional resources, to which he can become overwhelmingly 'committed' or on which he can become fully 'dependent'. But, at the same time, in the nature of the socialisation process, this dependency must be temporary rather than permanent. Therefore, it is very important that the socialising agents should not themselves be *too* completely immersed in their family ties. It is a condition equally important with facilitating dependency that a family should, in due course, help in emancipating the child from his dependency on the family. *Hence the family must be a differentiated sub–system of a society, not itself a 'little society' or anything too closely approaching it.* More specifically this means that the adult members must have roles other than their familial roles which occupy strategically important places in their own personalities. In our own society the most important of these other roles, though by no means the only one, is the occupational role of the father.

The second primary function of the family, along with socialisation of children, concerns regulation of balances in the personalities of the adult members of both sexes. It is clear that this function is concentrated on the marriage relation as such. From this point of view a particularly significant aspect of the isolation of the nuclear family in our society is again the sharp discrimination in status which it emphasises between family members and non-members. In particular, then, spouses are thrown upon each other, and their ties with members of their own families of orientation, notably parents and adult siblings, are correspondingly weakened. In its negative aspect as a source of strain, the consequence of this may be stated as the fact that the family of procreation, and in particular the marriage pair, are in a 'structurally unsupported' situation. Neither party has any other adult kin on whom they have a right to 'lean for support' in a sense closely comparable to the position of the spouse.

The marriage relation is then placed in a far more strategic position in this respect than is the case in kinship systems where solidarity with 'extended' kin categories is more pronounced. But for the functional context we are discussing, the marriage relationship is by no means alone in its importance. Parenthood acquires, it may be said, an enhanced significance for the emotional balance of the parents themselves, as well as for the socialisation of their children. The two generations are, by virtue of the isolation of the nuclear family, thrown more closely on each other. . . .

We suggest then that children are important to adults because it is important to the latter to express what are essentially the 'childish' elements of their own personalities. There can be no better way of doing this than living with and interacting on their own level with *real* children. But at the same time it is essential that this should not be an unregulated acting out, a mere opportunity for regressive indulgence. The fact that it takes place in the parental role, with all its responsibilities, not least of which is the necessity to renounce earlier modes of indulgence as the child grows older, is, as seen in this connexion, of the first importance. The circumstantially detailed analysis which alone can substantiate such a set of statements will be presented in the subsequent chapters. The general thesis, however, is that the family and, in a particularly visible and trenchant way, the modern isolated family, incorporates an intricate set of interactive mechanisms whereby these two essential functions for personality are interlocked and interwoven. By and large a 'good' marriage from the point of view of the personality of the participants, is likely to be one with children; the functions as parents reinforce the functions in relation to each other as spouses.

Glossary

Macroscopic taking a large-scale view.

Differentiated sub-system an integrated part of a wider whole which yet has its own separate identity.

Circumstantially detailed consisting of a close analysis of the circumstances of something.

Substantiate giving evidence to prove the truth of something.

Trenchant penetrating, decisive.

Questions

1 What has been happening to the family with the development of advanced industrial society according to Parsons?

2 What functions does the modern American family fulfil and why is it necessary that it should do so, according to this passage?

3 Parsons does not present any evidence to support this theory. In general his sociology is very much non-empirical.

(a) does this matter—should he present evidence to support his ideas?

(b) what sort of evidence would be necessary to substantiate the theory presented in this extract and how could it be collected?

R. D. Laing and A. Esterson

Sanity, Madness and the Family, 1970, pp. 109–10, 123–27

Family Four: The Danzigs

Clinical perspective

From the clinical psychiatric viewpoint, Sarah Danzig began to develop an illness of <u>insidious</u> onset at the age of seventeen. She began to lie in bed all day, getting up only at night and staying up thinking or brooding or reading the Bible. Gradually she lost interest in everyday affairs and became increasingly preoccupied with religious issues. Her attendance at commercial college became intermittent, and she failed to complete her studies. During the next four years Sarah failed to make the grade at whatever job or course of study she undertook.

When she was twenty-one her illness took a sudden turn for the worse. She began to express bizarre ideas, for instance that she heard voices over the telephone and saw people on television talking about her. Soon afterwards she started to rage against members of her family. After one outburst against her mother she fled the house and stayed out all night. On her return she was taken to an observation ward, where she remained for two weeks. Thereafter, she was listless, <u>apathetic</u>, quiet, withdrawn, and lacking in concentration. Although from time to time she made bizarre statements, for example that she had been raped, on the whole she was able to live quietly at home, and even return to work, this time in her father's office. She continued like this for fifteen months, and then relapsed. Once more she persistently expressed bizarre ideas. She complained that people at the office were talking about her, were in a plot against her, and did not wish her to work with them. She insisted they intercepted and tore up her letters. She also insisted that her letters were being intercepted at home. She complained to her father that his staff were incompetent, and quarrelled with him and his secretary over keeping the books. Eventually she refused to go to work, and took to lying in her bed all day, getting up only at night to brood or to sit reading the Bible. She spoke hardly at all except to make occasional statements about religion or to accuse her family of discussing her, or to complain that the telephone operators were listening in to her calls. She became irritable and aggressive, particularly towards her father, and it was following an outburst against him that she was again brought into hospital. . . .

Father: 'Well one of the reasons why I personally was interested in her social life is not because I was prying into her private affairs; I was mainly interested in watching that she shouldn't be impressed by funny stories, by all sorts of—all and sundry—I realised she was a very sensitive young lady, very highly impressionable, and that she should not be impressed, to get wrong impressions. Because there are so many young men around with glib tongues and fancy themselves to get hold of a girl like Sarah and tell her all sorts of funny stories, and can lead to a lot of complications—that was the main reason why I was interested in her social standing and social life. But I wasn't interested to pry into her private affairs.'

They did not forbid her to go out with boys, in fact they told her she should, but they watched her every move so closely that she felt she had no privacy at all, and when she objected, if they did not deny what they were doing, they reproached her for being ungrateful for their concern. She thus became muddled over whether or not it was right to want to go out with boys, or even to have any private life in the first place. Her father tried to investigate her boy-friends without her knowledge in various ways.

'I often used to tell her, I said, "I think you ought to go out and meet boys and meet girls. You should go out more and get dates and get to know people and go somewhere else. You meet them if you already know somebody. If you've seen them before you can approach them. You feel you've seen them once before, you know them and it doesn't make you so shy."'

Of course the relationship must be of the right kind. In other words, it was not only all right to go out with the opposite sex, it was a social obligation for all normal girls; but naturally nothing sexual must enter into the relationship.

'Well I would have liked her to go out with boys. I think it's very normal for young girls to go out with the opposite sex, and I think it's the right thing that she should go out with the opposite sex, in the right way of course, to go out socially, yes.'

Her parents, however, secretly investigated the boys she went out with, and regarded it as their right to listen in on her telephone calls—without, of course, admitting to her that they did so.

Glossary

Insidious progressing subtly.
Apathetic uninterested.

Questions

1 In what ways could the behaviour of Sarah's parents be said to have brought on her schizophrenia?
2 Compare the view of the family which this passage suggests with that put forward by Parsons in the previous passage.
3 In what sense is the work of Laing related to sociology rather than psychology or psychiatry?
4 What criticisms have you of Laing's theory as a general explanation of mental illness?

J. Bernard

The Wife's Marriage, in M. Evans (ed.) *The Woman Question*, 1982, pp. 112–13

The housewife syndrome

That it is being relegated to the role of housewife rather than marriage itself which contributes heavily to the poor mental and emotional health of married women can be demonstrated by comparing housewives, all of whom may be presumed to be married, with working women, three fifths of whom are also married. Marriage *per se* is thus at least partially ruled out as an explanation of differences between them. The comparison shows that wives who are rescued from the ioslation of the household by outside employment show up very well. They may be neurotic, but ... they are less likely than women who are exclusively housewives to be psychotic. And even the allegation of neuroticism can be challenged. For ... 'working mothers are less likely than housewives to complain of pains and ailments in different parts of their body and of not feeling healthy enough to carry out things they would like to do'. (Actually, in the earlier age brackets, twenty-five to forty-four, working women averaged more days of restricted activity or bed disability than housekeeping women, though in the later age brackets the reverse was true. Data from an unpublished table by the National Centre for Health Statistics.)

But the truly spectacular evidence for the destructive effects of the occupation of housewife on the mental and emotional health of married women is provided by the relative incidence of the symptoms of psychological distress among housewives and working women. In all except one of twelve such symptoms—having felt an impeding nervous breakdown—the working women were overwhelmingly better off than the housewives. Far fewer than expected of the working women and more than expected of the housewives, for example, had actually a nervous breakdown. Fewer than expected of the working women and more than expected of the housewives suffered from nervousness, inertia, insomnia, trembling hands, nightmares, perspiring hands, fainting, headaches, dizziness, and heart palpitations. The housewife syndrome is far from a figment of anyone's imagination.

If this chapter were a musical composition, Table 1 would be accompanied by a loud clash of symbols. And a long silence would ensue to give

Table 1

Selected Symptoms of Psychological Distress among White Housewives and Working Women

Symptom	Housewives	Working Women
Nervous breakdown	+ 1·16	− 2·02
Felt impending nervous breakdown	− 0·12	+ 0·81
Nervousness	+ 1·74	− 2·29
Inertia	+ 2·35	− 3·15
Insomnia	+ 1·27	− 2·00
Trembling hands	+ 0·74	− 1·25
Nightmares	+ 0·68	− 1·18
Perspiring hands	+ 1·28	− 2·55
Fainting	+ 0·82	− 2·69
Headaches	+ 0·84	− 0·87
Dizziness	+ 1·41	− 1·85
Heart palpitations	+ 1·38	− 1·56

Source: National Centre for Health Statistics, *Selected Symptoms of Psychological Distress*, US Department of Health, Education and Welfare, 1970, Table 17, pp. 30–1.

a chance for its emotional impact to be fully experienced. For table 1 provides one of the most cogent critiques yet made of marriage as it is structured today.

Dismissing the housewife syndrome, as some unsympathetic observers do, is like telling a man dying of malnutrition that he's lucky he isn't dying of cancer. Perhaps he is. But this is no reason to dismiss malnutrition because it is slower and less dramatic. The conditions producing both are worthy of attack as epidemiological challenges. In terms of the number of people involved, the housewife syndrome might well be viewed as Public Health Problem Number One.

Glossary

Neurotic suffering from 'nerves'.

Psychotic suffering from more serious mental illness, often based on insecurity.

Cogent convincing argument.

Epidemiological related to the scientific study of epidemics.

Questions

1 What is Bernard's main thesis in this passage?

2 Try to account in detail (i.e. by giving specific examples of activities in the home and responsibilities, for example) for the relationship between being a housewife and ill–health.

3 Sociologists should not accept statistical data uncritically. Try to account for the figures in Table 1 in away which undermines Bernard's argument; for example, suggest why the figures may be an incorrect picture of the real situation in one or both columns, or suggest other causes for the differences in the health of working women and housewives.

4 Bernard presents statistical evidence in support of her theory here. What other methodological techniques and sorts of evidence might be collected to lend the theory weight?

Questions on Parsons, Laing and Esterson, and Bernard extracts

1 'The nuclear family is the ideal form both for modern industrial society as a whole and for its individual members'. Explain and discuss.

2 What is meant by 'a functionalist analysis of the family'? What have been the main criticisms of this approach?

3 'In modern industrial society the family has been stripped of its functions'. Explain and discuss.

Bibliography

Source of extracts

M. Barrett, *Women's Oppression Today: Problems in Marxist Feminist Analysis* Verso, London, 1980

D. Gittins, *The Family in Question*, Macmillan, London, 1985

L. Segal, *What is to be Done About the Family?* Penguin, Harmondsworth, 1983

Social Trends 1985, HMSO, 1985, General Household Survey 1981, HMSO, 1983

C. Brown, *Black and White Britain: The Third Policy Studies Institute Survey* Heinemann, London, 1984

T. Parsons from T. Parsons and R. F. Bales, *Family, Socialisation and*

Interaction Process, Routledge & Kegan Paul, London, 1956, quoted in M. Anderson (ed.), *Sociology of the Family*, Second Edition, Penguin, Harmondsworth, 1980

R. D. Laing and A. Esterson, *Sanity, Madness and the Family*, Penguin, Harmondsworth, 1970, first published 1964

J. Bernard, *The Wife's Marriage* in M. Evans (ed.), *The Woman Question*, Fontana, London, 1982

Reference in the Introduction

G. P. Murdock, *Social Structure*, Macmillan, New York, 1949 in N. Bell and F. Vogel, *A Modern Introduction to the Family*, Free Press, New York, 1968

Reference in Gittins extract

R. T. Smith, *The Family and the Modern World System: Some Observations from the Carribean*, The Journal of Family History, Volume 3, 1978

References in Barrett extract

1 S. Firestone, *The Dialectic of Sex*, Women's Press, London, 1980
2 P. Ariès, *Centuries of Childhood*, Jonathan Cape, New York, 1972
3 A review of this literature is provided by A. Oakley's *Sex, Gender and Society*, Temple–Smith, London 1972
4 C. Lasch, *Haven in a Heartless World*, New York, 1977
5 M. McIntosh, *The Welfare State and the Needs of a Dependent Family*

Further reading

M. Barrett and M. McIntosh, *The Anti–Social Family*, Verso, London, 1982

S. Edgell, *Middle Class Couples*, Allen & Unwin, London, 1980

M. Evans and C. Ungerson, (eds), *Sexual Divisions: Patterns and Processes* Tavistock, London, 1983

S. Firestone, *The Dialectic of Sex*, Paladin, London, 1972

N. Hart, *When Marriage Ends*, Tavistock, London, 1976

D. H. J. Morgan, *Social Theory and the Family*, Routledge & Kegan Paul, London, 1975

R. Rapoport, *Families in Britain*, Routledge & Kegan Paul, London, 1982

E. Shorter, *The Making of the Modern Family*, Fontana/Collins, London, 1975

K. Young *et al.* (eds), *Of Marriage and the Market*, CSE Books, London, 1981

◪ Social Policy

Introduction   This chapter is divided into five sections, dealing with the effect of social policy on inequality in society; definitions of poverty; the four main perspectives on social policy (the social democratic, functionalist, Marxist and market liberal); the issue of decarceration (the policy of moving inmates out of institutions such as mental hospitals into the community) and social policy issues related urbanism.

The first two extracts, from George and Wilding's *The Impact of Social Policy* and Le Grand's *Making Redistribution Work*, examine the impact that social policy has had on inequality in society. In the earlier chapters of their book, George and Wilding discuss recent evidence on the effects of policy initiatives in a variety of areas. The authors discuss the nature of the initiatives taken and the impact they have had, firstly in creating a 'safety net', i.e a minimum standard of provision below which it should not be possible to fall, and secondly in reducing social inequality in each of the policy areas reviewed. They find that in terms of meeting minimum standards there has been a fair degree of success in some areas—notably health, housing and social security—and relative failure in others—personal social services and general provision for ethnic groups in particular. There is still much to be done before minimum standards are fully achieved but George and Wilding pessimistically comment that, 'minimum standards ... cannot possibly be achieved under a government as hostile to the very idea of a welfare state as is the Conservative government of 1983.'

As far as inequalities in society are concerned, the following are their main findings:

In *education* there have been improvements in terms of inequalities between the sexes but not between the social classes. Inequalities in *health* between the social classes have widened over the years, despite the advent of the NHS. In *housing* there has been a general improvement for all and a reduction in social inequalities in terms of basic standards. However, the middle class has benefited from government subsidies such as income tax relief and improvement grants and as a result inequalities in access to high standard and desirable housing remain. In *income* and *employment* George and Wilding note the 'extreme rigidity' in inequalities between manual and non–manual workers. Income differences and deprivations in the workplace for the working class compared to the middle class have remained broadly static. The extract from the book included here discusses the implications of these findings.

The second extract in this section, from J. Le Grand, makes some social policy proposals through which social and economic inequalities in areas such as health and housing may be reduced. Like George and Wilding, he finds that social policy initiatives in this direction have failed so far. In his earlier work *The Strategy of Equality*—so called after R. H. Tawney's term for the attempt to make society more equal through the 'back door' method of public spending on the Welfare State—he suggested that this was due to entrenched inequalities in the class system. He recommended that the rich ought to be persuaded to redistribute their wealth on humanitarian grounds in order to achieve the goal of equality in society directly. This proposal is criticised, with some justification, in the extract from George and Wilding (page 132). The recommendations Le Grand makes in this later work, however, suggest a more realistic approach to the problem of social inequalities and its solution.

The first extract in the second section is from Peter Townsend's *Poverty in the United Kingdom*. The second extract is a critique of some aspects of it by David Piachaud in an article in *New Society* entitled 'Peter Townsend and The Holy Grail', the Holy Grail being the holy relic which the knights of old sought. Like Townsend's search for an all–encompassing definition of relative poverty it was an impossible task. Townsend gives details of his methodology, the three definitions of poverty used, the incidence of poverty found as measured by each of the definitions of poverty, and proposals for policy measures which would eliminate it in the UK. Townsend's is the most recent and wide ranging non–governmental study of poverty we have available and its results have been universally recognised as being of great importance. Much criticism has been focused, however, on his third definition of poverty, the 'deprivation standard of poverty' as he calls it. This tries to go beyond deprivation measured solely in terms of income. It even goes beyound the concept of relative poverty (i.e. income levels insufficient to support the minimum standard of life considered acceptable in any given society), to include criteria of deprivation other than money. Townsend's argument in support of this much broader definition is that two people can be on the same income but one may have a wider circle of friends and much better amenities available than the other. Therefore, one is in poverty but the other is not, despite the fact that they are living on the same income.

The overall findings of Townsend's massive study of poverty in this country are as follows:

> By the state's standard (the basic supplementary benefit scales plus housing costs), 7% of households were found to be in poverty and 24% on the margins of poverty. The corresponding proportions of people [i.e. individuals, not households] were 6% and nearly 22%, representing 3,320,000 and 11,860,000 people respectively.
>
> By the relative income standard (households having an income of less than 50% of the mean for their type), 10.5% of the households and 9% of the people, representing 5 million, were in poverty.
>
> By the deprivation standard (households having an income of less than a level below which deprivation tends to increase disproportionately as income diminishes), 25% of the households and 23% of people in the sample, representing 12,460,000, were in poverty.

Townsend's formulation of a 'deprivation index' which takes into account non–economic factors is the subject of Piachaud's critique. Piachaud, like Townsend, is a well–known student of poverty and a

lecturer at the LSE. He suggests that Townsend's approach imposes on people an ideal style of life and counts any deviation from this as an indication of poverty. Piachaud argues that 'the reason for tackling poverty is not to create uniformity, but to push back the constraints and increase choice and freedom'. It is, in fact, impossible to find an index of relative poverty in terms of life style, he believes.
Townsend's reply to Piachaud's points can be found in *New Society*, 17 September 1981.

The third section contains four extracts concerning the major perspectives on social policy. These are the *social democratic*, here represented by Titmuss, the *functionalist*, represented by Marshall and discussed by Mishra, the *Marxist*, represented by Ginsburg, and the *market liberal*, represented by Friedman.

The social democratic approach is characterised by the belief that the free market system has a number of problems, or 'diswelfares' as Titmuss calls them. All members of the social democratic 'school' (for example, D. Donnison, B. Abel–Smith, P. Townsend, as well as Titmuss) suggest that the government is responsible for counteracting these problems through the agencies of the Welfare State. The old, the poor, the disabled, those who are the victims of prejudice or who cannot cope, those thrown out of work because of the need for profitability and others are all the victims of an inequitable system. The beneficiaries of the workings of the capitalist economy should be made to support such people through the mediation of the Welfare State. In this piece Titmuss discusses whether universal benefits or selective benefits are the best method for this. Universal benefits are those available to all within a certain category; for example, state pensions for the retired. Selective benefits are those which are available only to those most in need, as identified by a means test; for example Supplementary Benefit.

The next extract concerns functionalist theory. This approach to social policy sees society as an integrated set of institutions, each working in harmony with the others to fulfil functions for the whole. The primary function of social welfare institutions such as those which make up the Welfare State is seen to be integrative. Parsons, Durkheim and Marshall are agreed on this. These institutions serve to ensure that inequalities in income and status are kept to such a level that they do not threaten the stability of society. However, most functionalists concur that some social inequality is both inevitable and functional for society—see, for example, K. Davis and W. E. Moore and H. Gans on this—so that the Welfare State needs to establish an optimum level of social inequality, not entirely eliminate it. Functionalist theory is not far removed from the social democratic perspective, as both believe in the need only to mitigate the *worst* effects of capitalism through the Welfare State by reforms within the system. Indeed Titmuss and Marshall could be said to belong to both schools. This discussion of Marshall by R. Mishra neatly summarises his view of citizenship rights and the integrative function they perform in society. Mishra goes on to criticise Marshall's ideas and to point out the shortcomings of his historical account of the genesis of citizenship rights.

Ginsburg also examines the nature of the Welfare State and, in a

sense, the 'function' it fulfils. However, being a Marxist, he is
concerned with its function for the capitalist class rather than any
supposed function it may have for society as a whole. He examines
the competing views on the role of the Welfare State, including those
held by what he calls the 'anti–collectivist right', which refers to the
group of authors labelled here (following G. Room) as market liberals.
Ginsburg states his views on this matter which, while coming from a
Marxist perspective, may not represent the views of at least some
other Marxists. Later in his book he goes on to support these
comments by showing how the social security benefits scheme
reproduces and maintains a reserve army of labour for the capitalist
class.

The extract from the book by M. and R. Friedman articulates a
market liberal perspective. Market liberals acknowledge the failure of
the Welfare State to provide a safety net for those hurt by the
capitalist system and to reduce inequalities within it. The market
liberals' analysis of the reasons for this and their proposals to remedy
it are very different from those of Marxists such as Ginsburg and Le
Grand or social democrats like Townsend. Market liberals are highly
suspicious of government attempts to regulate the economic and social
system. Such intervention infringes civil liberties, and reduces
incentives to work; for example, by taxing income and giving
handouts to the idle. It creates artificial demands for goods and
services which society cannot afford, such as medicines provided
cheaply or free by the NHS. Such intervention is also unnecessary
because voluntary associations are much better at providing welfare
services. Finally, state intervention is subject to corruption and
subversion by the rich and powerful who find it easy to commandeer
it and use it in their own interests. These are precisely the people, of
course, who need it least. This last is the aspect of the market liberal
critique of the Welfare State which this extract from the Friedmans'
Free to Choose focuses on.

The fourth section contains two extracts which concentrate on the
question of the incarceration of the mentally ill, prisoners, and others
in asylums and institutions aimed at remedy or reform. The extract
from E. Goffman's *Asylums* summarises his critique of such 'total
institutions'. According to A. Scull, however, this sort of critique has
led to a policy of 'decarceration'. This means the ejection into the
community of inmates of institutions. Justified by the authorities as
being a more humane form of treatment than shutting them up in
asylums or homes for the handicapped and subnormal, such a policy is
in reality a means of cutting costs. Instead of providing proper
facilities and intermediate forms of treatment through which the
'ejectees' can gradually become used to being in the community again,
they are dumped and left to fend for themselves. For Scull this
hypocritical policy should be stopped immediately and, if
decarceration must continue, proper facilities should be provided.

Scull's critique is itself the subject of criticism in R. Mathews'
Decarceration and the Fiscal Crisis. In summary some of Mathews' main
arguments against Scull are:

1 Decarceration is too broad a term for a number of very different policies.
2 The number of people incarcerated in Britain has increased, not decreased, in the post–war period.
3 There has been no move to direct people who would otherwise have been incarcerated away from that path, either through 'decriminalisation' of some activities or through any other method, but:
4 The search for alternatives to incarceration has been going on for longer than the recent period of 'fiscal crisis' identified by Scull. This term refers to the fact that the government can no longer raise sufficient income to match its commitments and so looks for areas of saving.
5 Scull accepts the official statistics too uncritically and does not examine social changes which underlie them.

The final section contains one extract concerning what is generally considered to be a contemporary social problem: inner city decay and the problems which it gives rise to. This selection, from Marxist M. Castells' *City, Class and Power*, discusses what he calls the 'crisis of the Welfare State'. The symptoms of this are seen most clearly in the 'urban fiscal crisis', i.e. the financial crisis of city areas in which funds are increasingly inadequate to meet the cost of supplying services. This crisis is brought about by the need to control state expenditure in order to reduce inflation and public debt. State and local authority spending on public housing, urban transport, public facilities, open spaces, education, etc., is therefore cut. This generates social protest movements related to these issues. Castells groups these together under the general title 'ecological questions', i.e. issues related to the urban environment. Thus the urban fiscal crisis and the ecological question are closely linked, the first giving rise to the second. Together they form 'a new axis of social and political change in advanced capitalism'. According to Castells, community action groups, feminist organisations and rioting residents in such areas as Liverpool, Brixton and Birmingham are the beginning of social movements which will eventually give rise to fundamental change in capitalism.

Castells' view of the city, as the arena for political struggle between the interests of the capitalist class and those of the people, contrasts markedly with earlier theories of urbanism. These tended to compare the urban way of life to that of rural areas, concentrating on the way people and institutions adapted to population concentration. Thus Tonnies contrasted *Gesellschaft* and *Gemeinschaft* (association and community). The former is found in the city, with its impersonal relations between people, the latter in the rural areas where relationships are an end in themselves and people are close to each other. Similarly, L. Wirth discussed the 'fractionalised' roles in which individuals encounter one another in the city where relationships are impersonal and rational. In a similar vein T. Parsons' pattern variables highlight the differences between the typical types of action found in modern industrial society and those of simpler societies. The Chicago school's discussion of the ecology of the city (see the discussion of

Shaw and McKay, page 18) also sees relationships in the city as fundamentally different from those found outside it. Castells' approach, on the other hand, is different. He:

1 Recognises the links between the city and wider society. Capitalist relationships pervade the whole of society, they lead to the development of large cities due to the centralisation necessitated by the increasingly monopolised nature of capitalism.
2 Recognises the importance of affiliations within the city, such as feminist groups and neighbourhood associations, which tend to be ignored by the writers just mentioned who see the city as impersonal and lacking these sorts of organisations.
3 Recognises the fact that these organisations give rise not to disassociation in the city but to strong and effective oppositional groups there.

V. George and P. Wilding
The Impact of Social Policy, 1984, pp. 116–17

Apart from these various policies of positive discrimination for deprived areas, a series of Acts of Parliament during the 1960s and 1970s sought to strengthen the rights of workers against unfair dismissal, the rights of tenants against unfair eviction, and the rights of immigrants and women against discrimination in the areas of employment, finance, housing, etc. Both sets of policies were weakly enforced and, as far as the positive discrimination policies were concerned, very small amounts of money were spent. The economic recession of the late 1970s has meant not only that government funds have become even more scarce for such policies but also that government and public concern has shifted away from issues of inequality to concentrate on the problems of productivity and economic growth. Emphasis has been placed on increasing income inequalities as a means of boosting incentives for more work effort on an individual and corporate level. In brief, policies towards equality have been directed mainly towards geographical inequalities, they have been haphazardly applied, they have involved very small amounts of money and, during the present economic depression, they have, to all intents and purposes, been abandoned.

What conclusions can be drawn from the failure of social services to reduce substantially socioeconomic inequalities of access, use and outcome? The first conclusion must be that this failure is not unexpected because social services were not designed to reduce such inequalities. Conservative governments have never been concerned with reducing such inequalities, while Labour governments have been, at best, unclear and lukewarm and, at worst, as hostile or indifferent as Conservative governments. Our second tentative conclusion is that social services may have reduced people's subjective sense of inequality. The existence of substantially one education and one health service for the whole country reduces the obvious and blatant forms of inequality even if social class differences in opportunity survive substantially within it. The third conclusion is that the reduction of socioeconomic inequalities of use and outcome depends as much on government policies relating to the areas of work, the environment, income, etc., as on social policies. The importance of the inequalities in the work environment and in the incomes of people has been underestimated in social policy debates. Such inequalities have a pervasive effect on the power, attitudes and lifestyles of people, which have a strong bearing on their use of the social services. As Goldthorpe expressed it, any attempt to reduce inequalities via social policy reforms alone 'grossly misjudges the resistance that the class structure can offer to attempts to change it'. The fourth conclusion is that any government which is anxious to reduce the socio-economic inequalities discussed in this chapter will inevitably meet with resistance from the powerful groups in society whose economic and social privileges will be threatened. It will also meet with resistance from some of the groups that stand to gain from such policies because of the grip that the ideology of inequality has on British society. Le Grand, for example, insists that for egalitarian policies to succeed, 'it is necessary to reduce the hold of the ideology of inequality on people's values and beliefs and this can only be done by challenging the factual underpinnings of that ideology'[1]. He hopes that in the ensuing battle of ideas, the weakness of the arguments for inequality will be exposed and young people in particular will be converted to the idea of equality. While there is a great deal of merit in this argument, it over-estimates the importance of what individuals say or write on the shaping of ideology. People's values and attitudes arise out of their material environment and daily experiences as much as out of what they hear or read. The fifth and final conclusion, is that, left to itself, capitalism has an inherent tendency to exacerbate inequalities of condition. The road to an egalitarian society, therefore, lies not so much through the social services, even broadly defined and purposefully designed, but through changes in the economic and political institutions of the country which generate and shape inequality. This line of attack on inequality is not any easier than the social services approach. It is, indeed, politically more difficult for it threatens the very essence. of capitalism. It is not a panacea either—it simply provides an economic and political framework, where co-operation between the various groups in society is less conflict-ridden, a fact which makes the possibility of government egalitarian measures more possible. In the last analysis, egalitarian policies will only succeed if they are desired and supported by the general public. Without such public support, egalitarian governments have to resort to excessive authoritarianism which can destroy the very notion of true equality that it hopes to achieve.

---

[1]See Bibliography

Glossary

Positive discrimination the policy of giving preference to disadvantaged groups in society.

Individual and corporate level concerning both individual people and companies.

Egalitarian relating to equality.

Exacerbate to make more severe.

Panacea cure–all.

Authoritarianism governing like a dictator

Questions

1 Summarise George and Wilding's five conclusions in your own words.
2 In general terms, what policies do these authors recommend for the reduction of social inequalities? Why do they concentrate on these more than on social service provision?
3 Explain and discuss the idea that 'capitalism has an inherent tendency to exacerbate inequalities of condition'.
4 Can you find any evidence of left–wing bias in this passage?
5 Outline specifically the sorts of measures which you believe George and Wilding would like to see introduced to reduce social inequality.

J. Le Grand

Making Redistribution Work in H. Glennerster (ed.), *The Future of the Welfare State*, 1983, pp. 74–85

There was a time when many people, even within the Labour Party, believed that state provision of such services as health care, education, housing, even transport, free or at heavily subsidised prices, would *in itself* be a significant contribution to redistributing income to the poorest members of the community. Inequalities would diminish and a classless society would be a little nearer attainment. These dreams were not fulfilled and it is important to understand the reasons. Some lie in the tax structure which finances these services and that is discussed in another chapter, but there is also a large amount of evidence suggesting that most of the services we have mentioned actually benefit the well off at least as much as the poor, and in many cases more than the poor. . . .

Health care

The evidence concerning the distribution of public expenditure on the National Health Service suggests that the poor do not use the service, relative to need, as much as their middle–class counterparts. The reasons for this can only be summarised here. . . .

They include: the absence of good medical facilities in poorer areas; the poor having worse access to such facilities as do exist, due to their possessing fewer cars and telephones; manual workers, unlike the salaried middle class, losing money when they take time off to go to the doctor; and failures of communication between middle–class medical staff and working–class patients.

On the first of these, it is possible to make some progress. Following the report of the Resources Allocation Working Party, the last Labour Government did make a creditable attempt to relocate health service facilities away from the medically over–endowed and wealthy South to the under–endowed and poor North and East. . . .

Education

Education expenditure is broadly equally distributed prior to the school leaving age but subsequently it becomes highly unequal. One way to redress the balance would be to redirect education expenditure further towards schools. To some extent this has happened in the past

The Distribution of Public Expenditure on the Social Services

Service	Ratio of expenditure per person in top fifth to that per person in bottom fifth
Pro–poor	
Council housing (general subsidy and rent rebates)	0.3
Rent allowances	not available
Equal	
Nursery education	not available
Primary education	0.9
Secondary education, pupils under sixteen	0.9
Pro–rich	
National Health Service	1.4[a]
Secondary education, pupils over sixteen	1.8
Non-university higher education[b]	3.5
Bus subsidies	3.7
Universities	5.4
Tax subsidies to owner–occupiers	6.8
Rail subsidies	9.8

[a] Per person ill.
[b] Polytechnics, colleges of education and technical colleges.

decade. At the same time it is obviously desirable to preserve, so far as possible, the poor's access to education past the school leaving age and not to undermine university standards. The question is how best this can be done.

One proposal favoured by many on the left, including the TUC and the authors of *Manifesto*, is to *expand state nursery education*. Perhaps surprisingly, nursery schools and nursery classes in primary schools are already used broadly equally by different social groups. According to the 1978 General Household Survey, 38 per cent of children aged between three and four attended nursery or primary school, and there was relatively little difference in this proportion between the social classes. If this pattern were maintained following an expansion (and there seems little reason to expect it not to be), then the proportion of education expenditure that was equalising would be increased. Since the difference between the home and the school environments is likely to be greater for working–class than middle–class children, the academic and social gains for the former would be greater. . . .

A more controversial proposal is to *raise the school leaving age*. This would reduce the overall inequality in public expenditure, since it would expand the period of compulsory education which is equally spread between income groups. Quite apart from this 'statistical' gain it might also contribute to reducing inequality in access to post–compulsory education, and it might even contribute to greater equality in later earnings. . . .

A way of avoiding some of the unpleasant consequences of introducing full cost charges and loans (such as the difficulties faced by graduates who may want to engage in unpaid work such as looking after their children) is to introduce a *graduate tax*. As formulated by its proponents, this generally takes the form of a percentage tax on the earnings of graduates from all publicly funded institutions of further and higher education, the rate varying with the length of course and type of institution attended. The tax would be administered by the Inland Revenue as part of the income tax collection system. . . .

Housing

Housing policies are of two kinds: those designed to help owner–occupiers and those aimed at tenants (council or private). The first mostly consist of tax exemptions of one kind or another and favour the better off; the second take the form of direct grants or rebates and favour the worse off. An obvious way of improving the overall redistributive impact of housing policy is therefore to switch public expenditure from the first to the second. . . .

Mortgage interest relief is already widely perceived as an anomaly. Through the imposition of the £25,000 limit in 1974, it is already being reduced; that limit would now be over £60,000 if it had been raised in line with inflation. The people most affected by its withdrawal are on the whole those best able to pay: the better off with larger mortgages. Although the savings to the Exchequer might not be as great as if imputed income were taxed, they would nonetheless be sizeable: £1,110 million in 1978–9.

The savings made from closing this tax loophole could be used—in whole or in part—to raise the general subsidy to council housing, and to increase the generosity of the rent rebate and allowance schemes. If they were all used for this purpose they could have a considerable impact. If, for instance in 1978–9, mortgage interest tax relief had been abolished this would have permitted a doubling of the subsidies to the rent rebate and allowance scheme without any net increase in public housing expenditure. . . .

Public transport

Public subsidies to rail users (British Rail and the London underground) massively favour the better off. The subsidies to bus travellers are more equally distibuted, but even they do not benefit the poor as much as they do the rest of the population. A major reason for this is the existence of commuter services. Generally, the higher the income or occupational status, the further is the distance travelled to work. The very poor, the old, the unemployed and many single parents do not go to work at all. Manual workers often live close to their work. Professionals, employers and managers, on the other hand, usually live in the suburbs and travel into central city offices by rail, or a combination of rail and bus.

Commuter services are expensive to run. To cope effectively with the morning and evening peak periods, they need massive amounts of rolling stock and (in the case of the railways) a complex infra–structure of track and signalling. But all this capital equipment in only used intensively for about five hours of the twenty–four; for the rest of the day, much of it lies idle. Commuter services are therefore substantial loss makers.

An obvious way to improve redistribution, therefore, would be not to increase the subsidy to commuters (as did the GLC in 1981), but substantially to reduce it. Indeed, the only way to correct the pro–rich distribution of public transport subsidies would be to eliminate them entirely, and to run public transport on a break–even basis. . . .

The reason why there is excessive congestion on the roads is because road travel, as well as public transport, is also heavily subsidised. In particular, motorists travelling in the rush hour do not have to pay directly for the costs they inflict on other travellers at that time through their contribution to traffic congestion. They will tend to over-use the road system, particularly at peak hours. An obvious remedy therefore is to levy a charge that is directly related to their use of the system. This would discourage road use, reduce congestion, increase the use (and hence the revenues) of public transport and hence reduce the need for public transport subsidies. Moreover, the cost would be borne primarily by the better off; for car ownership and use (particularly in central cities) is still far more widespread among the wealthier parts of the community than it is among the poorer. . . .

An agenda for social services reform

Any review of the figures showing the distributional impact of the social services leaves at least one clear impression. Policies involving subsidies whose distribution is dependent upon people's decision to consume the goods or use the service concerned favour the better off. Public transport, health care, continuing education and owner-occupied housing, all are subsidised, all are distributed in whole or in part according to people's decisions to use or consume them, and all have a distribution that is pro-rich.

The reasons for this are not hard to find. Unless it is one of those rare commodities whose consumption falls as income rises, the better off will always purchase more of a commodity than the worse off, and hence, if it is subsidised, obtain more of the subsidy. This will be true even of goods provided free of charge, such as continuing education or health care under the National Health Service. There is always some private expenditure involved in using even a free service, if only in the form of income foregone during the period of use: expenditure that will weigh more heavily on the poor than the rich. Moreover, the better off, being generally better

educated, more articulate and more confident, will be more able to manipulate even those parts of the system ostensible not under their control, more able to ensure that the GP refers them to the specialist, that the hospital provides them with the appropriate facilities, that their children go to the right schools and the right universities.

Any reform designed to *improve* the redistributive power of the welfare state should not involve any increase in the *subsidies* for these services, and may well involve a decrease. Instead, it should concentrate scarce fiscal resources upon those areas of policy whose distribution is determined not simply by the individual's decision whether or not to consume, but by other criteria. More specifically, there should be:

(a) A strengthening of the RAWP process for re-allocating health care resources between regions;

(b) An extension of state-provided nursery education to all children aged between three and four;

(c) The raising of the school leaving age from sixteen to seventeen and/or the extension of industrial training on the lines advocated by the Labour Party;

(d) The introduction of a graduate tax;

(e) The gradual abolition of mortgage tax relief through the maintenance of the present £25,000 limit;

(f) An increase in the general subsidy to council tenants, and an expansion of the rent rebate and allowance system;

(g) A reduction in the current operating subsidies to commuter services;

(h) The levying of charges on vehicles entering cities at peak periods and using the revenue raised to subsidise capital expenditure on public transport.

Glossary   TUC Trades Union Congress.

Mortgage interest relief a tax concession to those home-owners who have a mortgage. They do not pay tax on that part of their income used to pay the interest of the loan (up to a current loan limit of £30,000).

GLC Greater London Council.

RAWP Resources Allocation Working Party. This was set up after the 1974 reorganisation of the NHS to examine the distribution of expenditure within the service.

Questions

1 In the table, which social service:
   (a) benefited the rich most
   (b) benefited the poor most?
2 Explain the phrase 'the poor do not use the service, relative to need, as much as their middle class counterparts'.
3 Explain why Le Grand thinks that raising the school leaving age would reduce inequalities in expenditure on education by social class.
4 Why is mortgage interest relief described an 'an anomaly'?
5 Why does Le Grand disagree with increasing subsidies to commuters?
6 What criticisms have you of Le Grand's proposed reforms in social services?

Questions on George and Wilding, and Le Grand extracts

1 Discuss the views that social services have very little effect on the inequalities which result from the nature of the capitalist system.
2 What is the role of the Welfare State in advanced industrial societies?

P. Townsend

Poverty in the United Kingdom, 1979, pp. 93–4, 237, 241–2, 247, 251, 255, 260–1

Methods of research

Four phases of work were planned: special pilot research into certain minority groups who had not been studied intensively hitherto; preparatory and pilot work on the main survey, the main survey itself and follow-up surveys in poor areas of four parliamentary constituencies: Salford, Neath, Glasgow and Belfast. The pilot research which was carried out between 1965 and 1968 helped to sharpen methods of measuring unemployment and sub-employment, disability and sickness, and styles of living, including amenities at home and in the locality. An international conference was held at the University of Essex in 1967, centring on methods of poverty research. During the autumn of 1967 a questionnaire running to 120 pages, which was planned for the main survey, was applied to 150 households scattered in and around London. The main survey was then launched and ran for twelve months during 1968–9 in each of fifty-one constituencies in the United Kingdom. The fieldwork was completed in the early weeks of 1969. During the same period, four local surveys of a parallel nature were carried out in Salford, Glasgow, Belfast and Neath over a much shorter span, in two waves of a few weeks each in Salford and Glasgow and one wave in Belfast and Neath. Data were successfully collected for 2,052 households and 6,098 individuals in the United Kingdom survey, and for 1,208 households and 3,950 individuals in the four local surveys. In total, therefore, there are data, mostly of a very elaborate kind, for 3,260 households and 10,048 individuals.

The questionnaire
The questionnaire (Appendix Ten) runs to thirty-nine pages and comprises nine sections on housing and living facilities, employment, occupational facilities and fringe benefits, cash income, assets and savings, health and disability, social services, private income in kind and style of living.

Three measures of poverty

The state's standard of poverty
For most practical purposes, attention can be concentrated on the ordinary scales according to which payments are made under public assistance schemes to families of different composi-

tion. By comparing the actual incomes of families with their public–assistance 'entitlement', it would be possible to show how many people were in poverty by the standard accepted by society itself. Income data have been analysed along these lines both for Britain and for some other countries. ...

With reservations, then, the supplementary benefit standard in any year can be regarded as being the state's or society's current definition of a poverty line. It is not an objectively or scientifically constructed standard, and it would be unwise to treat it as such. For example, some writers have argued that since its relationship to mean or median income varies slightly from year to year over even a short span of years, it should be standardised in relation to such income. This would be to convert a social (or administrative) contruct into one which is neither social nor scientific.

The relative income standard or poverty
We decided to define the relative income standard in terms, first, of a number of types of households, and secondly, of levels of 50 per cent (very low) and 80 per cent (low) of the mean income for each type.

The deprivation standard of poverty
A list of sixty indicators of the 'style of living' of the population was built up. This covered diet, clothing, fuel and light, home amenities, housing and housing facilities, the immediate environment of the home, the characteristics, security, general conditions and welfare benefits of work, family support, recreation, education, health and social relations. The list is set out in Appendix Thirteen.

For illustrative purposes, a summary 'deprivation index' was compiled to cover major aspects of dietary, household, familial, recreational and social deprivation. This is set out in Table 6.3.
... So far we have been able to show the relationship between diminishing income and increasing deprivation. But is there evidence of the existence of a 'threshold' of income for different types of household, below which people are disproportionately deprived? The evidence from this survey is inconclusive, but suggests that such a threshold may exist. ...

As income ... diminishes from the highest levels, so deprivation steadily increases, but be-

Table 6.3
The deprivation index

Characteristic	% of population
1. Has not had a week's holiday away from home in last 12 months	53·6
2. *Adults only.* Has not had a relative or friend to the home for a meal or snack in the last 4 weeks	33·4
3. *Adults only.* Has not been out in the last 4 weeks to a relative or friend for a meal or snack	45·1
4. *Children only* (under 15). Has not had a friend to play or to tea in the last 4 weeks	36·3
5. *Children only.* Did not have party on last birthday	56·6
6. Has not had an afternoon or evening out for entertainment in the last two weeks	47·0
7. Does not have fresh meat (including meals out) as many as four days a week	19·3
8. Has gone through one or more days in the past fortnight without a cooked meal	7·0
9. Has not had a cooked breakfast most days of the week	67·3
10. Household does not have a refrigerator	45·1
11. Household does not usually have a Sunday joint (3 in 4 times)	25·9
12. Household does not have sole use of four amenities indoors (flush WC; sink or washbasin and cold–water tap; fixed bath or shower; and gas or electric cooker)	21·4

low 150 per cent of the supplementary benefit standard, deprivation begins to increase swiftly. Above and below this point the graph falls into distinct sections.

Glossary

Pilot research preliminary studies used to guide later research.

Constituencies geographical areas, the population of which are represented in parliament by one MP.

Supplementary Benefit a non–contributory benefit payable to those out of work and not eligible for unemployment benefit.

Mean average.

Deprivation index a measure of deprivation which goes beyond merely financial conditions.

Questions

1 Why is a pilot study required before the main survey in this type of research?

2 Outline Townsend's three measures of poverty in your own words.

3 Why is 150 per cent above the supplementary benefit standard a significant level of income, according to Townsend's research?

4 Comment on Townsend's research methods. What alternative/additional research strategies would you recommend and why?

D. Piachaud

'Peter Townsend and the Holy Grail', *New Society*, 10 September, 1981, pp. 419–21

My purpose here is to examine critically Professor Townsend's central theme—his conception and measure of relative deprivation. His study rests on shaky foundations. . . .

The first paragraph begins, 'Poverty can be defined objectively and applied consistently only in terms of the concept of relative deprivation. That is the theme of this book.'

He suggests two steps 'towards the objectification of the measurement of poverty.' The first is: 'To endeavour to measure all types of resources, public and private, which are distributed unequally in society and which contribute towards actual standards of living. This will tend to uncover sources of inequality which tend to be proscribed from public and even academic discourse.' . . .

But Townsend's second step towards an 'objective' measurement of poverty is 'to endeavour to define the style of living which is generally shared or approved in each society, and find whether there is . . . a point in the scale of the distribution of resources below which, as resources diminish, families find it particularly difficult to share in the customs, activities and diets comprising their society's style of living.'

Thus Townsend attempted 'to provide an estimate of objective poverty on the basis of a level

of deprivation disproportionate to resources'— an index of relative deprivation. How he did this, and whether it stands up to examination, are my central concerns here.

First, how was it constructed? 'A list of 60 indicators of the "style of living" of the population was built up. This covered diet, clothing, fuel and light, home amenities, housing and housing facilities, the immediate environment of the home, the characteristics, security, general conditions and welfare benefits of work, family support, recreation, education, health and social relations. . . . The indicators can be expressed as indicators of deprivation—for example, lacking that amenity or not participating in that activity. By applying the indicators to individuals and families, a 'score' for different forms of deprivation can be added up: the higher the score the lower the participation.'

He then compiled a 'provisional' deprivation index, based on the twelve characteristics which are set out in Table 6.3. [See Townsend extract, p. 137].

His next step was to consider the relationship of the score on the deprivation index to income. Taking the mean deprivation index for different income groups, he found a clear relationship with income. . . .

Townsend continued: 'So far, we have been able to show a relationship between diminishing income and increasing deprivation. But is there evidence of the existence of a "threshold" of income for different types of household, below which people are disproportionately deprived? The evidence from this survey is inconclusive, but suggests such a threshold may exist.' ...

The first problem arises with the components of Townsend's deprivation index, as set out in Table 6.3 [see Townsend extract, p. 137]. It is not clear what some of them have to do with poverty, nor how they were selected. Some of the components may certainly have a direct link with poverty—the holiday (item 1), the evening's entertainments (6), the refrigerator (10) and the household amenties (12), but other components—fresh meat (7), cooked meals (8), cooked breakfast (9) and Sunday joint (11)—may be as much to do with tastes as with poverty. Not having a cooked breakfast, for example, is often a remedy for overindulgence on other occasions.

Still other components—involving adults or children providing or attending a meal or party (items 2 to 5)—are often linked with poverty. But if such arrangements are fully reciprocated, a person may entertain and be entertained by a relative or friend at no net cost (indeed, economies of scale may make this more economical). There is thus no prior reason why many of the components of the deprivation index should bear any relationship to poverty. Townsend's index offers no solution to the intractable problem of disentangling the effects of differences in tastes from those of differences in income.

That certain characteristics are related to income level tells us something about people's behaviour and social and cultural differences. But it might tell us little or nothing about deprivation. ...

The second problem arises from the diversity o the results. As I noted earlier, Townsend showec that the mean deprivation index rose as income fell. But this mean score concealed the extent o the variation between people at the same income level. ...

Thus, while there is a tendency for those on low incomes to score high on the deprivation index, there are considerable numbers with very low incomes who score very low on the index, and also many with high incomes who score high on the deprivation index. ...

The most strange and unsatisfactory feature in Townsend's conception of relative deprivation is its emphasis on style of living. His deprivation index concerns itself with a number of primarily private aspects of behaviour. He does not include in his index more social aspects, such as deprivation at work, of environment, or of public services. He does discuss these extensively elsewhere in his study: but the emphasis in his deprivation index on style of living serves to narrow, rather than broaden, the concept of relative deprivation.

It is an unsatisfactory feature of any conception of relative deprivation that, even if all inequality of incomes were removed, there would still be relative deprivation as long as people behaved differently. Taken to its logical conclusion, only when everyone behaved identically would no one be defined as deprived. Townsend's index of relative deprivation cannot cope with diversity.

It is no indicator of deprivation if someone chooses to stay at home, eating salads and uncooked breakfasts. But all these personal choices are 'extraordinary' and so add to the score on Townsend's deprivation index. But as patterns of living become more diverse, it becomes steadily harder and less useful to think in terms of 'ordinary membership of society.'

What surely matters most is the choice a person has, and the constraints he or she faces. To *choose* not to go on holiday or eat meat is one thing: it may interest sociologists, but it is of no interest to those concerned with poverty. To have little or no *opportunity* to take a holiday or buy meat is entirely different. ...

Questioning Peter Townsend's emphasis on styles of living in his conception of poverty and his measure of deprivation, is not (as I have acknowledged) to question that poverty is a relative concept, or that there is real poverty in the United Kingdom. Nor is it to accept that the state's poverty standard, the supplementary benefit level, is adequate. But it is to question the bold claim with which he starts his study: 'poverty can be defined objectively and applied consistently only in terms of the concept of relative deprivation.'

We can learn much from the attempt, which is in line with Peter Townsend's massive contribution, over the years, to understanding social policy. But he has not substantiated his claim of scientific objectivity, any more than the knights of old found the Holy Grail.

Glossary

Relative deprivation the feeling of being deprived relative to one's reference group, i.e. the people one compares oneself with.

Proscribed prohibited.

Reciprocated did or provided the same thing in return.

Questions

1 Why is this article entitled 'Peter Townsend and the Holy Grail'?
2 What objections has Piachaud got to the components of Townsend's deprivation index?
3 Explain in your own words Piachaud's 'second problem' with Townsend's deprivation index.
4 What does Piachaud mean when he writes that, 'taken to its logical conclusion, only when everyone behaved identically would no one be defined as deprived?

Questions on Townsend, and Piachaud extracts

1 If you were asked to conduct a survey on poverty in your locality would you use an absolute, a relative or a 'deprivation index' definition of poverty? Justify your choice. If you decide to use a deprivation index definition, list the things other than income which you would look for in order to decide whether a family was in poverty or not.

2 In formulating and administering social policy, have recent British governments used an absolute or a relative conception of poverty? Explain why you believe this is the case.

R. M. Titmuss

Welfare State and Welfare Society, in E. Butterworth and R. Holman, *Social Welfare in Modern Britain*, 1975, pp. 34–7

The emphasis today on 'welfare' and the 'benefits of welfare' often tends to obscure the fundamental fact that for many consumers the services used are not essentially benefits or increments to welfare at all; they represent partial compensations for disservices, for social costs and social insecurities which are the product of a rapidly changing industrial–urban society. They are part of the price we pay to some people for bearing part of the costs of other people's progress; the obsolescence of skills, redundancies, premature retirements, accidents, many categories of disease and handicap, urban blight and slum clearance, smoke pollution, and a hundred-and-one other socially generated disservices. They are socially caused diswelfares; the losses involved in aggregate welfare gains.

What is also of major importance today is that modern society is finding it increasingly difficult to identify the causal agent or agencies, and thus to allocate the costs of disservices and charge those who are responsible. It is not just a question of benefit allocation—of whose 'Welfare State'—but also of loss allocation—whose 'Diswelfare State'.

If identification of the agents of diswelfare were possible—if we could legally name and blame the culprits—then, in theory at least, redress could be obtained through the courts by the method of monetary compensation for damages. But multiple causality and the diffusion of disservices—the modern choleras of change—make this solution impossible. We have, therefore, as societies, to make other choices; either to provide social services, or to allow the social costs of the system to lie where they fall. The nineteenth century chose the latter—the *laissez faire* solution ... an answer which can hardly be entertained today by a richer society equipped with more knowledge about the dynamics of change. But knowledge in this context must not, of course, be equated with wisdom. ...

The next question that presents itself is this: can we and should we, in providing benefits and compensation (which in practice can rarely be differentially provided), distinguish between 'faults' in the individual (moral, psychological or social) and the 'faults of society'? If all services are provided—irrespective of whether they represent benefits, amenity, social protection or compensation—on a discriminatory, means–test basis, do we not foster both the sense of personal failure and the stigma of a public burden? The fundamental objective of all such tests of eligibility is to keep people out; not to let them in. They must, therefore, be treated as applicants or supplicants; not beneficiaries or consumers. . . .

In the past, poor quality selective services for poor people were the product of a society which saw 'welfare' as a residual; as a public burden. The primary purpose of the system and the method of discrimination was, therefore, deterrence (it was also an effective rationing device). To this end, the most effective instrument was to induce among recipients (children as well as adults) a sense of personal fault, of personal failure, even if the benefit was wholly or partially a compensation for disservices inflicted by society.

The real challenge in welfare
Today, with this heritage, we face the positive challenge of providing selective, high quality services for poor people over a large and complex range of welfare; of positively discriminating on a territorial, group or 'rights' basis in favour of the poor, the handicapped, the deprived, the coloured, the homeless, and the social casualities of our society. Universalism is not, by itself alone, enough: in medical care, in wage–related social security, and in education. This much we have learnt in the past two decades from the facts about inequalities in the distribution of incomes and wealth, and in our failure to close many gaps in differential access to and effective utilization of particular branches of our social services. . . .

At this point, considering the nature of the search in all its ramifying complexities, I must now state my general conclusion. It is this. The challenge that faces us is not the choice between universalist and selective social services. The real challenge resides in the question: what particular infrastructure of universalist services is needed in order to provide a framework of values and opportunity bases within and around which can be developed socially acceptable selective services aiming to discriminate positively, with the minimum risk of stigma, in favour of those whose needs are greatest. . . .

In all the main spheres of need, some structure of universalism is an essential pre–requisite to selective positive discrimination; it provides a general system of values and a sense of community; socially approved agencies for clients, patients and consumers, and also for the recruitment, training and deployment of staff at all levels; it sees welfare, not as a burden, but as complementary and as an instrument of change and, finally, it allows positive discriminatory services to be provided as rights for categories of people and for classes of need in terms of priority social areas and other impersonal classifications.

Without this infrastructure of welfare resources and framework of values we should not, I conclude, be able to identify and discuss the next steps in progress towards a 'Welfare Society'.

Glossary

Obsolescence going out of date or use.

Multiple causality having a number of causes, not just one.

Cholera an infectious disease, here used ina figurative sense.

Laissez–faire the doctrine of the free market, a lack of government intervention in the economy and society.

Means–test an enquiry into the financial circumstances of claimants of benefit in order to establish their eligibility.

Residual refers to a model of social welfare wjocj sees the poor as an outcast minority group who should be treated quite differently from normal citizens. They are not considered an integral part of society.

Universalism the provision of benefits to all in society, or at least a certain section of society (e.g. the old) without a means test.

Infrastructure basic necessities to allow operations to continue.

Questions

1 Explain in detail what Titmuss means when he says that welfare benefits are partial compensation for 'socially caused diswelfares'.
2 What are Titmuss' arguments against means–tested benefits and in favour of universal ones?
3 Give three examples of universal benefits and three of selective or means–tested benefits currently available in Britain.
4 What is meant by an 'infrastructure of universalist services'? What would the establishment of such an infrastructure involve in Britain?
5 Why isn't there substantial provision of universal benefits in the British version of the welfare state?

R. Mishra
Society and Social Policy, 1981, pp. 27–30

Marshall's analysis is chiefly concerned with the development of citizenship rights and its impact on social inequality. These rights, according to Marshall, consist of three different elements— civil, political and social. The first refers broadly to guarantees of individual liberty and equality before the law; the second to political enfran- chisement—the right to vote and to seek politi- cal office; the third, a good deal less specific than the other two, comprises a 'modicum of eco- nomic welfare and security' and the 'right to share to the full in the social heritage and life of a civilised being according to the standards pre- vailing in the society. The first of these rights inheres basically in the legal institutions, the second in the political institutions and the third in the social services. Marshall traces the deve- lopment of these rights in England in some detail down to the mid-twentieth century. The major development of each is located within a particu- lar period: civil rights in the eighteenth century, political rights in the nineteenth century and social rights in the twentieth century.

Implicit in Marshall's historical analysis is the idea of change from a pre-industrial to an indus- trial society—from a communally-based social order (*Gemeinschaft*) to one that is based on more formal and rational relationships (*Gesellschaft*). But this change is examined in the context of Britain, as an evolutionary development of a particular society. All three constituent rights of citizenship have roots going far back into English history. Essentially, their development involves a widening of scope, for example to include the whole population, and in this sense also their

democratisation and redefinition in the context of modern society. Thus political rights, initially restricted to the aristocracy, were extended first to the middle classes, then to the working classes and finally to women. Similarly social rights, in the form of the Poor Law, were at first restricted to the needy (further restricted to the destitute in the nineteenth century); as social services they were later extended to the working classes and eventually to the whole population.

The rights of citizenship are essentially norms that define the membership of a large-scale, democratic, industrial community. In other words, these rights have a direct bearing on social solidarity in modern societies. According to Marshall, modern societies require a bond different in kind from the traditional forms of solidarity based on 'ascribed' status typical of the pre-industrial societies. Solidarity in modern conditions entails 'a direct sense of community membership based on loyalty of free men endowed with rights and protected by a common law. Its growth is stimulated both by the strug- gle to win these rights and their employment when won.' Citizenship, then, is a form of equa- lity of status as a member of the 'societal com- munity'—the modern nation-state. Civil, politi- cal and social rights together form the basis for the full membership of a modern community. The relation between the three remains some- what unclear in Marshall's work. But civil and, especially, political rights help the development of social rights which in turn enable the full and proper exercise of the other two. A minimum of education and of income, health and housing is a necessary condition for the full exercise of civil and political rights. Social rights, so to speak, round off the other two; they contribute both to the sentiment of solidarity—the sense of belonging to a community—as well as to effective participation as a member of the community.

In examining the relation between social rights and social stratification Marshall returns to the theme of community. The starting point of his analysis here is the paradox that the growth of citizenship—which has to do with equality—has coincided with the development of capitalism, a system of inequality. However, the paradox is more apparent than real for, as Marshall observed, citizenship has to do with equality of status as a member of a community and not with equality in any other sense. Thus equal status as a citizen is quite compatible with inequality in other respects, for example—material rewards, resulting from the operations of the market and other structures of capitalism. Indeed, ... Marshall was one of the earliest among sociologists to recognise that the welfare state is not, primarily, an egalitarian measure. He wrote: 'the extension of the social services is not primarily a means of equalising incomes. In some cases it may, in others it may not. The question is relatively unimportant; it belongs to a different department of social policy.' Neither the primary objectives nor the consequences of state welfare are egalitarian in the sense of reducing class inequality. As Marshall pointed out, with the social services the redistribution of incomes and life-chances tends to be mainly horizontal (within classes) rather than vertical (between classes). Far from reducing class inequality, citizenship creates an equality of conditions in certain respects in order that a structure of social inequality may be built all the more securely. It provides 'the foundation of equality on which the structure of inequality could be built'. In this sense the welfare state makes inequality more acceptable and legitimate.

Marshall, however, recognised some tension between the equality of citizenship and the inequalities of capitalism. And referring specifically to post-war Britain he thought that the 'enrichment' of the status of citizenship was making 'the preservation of economic inequalities' more difficult. From the vantage of the 1980s, Marshall's main contribution appears to have been to show that social rights, like civil and political rights, are not incompatible with capitalism and its class structure. Here Marshall stands closer to the Marxists than to social-democrats, many of whom see (or have seen) the welfare state as a socialist and egalitarian measure. However, as we shall see later, with its emphasis on community and solidarity, the citizenship view of welfare is closer to the functionalist approach. It is no mere coincidence that Talcott Parsons, the high priest of modern functionalism, should employ Marshall's ideas to depict the growth and consolidation of the 'nation as societal community' in modern times.

The affinity with functionalism is also evident in Marshall's view of the *development* of citizenship rights. Thus group conflict, concerning values and interests, finds no place in his account of the growth of citizenship which is presented as an evolutionary process. True, conflict makes its appearance from time to time but only as conflict between the various 'rights'. On the whole the process of development is seen as linear and incremental. Now this fits the case of civil and political rights quite well but not that of social rights. For unlike the other two, which show a more or less steady, linear progression (from about the eighteenth and the early nineteenth centuries respectively), social rights in England have had a chequered career. Thus the Speenhamland system of poor relief (early nineteenth century) represents a sort of high water mark in the recognition of social rights within a pre-modern framework of welfare. But with the deterrent poor law policy of 1834, which was to last through the best part of the nineteenth century, social rights suffered a sharp setback. In Marshall's words they 'sank to vanishing point'. Their 'revival began with the development of public elementary education, but it was not until the twentieth century that they attained to equal partnership with the other two elements of citizenship'. Why social rights should have had these ups and downs is not explained. Or rather the explanation offered is circular—in terms of the individual history of each of the rights. In pre-modern (feudal) England all three rights were fused together in the matrix of custom and tradition. But with the passing of the old order they parted company and 'it became possible for each to go its separate way, travelling at its own speed under the direction of its own peculiar principles'. But these 'peculiar principles' are nowhere elaborated and what we are offered is a narrative, a historical sketch, of the separate development of each of the rights. Marshall's account reads essentially like the story of the gradual and inevitable realisation of a certain concept of citizenship inherent in the nature and development of English society. Despite some sociological under-pinning, it is strongly reminiscent of Dicey's 'explanation' of the growth of social legislation in England. For Dicey the changing currents of public opinion decided whether individualism or collectivism held sway. For Marshall the changing conception of rights won the day.

Glossary

Enfranchisement making a group or person eligible to vote.
Modicum a small amount.
Inheres exists in something.
Speenhamland system an early form of benefit available to poor people, the level of benefit being dependent on family size and the price of bread.
Matrix interconnecting structure.

Questions

1 Distinguish between civil, political and social rights, giving examples of each one.
2 Why are such rights found in modern societies but not in traditional ones?
3 What is the relationship between citizenship rights and egalitarianism in this theory?
4 Explain what is meant by 'functionalism'. What features of Marshall's theory identify it as a functionalist one?
5 Can you offer an explanation for why social rights in England have had what Mishra calls a 'chequered career'?

N. Ginsburg
Class, Capital and Social Policy, 1979, pp. 1–2

In any critical consideration of the welfare state, one must distance oneself from the barrage of ideological assumptions surrounding it, as it is continually reinforced by politicians, the media and the academic literature as well as by the agencies of the state themselves. The dominant view or ideology promotes the appearance of the state as neutral, representing a coalition of all classes and pursuing the common interest or 'the national interest'. This is particularly true of the welfare state, and it is a view shared in slightly different forms by a wide range of ideologues of social welfare, ranging from the anti–collectivist right to many socialists. It is a widespread belief, even amongst socialists, that the welfare state is essentially administered in the interests of its working–class consumers and is even to some extent 'under the control of' working–class politicians, and therefore capable of further reforms to satisfy the needs of the working class. It is true

that specific reforms have come about as the result of pressure from the organised working class, though the enlightened bourgeoisie and the threat of the unorganised working class have also been important sources of pressure. It is also true that the welfare state is a response to the democratically expressed aspirations of the working class. Nevertheless, it will be argued here that a detailed examination of the functioning and management of state welfare suggests that it remains part of a *capitalist* state which is fundamentally concerned with the maintenance and reproduction of capitalist social relations. It requires only the briefest acquaintance with Britain's social and labour history to discover how consistently and how effectively working–class struggle and demands for better living conditions and welfare have been thwarted and repressed.

Thus the welfare state is not considered here as

an untrammelled achievement of the working class in struggle, an oasis of socialism and hence a series of concessions by the bourgeoisie. Nor is it viewed as an institution shaped largely by the demands and requirements of the capitalist economy. The welfare state has been formed around the contradictions and conflicts of capitalist development in specific historical contexts. From the working–class point of view it is a response to their continual struggle to improve and secure their conditions of existence or standard of living. From the capitalist point of view state welfare has contributed to the continual struggle to accumulate capital by materially assisting in bringing labour and capital together profitably and containing the inevitable resistance and revolutionary potential of the working class. Hence it is suggested here that the social security system is concerned with reproducing a reserve army of labour, the patriarchal family and the disciplining of the labour force. Only secondarily and contingently does it function as a means of mitigating poverty or providing 'income maintenance'. It is similarly argued that housing policy is directed towards regulating the consumption of a vital commodity for the reproduction of the labour force, and only secondarily and contingently as an attempt at providing secure and adequate accommodation for the working class. Thus the possibility of securing a fundamental shift in the structure of class inequality in favour of the working class through administrative and policy reform or working–class political struggle within the state apparatus is severely constrained by the essential form and functions of the state as a capitalist state, which boil down to the reproduction of the relationship between capital and labour.

Glossary

Anti–collectivist right market liberals, those opposed to state intervention in the economy and society, i.e. to 'collectivist' rather than 'individualist' measures.

Untrammelled unconfined.

Reserve army of labour a Marxist term referring to a group of workers currently unemployed but ready to work if required to do so.

Patriarchal family a family dominated by a male.

Contingently dependent upon something else.

Mitigating relieving.

Questions

1 What are the sorts of things Ginsburg is referring to in discussing the 'ideological assumptions' surrounding the idea of the welfare state?

2 What explanation for the rise of the welfare state in capitalism does Ginsburg reject?

3 How could it be argued (as Ginsburg goes on to do in his book) that the social security system reproduces (i.e. maintains the continued existence of):
   (a) a reserve army of labour
   (b) the patriarchal family
   (c) the disciplining of the labour force?

4 Why is the continued existence of these three things of use to the capitalist class?

5 Would you agree that the welfare state is in:
   (a) the national interest, or
   (b) the interest of the working class, or
   (c) the interest of the capitalist class?
   Explain your view.

M. Friedman and R. Friedman
Free to Choose, 1980, pp. 115—19

The fallacy of the welfare state

Why have all these [welfare] programmes been so disappointing? Their objectives were surely humanitarian and noble. Why have they not been achieved?

At the dawn of the new era all seemed well. The people to be benefited were few; the taxpayers available to finance them, many—so each was paying a small sum that provided significant benefits to a few in need. As welfare programmes expanded, the numbers changed. Today all of us are paying out of one pocket to put money—or something money could buy—in the other.

A simple classification of spending shows why that process leads to undesirable results. When you spend, you may spend your own money or someone else's; and you may spend for the benefit of yourself or someone else. Combining these two pairs of alternatives gives four possibilities summarised in the following simple table:

You are the spender

	On whom spent	
Whose money	*You*	*Someone else*
Yours	I	II
Someone else's	III	IV

Category I in the table refers to your spending your own money on yourself. You shop in a supermarket, for example. You clearly have a strong incentive both to economise and to get as much value as you can for each dollar you do spend.

Category II refers to your spending your own money on someone else. You shop for Christmas or birthday presents. You have the same incentive to economise as in Category I but not the same incentive to get full value for your money, at least as judged by the tastes of the recipient. You will, of course, want to get something the recipient will like—provided that it also makes the right impression and does not take too much time and effort.

Category III refers to your spending of someone else'e money on yourself. . . .

Category IV refers to your spending someone else's money on still another person. . . .

All welfare programs fall into either Category III or IV. . . .

The lure of getting someone else's money is strong. Many, including the bureaucrats administering the programmes, will try to get it for themselves rather than have it go to someone else. The temptation to engage in corruption, to cheat, is strong and will not always be resisted or frustrated. People who resist the temptation to cheat will use legitimate means to direct the money to themselves. They will lobby for legislation favourable to themselves, for rules from which they can benefit. The bureaucrats administering the programme will press for better pay and <u>perquisites</u> for themselves—an outcome that larger programmes will facilitate.

The attempt by people to divert government expenditures to themselves has two consequences that may not be obvious. First, it explains why so many programmes tend to benefit middle- and upper-income groups rather than the poor for whom they are supposedly intended. The poor tend to lack not only the skills valued in the market, but also the skills required to be successful in the political scramble for funds. Indeed, their disadvantage in the political market is likely to be greater than in the economic. Once well-meaning reformers who may have helped to get a welfare measure enacted have gone on to their next reform, the poor are left to fend for themselves and they will almost always be overpowered by the groups that have already demonstrated a greater capacity to take advantage of available opportunities.

The second consequence is that the net gain to the recipients of the transfer will be less than the total amount transferred. If $100 of somebody else's money is up for grabs, it pays to spend up to $100 of your own money to get it. The costs incurred to lobby legislators and regulatory authorities, for contributions to political campaigns, and for <u>myriad</u> other items are a pure waste—harming the taxpayer who pays and benefiting no one. They must be suჲtracted from the gross transfer to get the net gain—and may, of course, at times exceed the gross transfer, leaving a net loss, not gain.

These consequences of subsidy seeking also

help to explain the pressure for more and more spending, more and more programmes. The initial measures fail to achieve the objectives of the well-meaning reformers who sponsored them. They conclude that not enough has been done and seek additional programmes. They gain as allies both people who envision careers as bureaucrats administering the programmes and people who believe that they can tap the money to be spent.

Category IV spending tends also to corrupt the people involved. All such programmes put some people in a position to decide what is good for other people. The effect is to instil in the one group a feeling of almost God-like power; in the other, a feeling of childlike dependence. The capacity of the beneficiaries for independence, for making their own decisions, atrophies through disuse. In addition to the waste of money, in addition to the failure to achieve the intended objectives, the end result is to rot the moral fabric that holds a decent society together.

Another by-product of Category III or IV spending has the same effect. Voluntary gifts aside, you can spend someone else's money only by taking it away as government does. The use of force is therefore at the very heart of the welfare state—a bad means that tends to corrupt the good ends. That is also the reason why the welfare state threatens our freedom so seriously.

What should be done

Most of the present welfare programmes should never have been enacted. If they had not been, many of the people now dependent on them would have become self-reliant individuals instead of wards of the state. In the short run that might have appeared cruel for some, leaving them no option to low-paying, unattractive work. But in the long run it would have been far more humane.

Glossary

Perquisites perks.
Myriad a very large number.
Atrophies wastes away through lack of use.

Questions

1 What are the objections which the Friedmans have towards state benefits for the poor?
2 Why would it have been 'far more humane' never to have enacted most of the present welfare programmes?
3 In the view of the Friedmans, what is the relationship between welfare programmes and freedom of the individual?
4 Do you agree or disagree with the Friedmans' market liberal perspective? In either case present evidence to support your view.

Questions on Titmuss, Mishra, Ginsburg, Friedman and Friedman

1 Complete the following table, according to the different theories represented:

	Social Democrat	Market Liberal	Functionalist	Marxist
Reasons for the continued existence of poverty				
Effect of state intervention on society				
Attitude to currently available means–tested benefits				

	Social Democrat	Market Liberal	Functionalist	Marxist
Attitude to currently available universal benefits				
Effects of state intervention in society				
Real reason for having a welfare state				
Relationship between welfare state and social inequality in contemporary industrial society				
Proposed reforms to improve the current situation with regard to the welfare state				

2 'In seeking security not merely against physical want but against all these evils [disease, ignorance, idleness, and squalor] in all their forms, and in showing that security can be combined with freedom and enterprise and responsibility of the individual for his own life, the British community and those who in other lands have inherited the British tradition have a vital service to render to human progress.' (The Beveridge Report 1942.) Explain and discuss these ideas.

E. Goffman
Asylums, 1984, pp. 22, 47–8, 51, 53, 61–3

The total institution is a social hybrid, part residential community, part formal organisation; therein lies its special sociological interest. There are other reasons for being interested in these establishments, too. In our society, they are the forcing houses for changing persons; each is a natural experiment on what can be done to the self. . . .
. . . total institutions disrupt or defile precisely those actions that in civil society have the role of attesting to the actor and those in his presence that he has some command over his world—that he is a person with 'adult' self-determination, autonomy, and freedom of action. A failure to retain this kind of adult executive competency, or at least the symbols of it, can produce in the inmate the terror of feeling radically demoted in the age-grading system. A margin of self-selected expressive behaviour—whether of antagonism, affection, or unconcern—is one symbol of self-determination. This evidence of one's autonomy is weakened by such specific obligations as having to write one letter home a week, or having to refrain from expressing sullenness. It is further weakened when this margin of behaviour is used as evidence concerning the

state of one's psychiatric, religious, or political conscience.

There are certain bodily comforts significant to the individual that tend to be lost upon entrance into a total institution—for example, a soft bed or quietness at night. Loss of this set of comforts is apt to reflect a loss of self–determination, too, for the individual tends to ensure these comforts the moment he has resources to expend.

Loss of self–determination seems to have been ceremonialised in concentration camps; thus we have atrocity tales of prisoners being forced to roll in the mud, stand on their heads in the snow, work at ludicrously useless tasks, swear at themselves, or, in the case of Jewish prisoners, sing anti-Semitic songs. A milder version is found in mental hospitals where attendants have been reported forcing a patient who wanted a cigarette to say 'pretty please' or jump up for it. In all such cases the inmate is made to display a giving up of his will. Less ceremonialised, but just as extreme, is the embarrassment to one's autonomy that comes from being locked in a ward, placed in a tight wet pack or tied in a camisole, and thereby denied the liberty of making small adjustive movements. . . .

While the process of mortification goes on, the inmate begins to receive formal and informal instruction in what will here be called the privilege system. In so far as the inmate's attachment to his civilian self has been shaken by the stripping processes of the institution, it is largely the privilege system that provides a framework for personal reorganisation. Three basic elements of the system may be mentioned.

First, there are the 'house rules', a relatively explicit and formal set of prescriptions and proscriptions that lays out the main requirements of inmate conduct. These rules spell out the austere round of life of the inmate. Admission procedures, which strip the recruit of his past supports, can be seen as the institution's way of getting him ready to start living by house rules.

Secondly, against this stark background, a small number of clearly defined rewards or privileges are held out in exchange for obedience to staff in action and spirit. . . .

The third element in the privilege system is punishments; these are designated as the consequence of breaking the rules. One set of these punishments consists of the temporary or permanent withdrawal of privileges or the abrogation of the right to try to earn them. In general, the punishments meted out in total institutions are more severe than anything encountered by the inmate in his home world. In any case, conditions

in which a few easily controlled privileges are so important are the same conditions in which their withdrawal has a terrible significance. . . .

The privilege system and the mortifying processes that have been discussed represent the conditions to which the inmate must adapt. These conditions allow for different individualistic ways of meeting them, apart from any effort at collective subversive action. The same inmate will employ different personal lines of adaptation at different phases in his moral career and may even alternate among different tacks at the same time.

First, there is the tack of 'situational withdrawal'. The inmate withdraws apparent attention from everything except events immediately around his body and sees these in a perspective not employed by others present. This drastic curtailment of involvement in interactional events is best known, of course, in mental hospitals, under the title of 'regression'. . . .

Secondly, there is the 'intransigent line': the inmate intentionally challenges the institution by flagrantly refusing to cooperate with staff. The result is a constantly communicated intransigency and sometimes high individual morale. Many large mental hospitals, for example, have wards where this spirit prevails. . . .

A third standard alignment in the institutional world is 'colonisation'; the sampling of the outside world provided by the establishment is taken by the inmate as the whole, and a stable relatively contented existence is built up out of the maximum satisfactions procurable within the institution. Experience of the outside world is used as a point of reference to demonstrate the desirability of life on the inside, and the usual tension between the two worlds is markedly reduced, thwarting the motivational scheme based upon this felt discrepancy which I described peculiar to total institutions. . . .

A fourth mode of adaptation to the setting of a total institution is that of 'conversion': the inmate appears to take over the official or staff view of himself and tries to act out the role of the perfect inmate. While the colonised inmate builds as much of a free community for himself as possible by using the limited facilities available, the convert takes a more disciplined, moralistic, monochromatic line, presenting himself as someone whose institutional enthusiasm is always at the disposal of the staff. . . .

Many total institutions, most of the time, seem to function merely as storage dumps for inmates, but, as previously suggested, they usually present themselves to the public as rational organisations designed consciously, through and through, as effective machines for producing a few officially avowed and officially approved ends. It was also suggested that one frequent official objective is the reformation of inmates in the direction of some ideal standard. This contra-diction, between what the instition does and what its officials must say it does, forms the basic context of the staff's daily activity. . . .

Glossary

Hybrid a mixture of two things of different types (in this case, social institutions).

Autonomy independence of action.

Mortification the process of killing an old personality in preparation for imprinting a new one. Mortification is achieved by removing the symbols of the old personality and the independence which went with it; e.g. by taking away personal possessions, cutting the hair, and so on.

Prescriptions recommendations as to what should be done about something.

Proscriptions prohibitions against doing something.

Abrogation repeal or cancel something (usually a right or duty).

Monochromatic having only one colour.

Avowed admitted.

Questions

1 What are the effects of loss of self–determination in a total institution, according to Goffman?

2 Describe, in your own words, what Goffman means by the 'privilege system' and the role it has in a total institution.

3 In what ways do inmates in total institutions adapt to their situation?

4 What is the 'contradiction' concerning total institutions which Goffman refers to in the last paragraph?

5 Goffman says that the central features of a total institution are:
(a) all aspects of life are conducted in the same place
(b) one is in the company of a large batch of similar others
(c) the day's activities are tightly scheduled by those in authority
(d) there is a single rational plan design (supposedly) to fulfil the official aims of the institution.
You may never have been in an institution which fulfils each of these criteria. However, you may have experienced similar situations to that described by Goffman. If so, does your experience tend to confirm or refute his ideas?

6 Goffman's perspective is an interactionist one. What evidence is there of this perspective in this passage?

7 Goffman's research was done at St. Elizabeth's hospital, Washington, during the year 1955–6. He says, 'I started out in the role of an assistant to the athletic director, when pressed avowing to be a student of recreation and community life, and I passed the day with patients, avoiding sociable contact with the staff and the carrying of a key. I did not sleep in the wards and the top hospital management knew what my aims were. . . . The limits, of both my method and my application of it, are obvious. . . .' What are they?

A. Scull

Decarceration: Community Treatment and the Deviant—A Radical View,
1984, pp. 1–2, 129–35

'Decarceration' is a word which has not yet entered the dictionary. But it is increasingly being used to designate a process with momentous implications for all of us. It is shorthand for a state-sponsored policy of closing down asylums, prisons, and reformatories. Mad people, criminals, and delinquents are being discharged or refused admission to the dumps in which they have been traditionally housed. Instead, they are to be left at large, to be coped with 'in the community'.

We are told by those who run programmes of this sort that keeping the criminal and the mentally disturbed in our midst is 'humane'. We are informed that it is a 'more effective' means of curing or rehabilitating such people. And, miracle of miracles, we learn that this approach is also 'cheaper'! With an alternative which embraces such an array of virtues, who can be surprised to learn that mental hospitals are emptying faster and faster, and that with each passing day the convicted felon's chances of going to prison grow more remote?

On closer examination, it turns out that this whole enterprise is built on a foundation of sand. The contention that treatment in the community is more effective than institutionalisation is an empty one. There is massive ignorance about what 'community treatment' actually involves, and about the likely effects of abandoning institutional controls. The claim that leaving deviants at large 'cures' or 'rehabilitates' them is just that—a claim. Little or no solid evidence can be offered in its support. Instead, it rests uneasily on a cloud of rhetoric and wishful thinking. Most people's conception of the 'humane' does not embrace placing senile men and women in the hands of rapacious nursing home operators or turning loose the perpetrators of violent crimes, under conditions which guarantee that they will receive little or no supervision. . . .

What has the new approach meant in practice? For thousands of the old, already suffering in varying degrees from mental confusion and deterioration, is has meant premature death. For others, it has meant that they have been left to rot and decay, physically and otherwise, in broken down welfare hotels or in what are termed, with Orwellian euphemism, 'personal-care' nursing homes. For thousands of younger psychotics discharged into the streets, it has meant a nightmare existence in the blighted centres of our cities, amidst neighbourhoods crowded with prostitutes, ex-felons, addicts, alcoholics, and the other human rejects now repressively tolerated by our society. . . .

For the criminal and the delinquent, 'community corrections' (as it is called) has meant a further erosion of the sanctions imposed on their conduct. Not only are they steadily less likely to be caught in the first place, but if they do have the misfortune to be apprehended and convicted, their chance of receiving a prison term grows ever more remote. Instead, they find themselves released on probation, 'supervised' by men coping with caseloads of one and two hundred persons. This allows the probation officer to give each case an average of ten or fifteen minutes' attention per week.

Excluded from the more desirable neighbourhoods by zoning practices and organised community opposition, the decarcerated deviants are in any case impelled by economics—the need for cheap housing and to be close to a welfare office—to cluster in the ghettos and the decaying core of the inner city. As for the criminal, he is also attracted by the tokenism of police operations in these areas and by the willingness of the wider (white) society to leave ghetto residents to fend for themselves. Decarceration thus forms yet one more burden heaped on the backs of those who are most obviously the victims of our society's inequities. And it places the deviant in those communities least able to care for or cope with him. . . .

Far from asylums having been 'altruistic institutions . . . detached from the social structures that perpetuate poverty', they were clearly important elements in sustaining these structures. For at this period, the influential classes in both England and America were all but unanimous in their unwillingness to insulate the population as a whole from the twin spurs of poverty and unemployment. Under the conditions characteristic of early industrial capitalism, relief threatened to undermine radically the whole notion of a labour market. It interfered with labour mobility. It encouraged the retention of 'a vast inert mass of redundant labour' in rural areas, where the demand for labour was subject to wide seasonal fluctuations. It distorted the operations of the labour market, not least by creating cost differentials between one town and one region and another. And the guarantee of subsistence had a pernicious effect on labour productivity and discipline. On the ideological level, this determination to restrict relief was at once reflected and strengthened by the hegemony of classical liberalism. The latter's insistence that every man was to be free to pursue his fortune and at the same time was to be held responsible for his own success or failure, coupled with its dogmatic certainty that interference with the dictates of the free market could only be counterproductive in the long run (a proposition which could even be 'proved' theoretically), rendered the whole notion of social protectionism an anathema.

Hence came the stress on the principle of 'less eligibility' (enforced in large part through the discipline of institutions like workhouses and asylums); and the abhorrence of payments to individuals in the community (so-called 'outdoor relief') as the two central elements in dealing with the problems of extreme incapacity of one sort or another. For despite the ferocity of their ideological proclamations, as a practical political matter, the upper classes were aware of the impossibility of adhering rigidly to the dictates of the market. But although 'the residuum of paupers could not, admittedly, be left actually to starve,' the pressures of the market place must be interfered with as little as possible. Here, an institutionally-based system allowed the maintenance of conditions of relief which ensured that no one with any conceivable alternatives would seek public aid. In such a context, the asylum played its part, removing from lower-class families the impossible burdens imposed by those incapable of providing for their own subsistence, and thus ensuring that a potent source of discontent could be neutralised without having to alter society's basic structural arrangements. . . .

To summarise my thesis briefly at the outset, I shall argue that with the coming of the welfare state, segregative modes of social control became, in relative terms, far more costly and difficult to justify. This is particularly clear in the case of the group we have given most attention to, the mentally disturbed, who were formerly confined in 'monasteries of the mad'. As we have just seen, until well into the twentieth century, there had been little or no alternative to keeping the chronically disabled cases of insanity in the asylum; for although the overwhelming majority were harmless, they could not provide for their own subsistence, and no alternative sources of support were available to sustain them in the outside world. However, with the advent of a wide range of welfare programmes providing just such support, the opportunity cost of neglecting community care in favour of asylum treatment—inevitably far more costly than the most generous scheme of welfare payments—rose sharply. Simultaneously, the increasing socialisation of production costs by the state, something which has been taking place at an increasing pace during and since the Second World War, and of which modern welfare measures are merely one very important example, produced a growing fiscal crisis, as state expenditures continuously threatened to outrun available revenue. In combination, a focus on the interplay of these factors enables us to resolve what at first sight is a paradox—namely the emergence and persistence of efforts to curtail expenditures for control of 'problem populations' at a time when general expenditures on welfare items were expanding rapidly. For it is precisely the expansion of the one which made both possible and desirable the contraction of the other.

Noninstitutional approaches are less immediately palatable when, instead of 'sick' people, their object is criminals and delinquents. Incarceration, after all, has come to be virtually synonymous with punishment over the past century and a half; and the notion that lawbreakers deserve to suffer (i.e., be imprisoned) for their offences is a belief not easily abandoned. However, as the fiscal pressures on the state have intensified during the 1960s nad 1970s, so noninstitutional techniques for coping with the criminal and the delinquent have come to exert an ever-greater fascination for criminal justice planners and policy makers. Diversionary programmes enjoy a mounting popularity as traditional convictions as to the value of imprisonment for purposes of retribution and deterrence not so coincidentally lose their longstanding hold —on policy makers, if not on the public at large.

Glossary   Rapacious grasping, predatory.

Orwellian euphemism this refers to George Orwell's book *1984*, the
  characters of which are encouraged to use a special form of English.
  In it many words mean their opposite—freedom = bondage,
  war = peace, etc. In this way, the unpleasant features of that society
  are disguised by euphemisms: the substitution of harsh or
  unpleasant words by mild ones.
Zoning practices the practice of putting undesirable residents in an
  area of their own, away from those who might object to their
  presence, usually the middle class.
Altruistic being unselfish.
Relief what today are called 'benefits', i.e. payments to those in
  unfortunate circumstances.
Pernicious destructive.
Hegemony of classic liberalism the dominance in people's minds
  (hegemony) of the ideas of classic liberalism, primarily the stress on
  individual freedom to pursue one's own interests without hindrance
  by the state.
Anathema a detested thing.
Less eligibility the principle that conditions for those receiving poor
  relief (i.e. welfare benefits of any kind) should be made worse than
  those of the working population in order to discourage
  'scrounging'.
Residuum that which remains; (here) the poor who are left after those
  who can work have been found work.
Segregative modes of social control methods of controlling people's
  behaviour by isolating those whose behaviour is unacceptable.
Opportunity cost an economic concept which refers to the idea that,
  in buying or doing one thing, one has lost the opportunity to buy
  or do something else.
Fiscal crisis the inadequacy of income raised by government to meet
  its expenditure needs.
Synonymous meaning the same as.

Questions

1 What is meant be 'decarceration' and why do governments find it
   an attractive policy?
2 What is the difference between the theory and the practice of this
   policy?
3 Why were total institutions such as workhouses and asylums set up?
4 Why is there now a pressure to decarcerate people when there was
   not such a pressure before?
5 What evidence would be necessary to test Scull's thesis 'Mad
   people, criminals and delinquents are being discharged or refused
   admission to the dumps in which they have been traditionally
   housed'? How could this evidence be collected?

Questions on Goffman and Scull extracts

1 In the light of Goffman's critique of incarceration and Scull's attack
   on decarceration as it is practised at the moment, what social policy
   measures would you advocate for the mentally ill, the criminal, the
   old and others who have traditionally been put in institutions?
2 '"Community care" is a euphemism for abdication of responsibility
   by government.' Explain and discuss.

M. Castells

City, Class and Power, 1978, pp. 175–8

The acquired knowledge of the practical and theoretical fields of the urban must now be more fully developed. In this double movement, it is the development of new historical practices which becomes decisive. How is this question posed at present? What makes it new, and what are the perspectives of its practices in advanced capitalism?

In the first place, the <u>urban fiscal crisis</u>, which has for a number of years been affecting most large cities, demonstrates the structural limits, within the framework of dominant capitalist relations, of the increasing socialisation of public services. State intervention in the maintenance of essential but unprofitable public services has effectively been carried out at the cost of an inflationary and growing public debt, for the financing of these growing and indispensable public expenses could not be achieved through an imposition on capital (which refused to yield part of its profits), or, completely, through increased taxation—the eventual social struggles and political oppositions spelled out the limits of such a strengthening of state power at the expense of wage-earners. But from the moment the economic crisis threatened the stability of the circulation of capital because of uncontrollable inflation, one could witness a sudden halt in public expenditure, particularly in the area of public services. This was exercised through two principal mechanisms:

(1) Increasing state control on communes and regions, raising the level of local <u>rates</u>, and considerably reducing public-services budgets.

(2) The refusal by public and private financial institutions to issue loans to local and regional institutions. It is within this perspective that one should examine the fiscal crisis of New York and other large American cities, the increase in local rates in the United Kingdom, the drastic reduction of municipal budgets imposed by the Italian government upon all large cities administered by the Left, the blocking of most social programmes in the Paris region, and so on. The first line of attack of the economic crisis has been that of a policy of austerity imposed by the dominant capitalist groups, and which has taken the form of a questioning of the socialised functions of production, exchange and consumption which were to have been undertaken by the local government of large cities. The urban fiscal crisis is, in reality, the crisis of the Welfare State, and appears as the most immediate expression of a fundamental transformation of the historical model of capitalist accumulation which had prevailed since the Second World War.

This phenomenon is linked to the appearance and development of the *ecological question*, which is increasingly situated at the centre of the debate on the characteristics and objectives of the mode of economic and social organisation. In fact, the criticisms of the ecologists, who are becoming increasingly influential, go beyond the problems of the preservation of nature. Despite their political ambiguity and their intellectual confusions, even at times their naïve naturalism, they denounce the growing contradiction between the characteristics of a model of accumulation and their resulting consequences at the level of social organisation. The more society emphasises, at the cultural level, use value over exchange value (that is, the more everyday happiness becomes more important than the acquisition of commodities) the more absurd it becomes to accumulate for accumulation's sake. But capital cannot stop itself, it must continue to invest, to produce <u>surplus value</u> and to realise it as commodities, even if it means crushing its own productive agents, and even if this includes the executive level. Metropolitan hugeness, the destruction of natural resources, the decline in living standards, the massification of <u>mores</u> and the individualistic savagery of practices thus appear as the side of the coin whose other side is minted in the hallucinating design of an uncontrollable world monopoly capitalism. Therefore, while the questions which the ecologists pose may seem naïve, they fundamentally question the social relations of exploitation and domination. It is a search for open spaces instead of shopping centres, solar energy instead of nuclear plants, social facilities instead of commercial ones, community interaction instead of the mass media, local autonomy instead of a technocratic pseudo-planning. These are not just the themes of professional <u>symposia</u>. They constitute a questioning of the material organisation of daily life by capital and by the state.

In this way the development of the ecological critique appears as an essential historical reference point which demands the formulation of new thinking on the organisation of relations between society and cities, between the mode of economic growth and the forms of social life.

Now, if these and other questions at the basis of urban policy are being strongly posed in the 1970s, it is because *new urban social movements* have given rise to them. At an initial level, the protest movements have extended to the sphere of social consumption the permanent battle engaged upon by the labour movement at the level of mass living standards. The housing crisis gave rise to tenants' organisations. Refusing to accept the transport crisis, commuters' associations put forward new proposals for transport in the large cities. Rejecting the lack of facilities and the centralisation of their management, neighbourhood associations have made their interests felt in urban development. But this questioning of urban organisation is not simply that of the defence of resident interests, it also relates to the opposition to relations of domination. For example, the feminist movement is threatening the very

logic of the urban structure, for it is the subordinate role of women which enables the minimal 'maintenance' of its housing, transport and public facilities. In the end, if the system still 'works' it is because women guarantee unpaid transportation (movement of people and merchandise), because they repair their homes, because they make meals when there are no canteens, because they spend more time shopping around, because they look after others' children when there are no nurseries, and because they offer 'free entertainment' to the producers where there is a social vacuum and an absence of cultural creativity. If these women who 'do nothing' ever stopped to do 'only that', the whole urban structure as we know it would become completely incapable of maintaining its functions. The contemporary city also rests upon the subordination of 'women consumers' to the 'men producers'. The subversive nature of the feminist movement is not due to its demand for more nurseries, but to the refusal henceforth onwards to look after anything at all!

Glossary

Urban fiscal crisis the financial crisis of city areas in which funds available are increasingly inadequate to meet the cost of providing services.

Rates a form of raising revenue for local government.

Ecological question (here) a set of problems relating to the urban environment.

Surplus value profit derived from exploiting workers.

Mores customs.

Symposia conferences at which views on one topic are collected.

Questions

1 What are:
  (a) the reasons for
  (b) the consequences of
  the urban fiscal crisis?
2 What evidence is there:
  (a) for
  (b) against
  Castells' view?
3 Comment on Castells' theory concerning the ecological questions and the groups which form to fight over them.

Bibliography

Source of extracts

V. George and P. Wilding, *The Impact of Social Policy*, Routledge & Kegan Paul, London, 1984

J. Le Grand, *Making Redistribution Work*, in H. Glennerster, (ed.), *The Future of the Welfare State*, Heinemann, London, 1983

P. Townsend, *Poverty in the United Kingdom*, Penguin, Harmondsworth, 1979

D. Piachaud, 'Peter Townsend and the Holy Grail', *New Society*, 10 September 1981

R. M. Titmuss, *Welfare State and Welfare Society*, reprinted in E. Butterworth and R. Holman, *Social Welfare in Modern Britain*, Fontana, London, 1975

R. Mishra, *Society and Social Policy*, Second Edition, Macmillan, London, 1981, reprinted 1984

N. Ginsburg, *Class, Capital and Social Policy*, Macmillan, London 1979

M. Friedman and R. Friedman, *Free to Choose*, Secker & Warburg, London, 1980

E. Goffman, *Asylums*, Penguin, Harmondsworth 1984, first published 1961

A. Scull, *Decarceration: Community Treatment and the Deviant—a Radical View* Polity Press, London 1984, first published 1977

M. Castells, *City, Class and Power*, Macmillan, London 1978

Reference in the Introduction

J. Le Grand, *The Strategy of Equality*, Allen & Unwin, London, 1982

D. Donnison, *The Politics of Poverty*, Martin Robertson, Oxford, 1982

B. Abel-Smith and P. Townsend, *The Poor and the Poorest*, G. Bell & Sons, London, 1965

T. Parsons, *The System of Modern Societies*, Englewood Cliffs, New Jersey, 1971

E. Durkheim, *The Division of Labour in Society*, The Free Press, New York, 1947

T. H. Marshall, *Sociology at the Crossroads and other essays*, Heinemann, London, 1963

K. Davis and W. E. Moore, *Some Principles of Stratification*, in R. Bendix and S. M. Lipset, (eds), *Class, Status and Power*, Routledge & Kegan Paul, London, 1967

H. Gans, *More Equality*, Pantheon, New York, 1973

R. Mathews, *Decarceration and the Fiscal Crisis*, in B. Fine *et al.*, (eds), *Capitalism and the Rule of Law*, Hutchinson, London 1979

F. Tonnies, *Community and Society*, Harper & Row, New York, 1887 and 1963

L. Wirth, *Urbanism as a Way of Life*, 1938 in R. Sennett, *Classic Essays in the Culture of Cities*, Appleton–Century Crofts, New York

C. R. Shaw and H. D. McKay, *Juvenile Delinquency in Urban Areas*, University of Chicago Free Press, Chicago 1942

Reference in George and Wilding extract

J. Le Grand, *The Strategy of Equality*, Allen & Unwin, London, 1982

Further reading

W. E. Baugh, *Introduction to the Social Services*, Macmillan, London, 1983

M. Castells, *The Urban Question*, Edward Arnold, London, 1977

C. Cockburn, *The Local State*, Pluto Press, London 1977 (a Marxist study of Lambeth's local politics)

B. Fay, *Social Theory and Political Practice*, Allen & Unwin, London 1980

F. Field *et al.*, *To Him Who Hath*, Penguin, Harmondsworth, 1977

V. George and P. Wilding, *Ideology and Social Welfare*, Routledge & Kegan Paul, London, 1976

S. Iliffe, *The NHS: A Picture of Health?*, Lawrence and Wishart, London 1983

R. Mellor, *Theories of Urbanisation* in R. J. Anderson and W. W. Sharrock, (eds), *Applied Sociological Perspectives*, Allen & Unwin, London 1984

C. Offe, *Dilemmas of the Welfare State*, Hutchinson, London, 1984

P. Saunders, *Urban Politics*, Penguin, Harmondsworth 1980 (a study of Croydon's local politics)

P. Townsend and N. Davidson, *Inequalities in Health*, Penguin, Harmondsworth, 1982

The Sociology of Youth Culture

The extracts in this chapter have been chosen to illustrate some of the different perspectives on youth culture adopted by sociologists and to illustrate how they relate to each other. The first selection is from G. Pearson's book *Hooligan*. It describes a subcultural style popular among working class youths of the late nineteenth century. Young people adopting this style were called (in London) 'hooligans' and essential aspects of their manner of dress and behaviour were found not only in the capital but across the nation. In Manchester they were not hooligans but 'scuttlers', in Birmingham 'peaky binders' or 'sloggers', while in Bradford there were gangs such as the 'grey mare boys' who adopted the style described here.

Pearson's general thesis is that complaints are unfounded about 'the youth of today' and the 'post–war generation' lacking the civility of their predecessors. He argues that people have always looked back to a Golden Age, which is usually assumed to have ended about twenty or thirty years ago, during which people behaved much better than they do today and when there was very little crime. He relies on evidence from newspapers and journals to show that this 'things ain't what they used to be' syndrome is found in every age and that the supposed good behaviour of people in the past is and always has been a myth. At the time of the moral panic about hooligans in the 1890s people looked back to the 1860s and 70s. However, a study of the press of *that* time reveals a moral panic then about garrotting. This involved the garrotter moving in on his victim from the rear. He then:

> flings his right arm around the victim, striking him sharply on the forehead. Instinctively he [the victim] throws his head back, and in that movement loses every chance of escape. His throat is fully offered to his assailant, who instantly embraces it with his left arm. . . . (Pearson, quoting the *Cornhill Magazine*, 1863)

The victim quickly becomes unconscious and the garrotter and accomplices can rob him. In 1863 the Press make the complaint which will be heard thirty years later: the streets of London are no longer safe.

Pearson's thesis appears to undermine theories which see youth culture (and the problems of crime and deviance associated with it in the minds of many critics) as essentially a post–World War Two development. We should, therefore, read with caution the words of authors who suggest that post–war social change has given rise to youth culture. Such writers have proposed a number of causal factors for the rise of post–war youth culture. These have included:

- the expansion of education (A. Coleman, *The Adolescent Society*).
- The lack of proper socialisation of the young following the war (T. Fyvel, *Insecure Offenders*).

- The rise of the mass media and pre–packaged entertainment from America and their degrading effect, especially on the young (P. Johnson, *The Menace of Beatleism* and R. Hoggart, *The Uses of Literacy*).
- The new affluence of the young (M. Abrams, *The Teenage Consumer* and others).
- The need for an intermediate stage between leaving the protection of the family, with its distinctive patterns of behaviour and entering the increasingly impersonal and competitive wider society (S. Eisenstadt, *From Generation to Generation*).

The second extract comes from a text central to the sociology of youth, *Resistance Through Rituals*, edited by S. Hall and T. Jefferson. The separate chapters by different authors in this book elaborate variations on the same neo–Marxist theme: that working class youth subcultures such as mods, Teds and skinheads are an attempt to win space from the dominant bourgeois ideas and institutions. These subcultures represent resistance to bourgeois hegemony, though not *actual* resistance; for example, in the form of revolution, but symbolic resistance, through rituals. For example:

> Skinheads reassert, but 'imaginarily', the values of a class, the essence of a style, a kind of 'fan–ship' to which few working class adults any longer subscribe; they 're–present' a sense of territory and locality which the planners and speculators are rapidly destroying: they 'declare' as alive and well a game which is being commercialised, professionalised and spectacular–ised. 'Skins Rule, OK'. OK?.

The extract chosen here concerns not skinheads but girls. Largely ignored in the literature of youth culture and subcultures (except as mothers, usually inadequate ones) and in a sense marginal to at least some of the subcultural styles. McRobbie and Garber, the authors, try to locate girls within the neo–Marxist theory put forward in *Resistance Through Rituals*.

The third extract comes from Stan Cohen's *Folk Devils and Moral Panics*. It is not a summary of the study itself, which is a well–known interactionist account of the creation of mods and rockers by media labelling. Rather it is a critique of approaches such as that taken in *Resistance Through Rituals* and D. Hebdige's *Subculture: The Meaning of Style* which attempt to read things into subcultural phenomena which are simply not there. This search for symbols of a deeper meaning (rejection of bourgeois hegemony, the attempt to capture 'space', etc.) involves a process known as semiotics. According to Cohen it is an enterprise fraught with dangers for the sociologist who attempts it. His criticisms of it are elaborated in this extract from the introduction to *Folk Devils and Moral Panics*.

The fourth extract, from *Policing the Crisis*, is related to S. Cohen's interactionist account of the rise of mods and rockers. Cohen suggested that mods and rockers should be seen as creations of the mass media. In order to sell papers and acquire listeners and viewers the media whip up a sense of outrage (a moral panic) against particular folk devils, in this case these youth subcultures. By doing so the media serve to amplify the deviance out of all proportion to its original state.

Reading accounts of 'riots' in seaside resorts by 'hordes' of mods and rockers who descend on them for bank holidays suggests to young people that this might be an exciting thing to do. Thus the prophecy creates its own fulfilment. The media soon find that there are *real* mods and rockers and *real* riots to report. However, it is the media themselves which are to blame for creating the styles adopted by mods and rockers and for suggesting 'appropriate' forms of behaviour to them. The neo–Marxist authors of *Policing the Crisis*, S. Hall *et al.*, agree that there is some truth in the notion of moral panics created by the media and in the fact that they amplify any original deviance that there may have been. However, these authors go further than Cohen does in looking for the causes of these panics. For Cohen the causes lie simply in the search by the media for exciting stories to sell newspapers and their invention of them where none exist. Hall *et al.*, though, suggest that the generation of moral panic is part of the way in which capitalist society deals with the economic and social crises which periodically affect it. Public feeling is whipped up against some 'enemy within' and this popular mood is used to justify a tightening–up of the control culture, for example, by giving greater powers to the police. Such a tightening–up is required in order to ensure that capitalism is able to ride the storm of economic and social crisis, clamping down on discontent and hence preventing unwanted social change, even revolution. Social concern about 'the youth of today' and other folk devils is, from this perspective, an artificially created prelude to a tightening of law, strengthening of police powers, harsher sentencing, and so on. The extract chosen here elaborates on this theory.

Marxists criticise interactionists for being blind to large scale socioeconomic forces because they, the interactionists, focus on small scale interaction between individuals and groups. A comparison of Hall's study with Cohen's illustrates this point. While Cohen has realised the importance of media labelling and the effect this can have on behaviour, he has missed the significance of this, specifically its role in propping up the capitalist system.

The final selection, from Marsh, Rosser and Harré's *The Rules of Disorder*, is a product of a detailed participant observation study of the fans of the Oxford United football team. Adopting a phenomenological perspective, they give an account of the world as seen by these fans and they try to show that the stereotypes the general public hold about such fans are misconceived. In particular the fans' reputation for mindless violence is almost completely unfounded (although it is a reputation fostered by the fans themselves) because there are clearly defined 'rules of disorder' which limit violence and channel it into well–defined paths. The authors make no attempt to 'read' working class subcultures as a response to capitalist society or in any other way. Their task is an ethnographic one: to make the world of the fan accessible to and understood by the rest of us by describing it from the fans' point of view. Their phenomenological perspective is quite different, therefore, from the neo–Marxist one of the contributors to *Resistance Through Rituals* and *Policing the Crisis*. It is different, too, from the more closely related interactionist perspective of Stan Cohen.

While both Cohen and the authors of *The Rules of Disorder* are concerned with the motives and meanings of young people, the latter do not see the fans' world as 'created' by outside forces. It is the product of the fans themselves.

G. Pearson

Hooligan: A History of Respectable Fears, 1983, pp. 74, 92–4

The word 'hooligan' made an abrupt entrance into common English usage, as a term to describe gangs of rowdy youths, during the hot summer of 1898. 'Hooligans' and 'Hooliganism' were thrust into the headlines in the wake of a turbulent August Bank Holiday celebration in London which had resulted in unusually large numbers of people being brought before the courts for disorderly behaviour, drunkenness, assaults on police, street robberies and fighting. One of the more alarming aspects of these Bank Holiday disturbances was that they highlighted fierce traditions of resistance to the police in working–class neighbourhoods, so that not uncommonly policemen attempting to make street arrests would be set upon by large crowds — sometimes numbering two or three hundred people — shouting 'Rescue! Rescue!' and 'Boot him!'

At first it was not entirely clear where the word 'Hooligan' had sprung from — and it remains unclear to this day — or exactly what it meant, other than some kind of novel reference to street violence and ruffianism. It seems most likely, however, that it was a word like 'Teddy Boy' or 'Mod' or 'Skinhead' which, coming out of the popular culture of working–class London, had been adopted by youths in some localities in order to describe themselves and what they took for the common identity. . . .

One thing that quickly became apparent in the aftermath of the Bank Holiday affair was that the Hooligans all looked alike. But it was not in the way that the poor had always looked alike — it was not, that is, because they were shabby, shoeless and grubby as moles — but because the gangs wished to look alike, and had adopted a uniform dress–style. 'Look at them well,' said *The Daily Graphic* (16 November 1900) when the dust had settled a little and the danger could be looked in the face, 'They are the genuine article — real Hooligans':

'The boys affect a kind of uniform. No hat, collar, or tie is to be seen. All of them have a peculiar muffler twisted around the neck, a cap set rakishly forward, well over the eyes, and trousers very tight at the knee and very loose at the foot. The most characteristic part of their uniform is the substantial leather belt heavily mounted with metal. It is not ornamental, but then it is not intended for ornament.'

There can be no doubt that the buckle–end of a belt could be a formidable weapon, but in fact the belts were often pricked out in fancy patterns or embellished with metal studs in much the same way that modern motor–bike boys adorn their jackets with stud designs. Newspaper cartoons depicting the London Hooligans added another small detail of fashion: the bell–bottom trousers were shown with a tasty buttoned vent in the side. Local gangs also improvised local variations in style — velvet caps in Battersea or plaid caps in Poplar, for example, as a badge of identity — and there were certainly trend–setters among the Hooligans. One way–out youngster appeared in court following the Bank Holiday disturbances with his hair dressed in what sounds remarkably like the 'Mohican cut' which had a brief moment of popularity among more outlandish Teds in the 1950s and which has reappeared with the Punks. 'The appearance of the witness caused some amusement in court,' observed *The Daily Graphic* (6 August 1898). 'His hair had been clipped as closely as possible to the scalp, with the exception of a small patch on the crown of the head, which was pulled down over the forehead to form a fringe.' It was probably no more than a daring exaggeration of the 'donkey–fringe' style which was the standard Hooligan haircut. But here was a youth so far ahead of his time that if he had turned up on the streets of London sixty or seventy years later, he would still have been recognised as a sure sign of an alarmingly unrivalled degeneration among the young.

Questions

1 Would you agree with Pearson's thesis that people tend to look back to a golden age? What evidence have you to support your view?

2 In what areas of social life, other than the behaviour of youth, are things generally considered not to be what they were? Is there any justification for this belief in any of these areas?

3 Attempt a 'reading' of the hooligan style, in other words try to explain why they adopted the particular manner of dress and attitudes they did.

A. McRobbie and J. Garber

Girls and Subcultures, in S. Hall and T. Jefferson (eds), *Resistance through Rituals*,1975, pp. 213, 219–21

Teddy boy culture was an escape from the family into the street and the cafe, as well as evening and weekend trips 'into town'. Girls would certainly dress up and go out, either with boyfriends or, as a group of girls, with a group of boys. But there would be much less 'hanging about' and street–corner involvement. In the working–class parental value system, boys were expected to 'have fun while they could' (though many working class parents regarded Teddy boy kinds of 'fun' as pretty peculiar): but girls suffered the double injunction of 'having fun' while not 'getting yourself into trouble'. The sexual taboo, and the moral framework and 'rules' in which it was embodied continued to work more heavily against girls than against boys. While boys could spend a lot of time 'hanging about' in the territory, the pattern for girls was probably more firmly structured between being at home, preparing (often with other girls) to go out on a date, and going out. Boys who had, sexually and socially, 'sown their wild oats' could 'turn over a new leaf' and settle down: for girls, the consequences of getting known in the neighbourhood as one of the 'wild oats' to be 'sown' were drastic and irreversible.

There was certainly more attention than, say, in pre–war youth culture to the teenage leisure market and its accompanying manifestations (concerts, records, pin–ups, magazines), and girls as well as boys would have shared this. But many of these activities would have been easily appropriated into the traditionally defined cultural space of a home or peer–centred girls' 'culture' — operated mainly within the home, or visiting a girl–friend's home, or at parties, without involving the riskier and more frowned–on path of hanging about the streets or cafes. There was

room for a good deal of the new teenage consumer culture *within* the 'culture of the bedroom'—experimenting with make–up, listening to records, reading the mags, sizing up the boyfriends, chatting, jiving: it depended, rather, on some access by girls to room and space within (rather than outside) the *home*—even if the room was uneasily shared with an older sister. ...

Some of what has been conjectured above may lead us to the conclusion that the majority of girls find alternative strategies to those of the boys' sub–cultures. The important question, then, may not be the absence or presence of girls in the male sub–cultures, but the complementary ways in which girls interact among themselves and with each other to form a distinctive culture of their own. One of the most significant forms of an alternative 'sub–culture' among girls is the culture of the Teeny Bopper. While this is in no way a new phenomenon (the girl/pop idol relationship has been in existence for the last twenty years), it is one of the most highly manufactured forms of available youth culture—it is almost totally packaged. Evidence of this can be cited throughout the entire pop trajectory, but what is significant about the Teeny Bopper syndrome of the 70s is that it was directed expressly at an even younger market, i.e. ten–fifteen year old girls, too young even to have heard the Beatles, and who were certainly not turned on by the new heavy rock (E.L.O., Yes, Led Zeppelin or Deep Purple) which their elder brothers and sisters listened to so avidly. The attractiveness of this market with its quick turnover potential (Mark Bolan this week, David Cassidy the next) offered ailing American film and broadcasting companies a chance to boost their profits too, Screengems and M.G.M. in particular.

Even in relation to so manufactured a network we can locate a variety of negotiative processes at work amongst the girls themselves.

(a) Teeny Bopper culture can easily be accommodated, for ten to fifteen year old girls, in the home, requiring only a bedroom and a record player and permission to invite friends; but in this capacity it might offer an opportunity for girls to take part in a quasi-sexual ritual (it is important to remember that girls have no access to the masturbatory rituals common amongst boys). The culture also offers a chance for both private and public manifestations—the postered bedroom or the rock concert.

(b) Teeny Bopper culture is sufficiently flexible to allow anybody to join; it does not operate any exclusion rules or qualification on entry—thus differing greatly from the girls' school environment, where participation in certain activities demands a fair degree of competence and money.

(c) There are no risks involving personal humiliation or degradation, no chance of being stood up or bombed out. Some Teeny Bopper girls we have talked to show a remarkable awareness of the fact that boys are all out for 'the one thing', and that girls lose all the way along in that game. Involvement in Teeny Bopper culture, then, can be seen as a kind of defensive retreat away from the possibility of being sexually labelled, but also as displaying a high degree of self-sufficiency within the various small female groupings; 'we have a great laugh with the girls'.

(d) The obsession with particular stars, Donny Osmond etc., can be viewed as a meaningful reaction against the selective and authoritarian structures which control the girls' lives at school. That is, 'obsessions' can be a means of alienating the teacher, and, if shared, can offer a defensive solidarity, especially for those who are conscious of themselves as being academic failures.

While there may certainly be elements in Teeny Bopper culture which enable girls to negotiate a space of their own, it has also to be said that the relationship between the girls and the idols conjured up, and, as far as one can tell, reciprocated, is suffused with fantasy elements—the displacement—and to some degree de-sexualising of what are patently commercial and sexually-manipulative icons of the Teeny Bopper market. Here the element of fantasisation and fetishisation which is present, at all times, to some degree in the heavy involvement—boys and girls—with the 'presentational images' of commercial pop culture, is raised to a peculiarly high and powerfully charged pitch. There seems little doubt that the fantasy relationships which characterise this resistance depend for their very existence on the subordinate, adoring female in awe of the male on a pedestal. The culture also tends to anticipate the form of future 'real' relationships, and in so far as these are articulated in the magazine articles and stories, directs the girls hopefully towards romance and eventually an idealised version of marriage. All the way through the Teeny Bopper spectrum then, the dialectic is, as it were, tighter. The small, structured and highly manufactured space that is available for ten to fifteen year old girls to create a personal and autonomous area seems to be offered only on the understanding that these strategies also symbolise a future general subordination—as well as a present one.

Our focus on this piece, then, has been one which tends to move away from the Subcultural group phenomena simply because, in our view, the sub-cultural group may not be the most likely place where those equivalent rituals, responses and negotiations will be located. We feel that when the dimension of sexuality is included in the study of youth subcultures, girls can be seen to be negotiating a different space, offering a different type of resistence to what can at least in part be viewed as their sexual subordination.

Glossary Injunction order or instruction.

Jiving dancing, especially to jazz.

Negotiative processes methods of coming to agreement.

Icons images or symbols.

Fetishisation making something the object of worship.

Questions

1 What reasons are suggested for the fact that girls' participation in youth subcultures is different from that of boys?
2 Why are girls' subcultures oriented around the bedroom, according to these authors?
3 What is meant by the phrase 'girls can be seen to be ... offering a different type of resistance to ... their sexual subordination'?
4 If the girls' 'Teeny Bopper' culture is largely a product of the capitalist economy, as the authors suggest, why is it chosen to 'negotiate space' for these girls?
5 Do you agree with the authors' description of girls' subcultures and their 'reading' of them?

S. Cohen
Folk Devils and Moral Panics, 1980, pp. xvii–ix

Let me conclude this section by giving an example of the dangers of searching the forest of symbols without such a method—or indeed any method. This is the example often used by Hebdige and other theorists of punk: the wearing of the swastika emblem. Time and time again, we are assured that although this symbol is 'on one level' intended to outrage and shock, it is *really* being employed in a meta–language: the wearers are ironically distancing themselves from the very message that the symbol is usually intended to convey. Displaying a swastika (or singing lyrics like 'Belsen was a gas') shows how symbols are stripped from their natural context, exploited for empty effect, displayed through mockery, distancing, irony, parody, inversion.

But how are we to know this? We are never told much about the 'thing': when, how, where, by whom or in what context it is worn. We do not know what, if any, difference exists between indigenous and sociological explanations. We are given no clues about how these particular actors manage the complicated business of distancing and irony. In the end, there is no basis whatsoever for choosing between this particular sort of interpretation and any others: say, that for many or most of the kids walking around with swastikas on their jackets, the dominant context is simply conformity, blind ignorance or knee–jerk racism.

Something more of an answer is needed to such questions than simply quoting Genet or Breton. Nor does it help much to have Hebdige's admission (about a similar equation) that such interpretations are not open to being tested by standard sociological procedures: 'Though it is undeniably there in the social structure, it is there as an immanence, as a submerged possibility, as an existential option; and one cannot verify an existential option scientifically—you either see it or you don't.'

Well, in the swastika example, I don't. And, moreover, when Hebdige does defend this particular interpretation of punk, he does it not by any existential leap but by a good old–fashioned positivist appeal to evidence: punks, we are told, 'were not generally sympathetic to the parties of the extreme right' and showed 'widespread support for the anti–Fascist movement'. These statements certainly constitute evidence, not immanence—though not particularly good evidence and going right against widespread findings about the racism and support for restrictive immigration policies among substantial sections of working–class youth.

I do not want to judge one reading against the other nor to detract from the considerable interest and value of this new decoding work. We need to be more sceptical though of the exquisite aesthetics which tell us about things being fictional and real, absent and present, caricatures and re–assertions. This language might indeed help by framing a meaning to the otherwise meaningless; but this help seems limited when we are drawn to saying about skinhead attacks on Pakistani immigrants: 'Every time the boot went in, a contradiction was concealed, glossed over or made to disappear.' It seems to me—to borrow from the language of contradictions—that both a lot more and a lot less was going on.

Time indeed to leave the forest of symbols; and '... shudder back thankfully into the light of the social day'....

Mundane day–to–day delinquency is and always has been predominantly property crime and has little to do with magic, codes or rituals. I doubt that many of the intricate preoccupations of these theorists impinge much on the lives, say, of that large (and increasing) number of juveniles in today's custodial institutions: the 11,638 sent to detention centres, 7,067 to Borstals, 7,519 to prisons in 1978.

I fear that the obvious fascination with these spectacular subcultures will draw attention away from these more enduring numbers as well as lead to quite inappropriate criticisms of other modes of explanation. This, of course, will not be entirely the fault of the theorists themselves: the Birmingham group, for example, makes it absolutely clear that they are only concerned with subcultures which have reasonably tight boundaries, distinctive shapes and cohere around specific actions or places. As they are very careful to point out, the majority of working-class youth never enter such subcultures at all: 'individuals may in their personal life careers move into one and out of one, or indeed, several subcultures. Their relations to the existing subcultures may be fleeting or permanent, marginal or central.'

Despite these disavowals though, the *method* used in most of this work detracts us from answering the more traditional, but surely not altogether trivial sociological questions about these different patterns of involvement. Why should some individuals exposed to the same pressures respond one way rather than another or with different degrees of commitment? As one sympathetic criticism suggests, the problem arises from *starting* with groups who are already card–carrying members of a subculture and then working backwards to uncover their class base. If the procedure is reversed and one starts from the class base, rather than the cultural responses, it becomes obvious that an identical location generates a very wide range of responses and modes of accommodation.

Glossary

Meta–language a higher or second order form of language, a language within a language.

Indigenous explanations (here) explanations given by the people involved; in this case, punks.

Genet and Breton French authors who helped found the school of semiotic analysis.

Immanence an inherent part of something.

Existential option a possibility that one can choose to bring into existence.

Existential leap a leap of faith, a decision to believe in something even though its existence is uncertain or unprovable.

Exquisite aesthetics taste and awareness which is refined to an exceptional degree.

Birmingham group the Centre for Contemporary Cultural Studies at Birmingham University.

Disavowals denials of belief.

Questions

1 What, in your own words, is the point that Cohen is making in this passage?
2 What problems does he see with 'semiotics', the technique of reading social phenomena for hidden meanings and messages?
3 Attempt a reading of a subculture you know well.
4 In general, would you agree that a semiotic analysis of youth subcultures is a useful exercise for the sociologist?

S. Hall *et al.*
Policing the Crisis, 1978, pp. 221–22

The concepts of 'state' and 'hegemony' appear, at first sight, to belong to different conceptual territory from that of the 'moral panic'. And part of our intention is certainly to situate the 'moral panic' as one of the forms of appearance of a more deep-seated historical crisis, and thereby to give it greater historical and theoretical specificity. This relocation of the concept on a different and deeper level of analysis does not, however, lead us to abandon it altogether as useless. Rather, it helps us to identify the 'moral panic' as one of the principal surface manifestations of the crisis, and in part to explain how and why the crisis came to be *experienced* in that form of consciousness, and what the displacement of a conjunctural crisis into the popular form of a 'moral panic' accomplishes, in terms of the way the crisis is managed and contained. We have therefore retained the notion of the 'moral panic' as a necessary part of our analysis: attempting to redefine it as one of the key ideological forms in which a historical crisis is 'experienced and fought out'. One of the effects of retaining the notion of 'moral panic' is the penetration it provides into the otherwise extremely obscure means by which the working classes are drawn into processes which are occurring in large measure 'behind their backs', and led to experience and respond to contradictory developments in ways which make the operation of state power legitimate, credible and consensual. To put it crudely, the 'moral panic' appears to us to be one of the principal forms of ideological consciousness by means of which a 'silent majority' is won over to the support of increasingly coercive measures on the part of the state, and lends its legitimacy to a 'more than usual' exercise of control.

There is a tendency, in the early years of our period, for there to develop a succession of 'moral panics' around certain key topics of controversial public concern. In this early period, the panics tend to be centred on social and moral rather than political issues (youth, permissiveness, crime). Their typical form is that of a dramatic event which focuses and triggers a local response and public disquiet. Often as a result of local organising and moral entrepreneurship, the wider powers of the control culture are both alerted (the media play a crucial role here) and mobilised (the police, the courts). The issue is then seen as 'symptomatic' of wider, more troubling but less concrete themes. It escalates up the hierarchy of responsibility and control, perhaps provoking an offical enquiry or statement, which temporarily appeases the moral campaigners and dissipates the sense of panic. In what we think of as the middle period, in the later 1960s, these panics follow faster on the heels of one another than earlier; and an increasingly amplified general 'threat to society' is imputed to them (drugs, hippies, the underground, pornography, long-haired students, layabouts, vandalism, football hooliganism). In many instances the sequence is so speeded up that it bypasses the moment of *local* impact; there was no upsurge of grass-roots pressure required to bring the drugs squad crunching in on cannabis smokers. Both the media and the 'control culture' seem more alerted to their occurrence—the media quickly pick up the symptomatic event and the police and courts react quickly without considerable moral pressure from below. This speeded-up sequence tends to suggest a heightened sensitivity to troubling social themes.

There is indeed in the later stages a 'mapping together' of moral panics into a *general panic* about social order; and such a spiral has tended, not only in Britain, to culminate in what we call a 'law-and-order' campaign, of the kind which the Heath Shadow Cabinet constructed on the eve of the 1970 election, and which powered Nixon and Agnew into the White House in 1968. This coalescence into a concerted campaign marks a significant shift in the panic process, for the tendency to panic is now lodged at the heart of the state's political complex itself; and from that vantage-point, all dissensual breaks in the society can be more effectively designated as a 'general threat to law and order itself', and thus as subverting the general interest (which the state represents and protects). Panics now tend to operate from top to bottom. Post-1970, the law-and-order campaigners seem to have effectively sensitised the social-control apparatuses and the media to the possibility of a general threat to the stability of the state. Minor forms of dissent seem to provide the basis of 'scapegoat' events for a jumpy and alerted control culture; and this progressively pushes the state apparatuses into a more or less permanent 'control' posture. Schematically, the changing sequence in moral panics can be represented as follows:

(1) *Discrete moral panics* (early 1960s, e.g. 'mods' and 'rockers')
Dramatic event → public disquiet, moral entrepreneurs (sensitisation) → control culture action
(2) *'Crusading'—mapping together discrete moral panics to produce a 'speeded-up' sequence* (late 1960s, e.g. pornography and drugs)
Sensitisation (moral entrepreneurship) → dramatic event → control culture action
(3) *Post-'law-and-order' campaign: an altered sequence* (post–1970), e.g. mugging)
Sensitisation → control culture organisation and action (invisible) → dramatic event → control culture intensified action (visible)

Glossary

Hegemony the dominance in men and women's minds of a particular set of ideas.

Moral panic an outcry amongst the public about some social issue which seems to be threatening the fabric of society at a particular time.

Moral entrepreneurship acting as a definer of public morality, establishing the acceptable and the unacceptable.

Control culture consists of those institutions which act as agents of social control, for example the police, courts and the media.

Symptomatic indicating the presence of an underlying problem or disease.

Mapping together seeing something not as discrete but as part of a larger whole.

Coalescence the process of coming together or combining.

Dissensual lacking in agreement or consensus.

Subverting undermining.

Sensitisation the process of becoming sensitive to something, (here) a social problem.

Questions

1 What is the function of moral panics in capitalism, according to this passage?
2 Distinguish between a moral panic and a general panic.
3 Elaborate on what happens when the 'state apparatuses' adopt a 'control posture'.
4 Have any recent events occurred which might be used to confirm this theory of the relationship between moral panics and the control culture?
5 Generally, what problems can you identify with this theory?

P. Marsh, E. Rosser and R. Harré
The Rules of Disorder, 1978, pp. 97–9

The theme of this book has been that apparently disordered events on the football terraces and in the classroom can be seen as conforming to a very distinct and orderly system of roles, rules and shared meanings. Action is neither chaotic nor senseless but rather is structured and reasoned. Later we will argue that in the case of football fans this order derives from the very basic need of any society to possess social mechanisms by which aggression among its members can be controlled and managed. At this point in the development of the theme, however, we need to consider some expected consequences of order. One such consequence, we believe, is a conspiracy on the part of members of an orderly sub-culture to deny that order exists.

In conspiring to construct a reality which seems to be at variance with their tacit knowledge of orderly and rule–governed action, fans are engaged in the active creation (and adoption from the outside) of excitement. For fans, regularity and safety are things to be avoided. They are quite simply 'a drag'. What the soccer terraces offer is a chance to escape from the dreariness of the weekday world of work or school to something which is adventurous and stimulating. But in order to achieve the contrast it is necessary to construe, at least at one level, the soccer terraces as being radically different from the weekday world. School and work are safe and regular. *Ergo*, soccer terraces are potentially dangerous and unpredictable. Since fans 'know' that this is not the case—they are aware and can tell you that few people get hurt even when things 'get out of hand'—they must conspire to construct disorder. And because there is an easy rhetoric to hand—the rhetoric of the media which insists that events at football matches are *in fact* disordered, the conspiracy is an easy one to conduct.

Not only is such a conspiracy instrumental in achieving excitement and anticipation, it is also essential in the establishment and maintenance of careers. Certain roles would clearly not be available to fans unless conflict situations were capable of being perceived as requiring acts of courage and determination. If fights were seen as being purely ceremonial affairs involving no risk of injury, then the status of a fighter would be of very little value at all. But the status of aggro leader, as we have seen, affords the occupant a good deal of deference and kudos. There is a strong belief that such a person is ready to deal with any of the consequences that arise in challenging rival groups of fans. The emptiness of this belief is only removed if there exists a reality in which conflicts do indeed regularly lead to bloody end–products.

The idea of a conspiracy of this kind, then, is theoretically very plausible. Not only is it to be expected, it can be seen as a necessary consequence of an orderly system such as the one with which we are concerned. But besides being theoretically possible, the conspiracy process can actually be observed. Many examples are evident from conversations between fans in a variety of settings. The one we offer here is taken from talk between four fans on a special coach. The conversation is reconstructed from notes made at the time and although it is not reported verbatim it is a good representation of what was said.

A note concerning the background to the story is required. A coach had been hired by fans, under the management of one of the organisers, to take them to a match against Southampton. On arriving fans found to their dismay that the game had been cancelled because the ground was waterlogged. (The organiser was the subject of some censure for not having checked on this before setting out.) The Oxford fans, faced with the prospect of a wasted Saturday, persuaded the coach driver to take them to Swindon, who happened to be at home to Walsall. Swindon are Oxford's arch rivals from the days when they used to play in the same division and the prospect of having a rare opportunity to 'have a go' at them almost compensated for not being able to see Oxford play. The coach arrived at Swindon just after the kick-off and about fifty Oxford fans entered the ground chanting insults and imprecations at the Swindon 'wankers' and threatening to take their End. Walsall supporters were much bemused at having such uninvited allies but having as little love for them as they had for the Swindon fans, refused to join them in their assault on Swindon's End. Even on a bad day in the Third Division, an End can hold several hundred Rowdies and the odds against the fifty Oxford fans making more than a mere token gesture for occupying the End were rather high. There was a brief pushing scuffle as about twenty of the fitter Oxford boys tried to squeeze their way into the crowd, but they were pushed out again and sent back to the other end of the pitch. The rest of the match passed without incident and some fans even went back to the coach early because it was raining quite hard. Out of such an uninspiring day, however, fans were able to construct a very much more exciting reality.

Keith: Did you see that big fat cunt of a copper when we was in the Swindon End? There's this Swindon boy with a beer can and he chucks it at us—but when we tries to get him the copper grabs me by the hair and slings me out.

Danny: Yeah—if it weren't for the coppers we could have walked in there—right over them.

Keith: Cunts.

Dave: That kid on the floor though—old John gave him a real good kicking—lost some teeth I reckon.

Ross: Was that the kid with blood on his face— sort of ginger hair—stupid looking?

Dave: No—he had black hair—had black hair, didn't he Keith?

Keith: I dunno—I didn't see it.

Dave: You must have done. We were right together. The kid on the floor getting kicked.

Keith: Oh him. But what about when we first run in and this old boy makes a grab at—at Terry wasn't it? Hey Terry—what happened to that old boy who made a grab at you?

[*Terry doesn't hear because he's sitting much further back in the coach*]

Keith: Deaf cunt. No, but I saw this old boy and he's sort of holding his head like he got nutted or something.

[*John, sitting in the seat behind Keith and Dave has been quietly listening*]

John: You bullshitter, Matthews.

Keith: No, straight John—he got hit on the head or something. Terry really got him I reckon.

Dave: Swindon are bloody easy—if they were to come up to the Manor still we'd kick shit out of them.

Danny: Just one bus load of us and we walked straight in there. If it weren't for the coppers we could have just stayed there.

A song starts up . . .

> We took Swindon and all them in it,
> We took Swindon in half a minute.
> With hatchets and hammers,
> Carving knives and spanners . . .

The example is not more than a slightly comic vignette and yet it shows up quite clearly the way in which conspiracies are managed. Fans 'knew' that very little had happened and in fact said so when asked to talk about the match during the following week. But by the time the coach had arrived back in Oxford on the Saturday evening the day had been made remarkable and worthy of being talked about.

Glossary

Ergo therefore.
Kudos glory, status.
Verbatim words reported literally.
Vignette short description to illustrate or give a picture of something.

Questions

1 (a) Why is there a myth that football terraces are violent places, according to the authors?
(b) Why are the terraces not *really* violent?
2 The method in this study was participant observation. In what ways might the choice of this research method have influenced the findings?
3 Critically assess the authors' theory concerning the 'rules of disorder'; you could refer to the quality of their explanation, the nature of their evidence, any evidence to the contrary which they might find difficult to explain and so on.

Questions on all the extracts

1 Discuss the view that any sociological explanation of youth subcultures must be recognised as a valid one by those who participate in them.
2 Examine the relationship between youth subcultures and the larger, adult, society.
3 By concentrating their attention on those young people who have joined youth subcultures, sociologists have ignored those who have not. This omission has led to a serious misunderstanding of the importance and role of youth subcultures in modern industrial societies. Explain and discuss.

Bibliography

Source of extracts

G. Pearson, *Hooligan: A History of Respectable Fears*, Macmillan, London, 1983

A. McRobbie and J. Garber, *Girls and Subcultures* in S. Hall and T. Jefferson, (eds), *Resistance Through Rituals*, Hutchinson, London, 1975

S. Cohen, *Folk Devils and Moral Panics*, Second Edition, Martin Robertson, Oxford, 1980

S. Hall et al., *Policing the Crisis*, Macmillan, London, 1978

P. Marsh, E. Rosser and R. Harré, *The Rules of Disorder*, Routledge & Kegan Paul, London, 1978

References in the Introduction

A. Coleman, *The Adolescent Society*, Glencoe Free Press, New York, 1961

T. Fyvel, *Insecure Offenders*, Penguin, Harmondsworth, 1966

P. Johnson, 'The Menace of Beatleism', *New Statesman*, February 1964

R. Hoggart, *The Uses of Literacy*, Penguin, Harmondsworth, 1958

M. Abrams, *The Teenage Consumer*, London Press Exchange, 1959

S. Eisenstadt, *From Generation to Generation*, New York Free Press, 1956

D. Hebdige, *Subculture: The Meaning of Style*, Methuen, London, 1979

Further reading

E. Cashmore and B. Troyna, *Black Youth in Crisis*, Allen & Unwin, London, 1982

P. Corrigan, *Schooling the Smash Street Kids*, Macmillan, London, 1979

S. Lees, *Losing Out: Sexuality and Adolescent Girls*, Hutchinson, London, 1986

G. Mungham and G. Pearson, *Working Class Youth Culture*, Routledge & Kegan Paul, London, 1976

D. Robins and P. Cohen, *Knuckle Sandwich: Growing up in the Working Class City*, Penguin, Harmondsworth, 1978

◪ The Sociology of Work

Introduction The main theme in this section is the influence of technology on workers' attitudes and behaviour. The first extract, from R. Blauner's famous *Alienation and Freedom*, puts the view that technology is an extremely important determinant of attitudes. He is particularly concerned with the effect technology can have in giving rise to, or protecting the worker from, alienation.

In his study Blauner 'operationalises' the concept of alienation (i.e. makes it amenable to empirical study) by isolating what he considers to be its four essential components. These are *powerlessness, meaninglessness, isolation* and *self-estrangement* at work. He then uses data he has collected in the field and secondary data (i.e. from other studies) in order to establish the presence or absence of these components. He studies occupations which employ varying levels and different types of technology.

The findings of the study, which are not included in detail in this extract, are as follows: the simplest level of technology engenders only a low level of alienation. This is due to the substantial degree of control the craftsman has over the production process, the fact that he/she is faced with interesting challenges in the work, the ample opportunities for socialising with other workers and finally the fact that the production process allows the craftsman to identify with the product he/she has created.

The next technological level, machine tending, has a considerably higher level of alienation. Here machines determine the nature of the work and its pace. The job is repetitive and tedious. It is difficult to communicate with the other workers and one cannot identify with the finished product. Nonetheless, the workers are not completely alienated because such technology is usually found in areas where there is a pre–existing community and so workers have a range of kin and friends at work. They can derive substantial satisfaction from this. The level of technology which follows machine minding, assembly line production, has no such advantage. Now the community has been broken down by geographical mobility. In their search for jobs in the developing industries, people have had to leave their traditional communities. In the assembly line factory the worker has no power, derives no meaning from the work, is socially isolated and estranged from him/her self.

At the highest level of technology, however, automation has been introduced. The workers supervise the production process and they have power over it. Blauner calls this type of production 'continuous process production'. Now the workers consider themselves to be important to the whole operation. They have the freedom to socialise with each other and derive satisfaction and a sense of purpose from the job. This is the type of technology which will be introduced in virtually all fields of production eventually, argues Blauner. As a result we can be optimistic about the satisfaction that people will derive from work in the future.

The second extract is from D. Wedderburn and R. Crompton's *Workers' Attitudes and Technology*. This study was designed as 'part of an investigation into the nature and extent of differences in the terms and conditions of employment of manual and non–manual workers and of attitudes towards these differences'. They were particularly interested in whether the introduction of high technology meant that the fringe benefits received by the non–manual workers would also be received by the manual workers. The authors collected their data mainly in 1965 with subsequent fieldwork in 1967 and 1968. This was done at the 'Seagrass' site, a large chemical complex in the north east of England where a number of technologies were in use. It was a site of about 900 acres with approximately 10,000 employees. Among other methodological techniques, Wedderburn and Crompton carried out a large scale attitude survey of a sample of manual workers and their immediate supervisors (foremen and assistant foremen). They believed that earlier studies such as Blauner's had tended to see technology as virtually the sole determinant of workers' attitudes and behaviour and that this was incorrect. Their findings bear this out. Workers' attitudes appeared to be conditioned at least as much by the level of pay, job security, attendant welfare benefits and good working conditions as by technology. Other factors, such as the nature of the supervisory system, were found to influence attitudes, though they were conditioned by the nature of the technology being used.

The third extract, from H. Beynon's *Working for Ford*, illustrates a socialist position on the question of workers' attitudes. While he recognises the importance of technology in influencing attitudes, he also believes it to be vital that we take into account the nature of the economic system in which the technology is being employed. In order to understand this more clearly we should examine Marx's view on this question. For Marx, work should be a satisfying and humanising activity. Indeed without work we would not develop culturally, physically or intellectually as individuals or as a species. In capitalism, however, work is degraded. It is not a pleasurable end in itself. Rather it is a means to an end; earning enough money to buy the necessities of life. The products of our labour do not belong to us in capitalism, they are expropriated for profit by the owners of the means of production. Work is forced upon us so that we can satisfy our needs and wants (which are artificially created). In the workplace the capitalist's search for profit directly conflicts with the workers' interest in high rewards and interesting work. Thus, Marx believed, there will be alienation, dissatisfaction and conflict within the capitalist system regardless of the level of development of technology it has reached.

Beynon's book documents the brutalising nature of the job at Ford's Halewood plant in Liverpool. He notes the attempts by management to squeeze more and more profit out of the workers there and the method by which the workers try to make the job bearable. Beynon agrees with Marx that trade unions have limited success in resisting the ill effects of capitalism on the workers. This is because, rather than trying to change the capitalist system, unions limit themselves:

> to a guerrilla war against the effects of the existing system instead of simultaneously trying to change it, instead of using their organised forces as a lever for the emancipation of the working class, that is to say the ultimate abolition of the wages system. (Marx, quoted by Beynon)

The history of Ford's is a history of guerrilla war between management and workers, yet there have not been any radical political demands, or attacks upon the dominant logic of capitalist production. Beynon regrets this fact, but as he says himself, 'Radical intellectuals may put their hands to their heads in despair but that doesn't help either'. The information contained in the book was collected in the late 1960s when Beynon was a research student at Liverpool University. He conducted a detailed participant observation study of the factory, intending that it should, 'situate the events that took place in one factory in the 1960s within a broader, historical framework'. This extract gives an insight into conditions on the shop floor for workers at the Halewood plant.

The fourth extract comes from R. Crompton and R. Jones' recent book *White Collar Proletariat*. The overall aim of this study was to test the Marxist theory of proletarianisation. This was expressed most famously in the mid–1970's by H. Braverman in *Labour and Monopoly Capital*. It suggested that the terms and conditions of employment of the middle class were becoming like those of the working class. The proposed causes of this phenomena are, amongst other things, the capitalists' search for profit and the deskilling of middle class jobs resulting from the introduction of high technology. This proletarianisation of the middle class will lead, according to Braverman and other Marxists, to an alliance between or fusion of manual and non–manual workers and this will have important political consequences, even revolutionary ones.

To test the thesis of proletarianisation, Crompton and Jones studied clerical workers in three organisations: Cohall (a county council HQ), Lifeco (a life insurance company) and Southbank (a bank). Each institution had introduced computers to differing extents (Cohall to a small degree, Lifeco quite thoroughly). Thus it was possible to test the effect of computerisation on skill levels. The most recent technology allows the computer operator to be 'on line', i.e. to feed information into and get information out of the central computer's data banks. The effects of this more recent development on skill levels were also tested.

The clerical staff were interviewed in each of the three organisations. The authors were able to ask the older staff to compare their job before and after computerisation in order to evaluate the perceived impact of the computers' arrival. Crompton and Jones' findings on the impact of technology on the clerical workers' jobs are summarised here. The stratification chapter contains an extract relating to their general findings on the validity of the proletarianisation thesis as a whole.

The final extract, from R. Hyman's *Strikes*, also concerns the influences on workers' attitudes and behaviour, most notably, of course, on the factors which impel them to go on strike. This extract neatly summarises a variety of theses about the reasons for strikes and associated explanations as to why some industries are more strike prone than others. These include the technology used in the workplace, the nature of the community around it, the management structure, and so on. Hyman criticises such theories as being purely *structural* in their focus, i.e. they see strikes as caused by factors which are external to the worker. Hyman wishes to introduce a phenomenological element into the study of industrial unrest. Workers' own motives and meanings, previously ignored by many writers on the subject, need to be explored in addition to structural factors. Both the subjective viewpoint and the objective conditions must be taken into account. The student may find it interesting to explore the similarities between Hyman's comments and those of S. Cohen in the youth culture chapter.

R. Blauner
Alienation and Freedom, 1964, pp. 6–7, 11–15, 32–33, 182

The most important single factor that gives an industry a distinctive character is its *technology*. Technology refers to the complex of physical objects and technical operations (both manual and machine) regularly employed in turning out the goods and services produced by an industry.

Of course, no industry has a completely homogeneous technology. Even within the same factory there may be different technological processes that carry out various stages of production. Yet most individual industries have their characteristic forms of production. The four compared in this study have distinctive technological arrangements. Since relatively unique products are manufactured in printing, there is little standardisation of production. The level of mechanisation is low. Much work is done by hand rather than by machines. These are the characteristics of a *craft* technology. The textile industry is more highly mechanised and its work processes are more standardised. Since the bulk of the productive process is carried out by workers who 'mind' machines, it may be called a *machine-tending* technology. The automobile industry is dominated by an *assembly-line* technology and highly rationalised work organisation. The conveyor belt carries cars in the process of completion past lines of "semiskilled" operatives, each of whom makes his contribution to the assembly of a particular part on the body or chassis. The industrial chemical industry is based on the most advanced kind of technology, *continuous-process* production, a form of automation. Since all production processes are carried out automatically in a series of chemical reactors through which the product flows continuously, the relatively few blue-collar workers in this industry either monitor instruments on panel boards or repair automatic machinery when necessary. ...

Data and methods
The present study brings together empirical evidence from a variety of sources. My most important source of comparative quantitative data on the alienation process in the four industries is a job–attitude survey carried out by Elmo Roper for *Fortune* magazine in 1947. This was a representative sample of 3,000 blue-collar factory workers in sixteen different factory industries. It is the only major study of workers I have seen that divides the sample according to specific industries, as compared to such general industrial categories as manufacturing, mining, construction, and transportation. The sample included 118 printing workers, 419 textile workers, 180 automobile workers, and 78 chemical workers. 'Within the universe defined, the sample was stratified so as to contain the proper distribution of respondents by sex, geographic area, race, and age according to the Census of 1940.' Although

not a random probability sample, it was, according to Elmo Roper, 'a pretty carefully controlled quota sample,' and therefore representative of a population much larger than the 3,000 workers interviewed. . . .

Although the Roper survey provides the chief statistical attitude data, I have relied on industrial case studies and published accounts for additional descriptive and analytic material. Because of the lack of research on continuous-process workers, I conducted a field study in a chemical plant in the California bay area, during the winter of 1961. The plant, which had 400 blue–collar and 250 white–collar employees, is a branch of a large national industrial company. It produces heavy industrial organic and inorganic chemicals and is therefore typical of the most advanced section of the industry, although the bay area plant is not as new and as highly automated as some chemical factories. I interviewed 21 blue-collar workers in this plant, which shall be referred to as the Bay Chemical Company. The respondents were chosen at random among employees in the three major divisions—operations, maintenance, and distribution—who had worked in other industries. The interviews lasted from one hour to an hour and a half and took place on company property, with the co-operation of the local union. In addition to formal interviews in 1961, I spent several days and nights in various departments of the plant in the summer of 1962, observing the work process and discussing the operators' work situations. . . .

Alienation exists when workers are unable to control their immediate work processes, to develop a sense of purpose and function which connects their jobs to the over-all organisation of production, to belong to integrated industrial communities, and when they fail to become involved in the activity or work as a mode of personal self-expression. In modern industrial employment, control, purpose, social integration, and self-involvement are all problematic. . . .

The split in man's existence and consciousness into subject and object underlies the idea of *powerlessness*. A person is powerless when he is an object controlled and manipulated by other persons or by an impersonal system (such as technology) and when he cannot assert himself as a subject to change of modify this domination. The non–alienated pole of the powerlessness dimension is the state of freedom and control.

Meaninglessness alienation reflects a split between the part and the whole. A person experiences alienation of this type when his individual acts seem to have no relation to a broader life–programme. Meaninglessness also occurs when individual roles are not seen as fitting into the total system of goals of the organisation but have become severed from any organic connection with the whole. The non-alienated state is understanding of a life–plan or of an organisation's total functioning and activity which is purposeful rather than meaningless.

Isolation results from a fragmentation of the individual and social components of human behaviour and motivation. Isolation suggests the idea of general societal alienation, the feeling of being in, but not of, society, a sense of remoteness from the larger social order, an absence of loyalties to intermediate collectivities. The non-alienated opposite of isolation is a sense of belonging and membership in society or in specific communities which are integrated through the sharing of a normative system.

Self-estrangement is based on a rupture in the temporal continuity of experience. When activity becomes a means to an end, rather than an end in itself, a heightened awareness of time results from a split between present engagements and future considerations. Activity which is not self-estranged, but self-expressive or self-actualising, is characterised by involvement in the present-time context. Self-estrangement also entails a separation between work life and other concerns. When work is self-estranging, occupation does not contribute in an affirmative manner to personal identity and selfhood, but instead is damaging to self-esteem.

Alienation trends: the long view

The historical perspective on alienation and freedom in the factory reveals a clear and consistent pattern. Because secular developments in technology, division of labour, and industrial social structure have affected the various dimensions of alienation largely in the same direction, there is a convergence of long-range trends in the relation of the factory worker to his work process. Alienation has travelled a course that could be charted on a graph by means of an inverted U-curve.

In the early period, dominated by craft industry, alienation is at its lowest level and the worker's freedom at a maximum. Freedom declines and the curve of alienation (particularly in its powerlessness dimension) rises sharply in the period of machine industry. The alienation curve continues upward to its highest point in the assembly-line industries of the twentieth century. In automotive production, the combination of technological, organisational, and economic factors has resulted in the simultaneous intensification of all dimensions of alienation. Thus in this extreme situation, a depersonalised worker, estranged from himself and larger collectives, goes through the motions of work in the regimented milieu of the conveyor belt for the sole purpose of earning his bread. Assuming that the industries compared in this book are to some degree prototypes of the historical epochs of manufacturing, the dominant and most persistent long-range trend is an increase in alienation and a corresponding decline in freedom.

But with automated industry there is a counter-trend, one that we can fortunately expect to become even more important in the future. The case of the continuous-process industries, particularly the chemical industry, shows that automation increases the worker's control over his work process and checks the further division of labour and growth of large factories. The result is meaningful work in a more cohesive, integrated industrial climate. The alienation curve begins to decline from its previous height as employees in automated industries gain a new dignity from responsibility and a sense of individual function—thus the inverted U.

Glossary

Homogeneous consisting of parts all of the same kind.
Mechanisation the introduction of machines to the work task.
Automation the replacement of workers by machines completely.
Empirical based on observation or experiment, not theory.
Normative system shared set of ideas and behaviour.
Rupture in the temporal continuity of experience a break in living—here refering to the idea that time at work is 'lost' or 'dead' time.
Milieu environment.
Prototypes an original, as opposed to a copy of something.

Questions

1 Distinguish between the four types of technology Blauner identifies.
2 Express Blauner's definition of alienation in your own words.
3 What will the future bring in terms of the alienation of workers and why does Blauner believe this to be the case?
4 Would you describe Blauner as a technological determinist? (See p. 182 for a definition of this.)
5 Criticise Blauner's methodology.
6 What is your general view of:
   (a) Blauner's definition of alienation.
   (b) His theory on the future of alienation in a society where process production is virtually the only type?

D. Wedderburn and R. Crompton
Workers' Attitudes and Technology, 1972, p. 151

One major limitation of the Seagrass study is that it stopped at the factory gate. We cannot even begin to suggest what impact the work experience of the men we studied had on their lives outside of work, upon their family and social life, their aspirations for the future, or their political attitudes. And we can only indicate one

or two directions in which their experience in the community reacted upon their attitudes and behaviour at work.

This case study has, however, provided a further understanding of the dynamics outside and within the workplace. At one level of analysis what was happening at Seagrass must be understood in terms of a group of workers with primarily instrumental attitudes to work, committed for the most part to collective action through their trade union representation, not apparently holding any clear ideological position about the power structure in the industrial situation or in the total society, but directly experiencing conflicts of interest between themselves and their employers which had to be bargained about. The significant variation in this general position was that of the tradesmen, who were far more independent in their attitude to management than the general workers. At another level of analysis, that is within the specific work setting, other differences of attitude and behaviour emerged in response to the specific constraints imposed by the technology and the control system. These made themselves felt through two channels, the structuring of the job itself on the one hand, and, on the other, through the way in which supervisor and operator relationships were shaped. Thus it would seem that an approach to the study of behaviour in organisations which uses a comparative approach may still fruitfully take as *its starting point* technology and the systems which management devise for the planning and execution of the task. We would expect such an approach to shed light on certain aspects of behaviour related to the immediate organisational situation. For explanations of industrial behaviour at a more general societal level other starting points are required.

Glossary

Instrumental attitudes attitudes which stress only financial rewards given by work rather then the value of the work itself.
Ideological based upon a coherent set of strongly-held beliefs.

Questions

1 Describe the type of attitudes held by most workers at Seagrass.
2 How did technology influence attitudes? Give examples of what the authors mean.
3 Would you describe Wedderburn and Crompton as technological determinists? Give reasons for your answers.
4 Elaborate on the final sentence of the passage.

H. Beynon
Working for Ford, 1975, pp. 109, 138–9

Working in a car plant involves coming to terms with the assembly line. 'The line never stops', you are told. Why not? '. . . don't ask. It *never* stops'. The assembly plant itself is huge and on two levels, with the paint shop on the one floor and the trim and final assembly departments below. The car shell is painted in the paint shop and passed by lift and conveyor to the first station of the trim assembly department. From this point the body shell is carried up and down the 500-yard length of the plant until it is finally driven off, tested, and stored in the car park.

Few men see the cars being driven off the line. While an assembly worker is always dealing with a moving car it is never moving under its own steam. The line—or 'the track' as some managers who have been 'stateside' refer to it—stands two feet above floor level and moves the cars monotonously, easily along. Walking the floor of the plant as a stranger you are deafened by the whine of the compressed air spanners, you step gingerly between and upon the knots of connecting air pipes which writhe like snakes in your path, and you stare at the moving cars on either side. This is the world of the operator. In and out of the cars, up and over the line, check the line speed and the model mix. Your mind restlessly alert, because there's no guarantee that the next car will be the same as the last, that a Thames van won't suddenly appear. But still a blank—you keep trying to blot out what's happening. 'When I'm here my mind's a blank. I *make* it go blank.' They all say that. They all tell the story about the man who left Ford to work in a sweet-factory where he had to divide up the reds from the blues, but left because he couldn't take the decision–making. Or the country lad who couldn't believe that he had to work on *every* car: 'Oh no. I've done my car. That one down there. A green one it was.' If you stand on the catwalk at the end of the plant you can look down over the whole assembly floor. Few people do, for to stand there and look at the endless, perpetual, tedium of it all is to be threatened by the overwhelming insanity of it. The sheer <u>audacious</u> madness of a system based upon men like those wishing their lives away. I was never able, even remotely, to come to terms with the line. Mind you, I never worked on it. But that's another story. . . .

The history of the assembly line is a history of conflict over speed–up—the process whereby the pace of work demanded of the operator is syste–matically increased. This can be obtained in a number of ways, the most simple involving a gradual increase in the speed of the line *during* a shift. In other words a man may start a shift with a work allocation of two minutes to coincide with a line speed of thirty cars an hour and then find that he is working on a line that is moving at thirty–five cars an hour. He gets suspicious after a bit because he finds that he can't make time on the job. He can't get those few stations up the line which allow him a break and half a ciggie now and then. We have already seen that this practice was common in the pre–union era of the American motor industry and also at Dagenham. The long–serving stewards and workers at

Halewood insist that plant management made frequent use of this type of speed–up in the early days of the plant. Production managers out to make a name for themselves can only do it through figures—through their production and their costs. They abuse their supervision to this end. To service the god of production is also to serve yourself and in this climate a few dodges are all part of the game. These dodges could be controlled though. They provoked a number of unofficial walkouts on the trim lines. 'The lads said "Sod you. We're not doing it, we're just not doing it." It worked as good as anything else y'know. We just said no and if they pushed it we went home.' No procedure could sort out issues like these. This was naked aggression being met with violent defiance. Management was trying to force the lads to do the unthinkable and they weren't having it. An agreement had to be reached and management conceded to the stew–ards the right to hold the key that locked the assembly line. Little Bob Costello had the key on the A shift, and the line speeds were changed with great ceremony, watched and cheered by the workers on the line. This wasn't enough for some sections. Some stewards had been able to obtain an additional safeguard. The first man on these sections was given an extra time allowance for counting the cars that entered the section. If the number of cars in any hour exceeded the stipulated line speed he was able to stop the line.

Glossary   <u>Stateside</u> in the United States of America.
<u>Audacious</u> bold.

Questions

1 Describe the attitude Beynon had towards Ford.
2 Beynon used participant observation to study the Ford plant. Does this passage provide any evidence that this was:
(a) an appropriate method or
(b) an inappropriate method.
3 Would you describe Beynon as a technological determinist?

R. Crompton and G. Jones
White Collar Proletariat, 1984, pp. 53, 73

In summary, therefore, our case–study evidence indicates that, as far as clerical work is concerned, computerisation 'deskills' tasks, enhances the

level of <u>functional specialisation</u>, and centralises control within the organisation. The clerical workforce, therefore, is increasingly stratified. In the bank, for example, there has been a clear and recognised trend towards an occupational structure comprising, on the one hand, routine clerks (largely grades 1 and 2) who input and process data according to tightly specified procedures, and on the other, a much smaller proportion of higher–level staff who actually use the information in the course of their work. In the case of banking and insurance, there seems to be little indication from the evidence of our case studies, that the development of on–line systems associated with 'new' technology will reverse this trend. In our interviewing, we collected details of the pattern of computer use among clerks and lower–level supervisory and administrative grades. . . .

The greater the level of mechanisation within both departments and organisations, the more likely was the work of the lower clerical grades to be rated as unskilled or semi–skilled in terms of the work–description code we described. Excluding programmers and systems analysts, over 90 per cent of those on clerical grades were in jobs that were entirely rule–bounded—although the complexity of the rules varied—and required no discretion or autonomy in carrying out the various job tasks. Of course, many clerical jobs before computerisation will have been rule–bounded and routine—although we can make no estimate as to what extent. (We have seen that Lockwood, writing of a previous era, suggested that most were not.) 'Optimistic' commentators have argued that the computer has effectively 'taken the drudgery' out of such jobs; but what may seem as 'drudgery' to some may be a source of pride and satisfaction to others. As one bank employee commented:

When I first started here there were massive ledgers—I was given responsibility for two of them. There was much personal pride in keeping these straight, neat and accurate—competition between the girls about who's got the best ledger. Now you just 'blame the computer'.

Glossary

Functional specialisation the division of tasks so that only one person performs one function in an organisation.

Programmers those who write computer programs.

Systems analysts those who study the nature of tasks to be computerised and set the framework of the program.

Autonomy freedom to make decisions.

Ledgers books in which records of transactions are kept.

Questions

1 What has been the effect of the introduction of technology on the clerical jobs studied by these authors?

2 What social consequences may result if these effects occur generally? You might think in terms of trade unions, political effects, effects on attitudes, etc.

3 Having read the description of the methodology of this study in the introduction to this and the stratification chapter, write a critique of this, suggesting improvements.

R. Hyman
Strikes, 1984, pp. 59–76, 110–11, 120–22

Explanations of strike–proneness

There are two main ways in which sociologists can try to account for strikes. The first is to examine variations in strike–proneness: to consider why the incidence of industrial conflict differs between work groups, between firms, between industries, or between regions and even nations. Industrial sociologists have devoted considerable ingenuity to efforts to explain these variations, and the 'man in the street' tends to hold some sort of theory about this also. The second approach involves a different level of analysis: examining the causes of strikes in general, and exploring the rationale behind them.

Questions of this order will be considered later in this book; in the present section, some theories of the first type are examined.

Agitators

A widespread assumption about strikes, even if rarely coherently formulated, is that disputes are fomented by agitators. . . .

The shop steward is the usual target for the 'agitator' label; but as was seen previously, the steward's role is more often associated with attempts to prevent strikes than to foment them.

To attribute industrial disputes to agitators is therefore, at best, to point to the instrument of conflict rather than its cause. More often it is to imply that strikes are of such questionable rationality that evil machinations must lie at their root. This thesis is thus profoundly *un*sociological, seeking to explain social processes exclusively in terms of the interventions of 'influential' individuals. It is the mirror image of that approach to history which relates events of major social significance solely to the actions of 'great men'. The sociologist, by contrast, is aware of the constraints which the social situation itself normally imposes on the influence of any individual, and it is this which she or he seeks to analyse.

Communications

The 'human relations' school is the title commonly applied to a loosely knit group of American industrial sociologists and social psychologists, who developed their main theories in the 1930s and 1940s and were particularly influenced by the ideas of Elton Mayo. The name indicates their central argument: that the key to workers 'morale', high productivity, and industrial peace lies in the quality of 'human relations' in industry. Exponents of this approach insisted that employers could best attain their objectives by encouraging cohesive social relationships within the labour force, by providing workers with 'supportive leadership', and by ensuring the existence of effective channels of communication between management and employees.

This approach has long attracted hostile criticism. Its advocates have been charged with managerial bias, a manipulative approach to workers, the treatment of the factory as a closed community, the denial of the rationality of industrial conflict, the neglect of the role of trade unions. . . .

Social phenomena are, in the last analysis, products of the actions and interactions of individuals; industrial relations are also interpersonal relations; and undeniably the attitudes and actions of specific individuals can in certain circum-stances have far-reaching repercussions. But individual influence over social events is usually more limited. Bad human relations are more often a symptom of industrial conflict than its cause.

Community integration

By contrast, Kerr and Siegel see workers with a lower propensity to strike as more closely integrated into the wider society. 'They are more likely', they argue, 'to live in multi-industry communities, to associate with people with quite different working experiences than their own, and to belong to associations with hetero-geneous memberships. In these communities their individual grievances are less likely to coalesce into a mass grievance which is expressed at the job level' (pp. 193–4)[1].

This is a persuasive explanation of the exceptional strike records of workers in a small number of industries. As a more general theory of industrial conflict it is less satisfactory. For there are industries—such as steel manufacture—which are highly strike-prone in some countries but not in others; while there are also significant variations in strike activity within industries in a single country (Eldridge, 1968: 38–9)[2]. Since the majority of workers in any industrialised nation fall within Kerr and Siegel's single undifferentiated category of 'community integration', their theory—as they themselves recognise—is necessarily unable to explain contrasts in the experience of conflict of different sections of these 'integrated' workers. (Their argument could, however, be extended to suggest that certain types of worker, while residentially integrated within an urban community, may because of a strong craft tradition or unusual working hours form a cohesive occupational community; they may therefore possess unusual solidarity and show a particular readiness to engage in collective conflict.)

Technology

This approach is generalised by Woodward[3], who has analysed the implications for management of different degrees of technical complexity: unit and small batch manufacturing, mass production, and process technology. She suggests that:

'the attitudes and behaviour of management and supervisory staff and the tone of industrial relations . . . seemed to be closely related to . . . technology. In firms at the extremes of the scale, relationships were on the whole better than in the middle ranges. Pressure on people at all levels of the industrial hierarchy seemed to build up as technology advanced, became heaviest in assembly-line production and then relaxed, so reducing personal conflicts. Some factors—the relaxation of pressure, the smaller working groups ..., and the reduced need for labour economy—were conducive to industrial peace in process production. ...'

It is indisputable that the technology of a firm or industry can have an important conditioning effect on worker-management and union-management relations. But a theory which sees technology as *all*-important is demonstrably inadequate. (This has been recognised, for example, in more recent work by Woodward.) Why is the steel industry strike-prone in some countries when—as was noted earlier—in others, under the same technological conditions, it is relatively peaceful? Or why does the strike record of the British motor industry contrast so markedly with the comparative harmony in Germany or Japan, when the technology of car assembly is internationally uniform? Single-factor explanatory theories, it is clear, do scant justice to the complexity of social reality. ...

The industrial relations system
While the socio-technical approach is considerably more sophisticated than simple technological determinism, its analysis stops at the factory gates; it ignores all influences on the nature of industrial relationships which derive from a wider society. A theoretical framework designed to overcome this limitation is Dunlop's concept of the 'industrial relations system' (1958). ...[4]

'An industrial-relations system is comprised of three groups of actors—workers and their organizations, managers and their organizations, and governmental agencies concerned with the work place and work community. These groups interact with a specified environment comprised of three interrelated contexts: the technology, the market or budgetary constraints and the power relations in the larger community and the derived status of the actors. An industrial-relations system creates an ideology or a commonly shared body of ideas and beliefs regarding the interaction and roles of the actors which helps to bind the system together' (p. 383). ...

Explicitly or otherwise, this theoretical perspective has tended to underlie a number of post-war studies of industrial conflict. The account given by Knowles[5], for example, of the strike-proneness of various British industries would fit comfortably within Dunlop's conceptual framework. And since the publication of his volume in 1958,

the notion of an industrial relations *system* has become widely adopted within the academic study of the subject—even if some of its implications are not always fully appreciated.

The limits of structural explanation
All the sociological theories considered so far (with the exception of the human relations school) have focused on *structural* determinants of industrial relations. ...
Yet this basic truth is often overstated. Many social theorists view human behaviour as mechanically determined by the social structure. This common fallacy is known as '*positivism*'. Such terms as 'role' or 'social institution' or even 'society' are used by sociologists to refer to the stable patterns of relationships which they discover; but positivism involves treating such concepts as real entities with an independent existence over and above the activities and relationships of human individuals. People are treated, in effect, as wholly passive: the helpless playthings of 'social forces'. ...
Humans are not puppets; they consciously interpret the situations in which they find themselves, and in the light of these interpretations they select their responses in accordance with the goals which they wish to achieve. Only by exploring the subjective dimension—human consciousness and the interrelation of people's definitions and responses—is it possible to understand the regularities and patterns which exist in industrial relations or in any other area of social life.
In recent years, the neglect of the subjective viewpoint—which is so characteristic of sociological orthodoxy—has led to something of a reaction. ...
The current emphasis on the 'action frame of reference' is not, however, without its dangers: for some sociologists, in their reaction against positivism, have neglected the structural influences of which the actors themselves may be unconscious. In effect, the views and definitions of the actors are treated as a sufficient explanation of the social situation being investigated.
This approach is itself misguided. Our consciousness does have a certain independence from such structural factors as the level of technology, the system of economic relations, and the institutions of political and industrial control; and it can influence the development of these components of the social structure. Yet consciousness is not wholly autonomous. Definitions of reality are themselves socially generated and sustained, and people's ability to achieve

their goals is constrained by the objective characteristics of their situation.

Put technically, it might be said that there exists a 'structured <u>dialectic</u> of social structure and social consciousness' (Coulson and Riddell, 1970, p. 93)[6]. There is, in other words, a complex two-way process in which our goals, ideas and beliefs influence and are influenced by the social structure. To do justice to its complexity, industrial sociologists must be attuned to this dynamic interaction between structure and consciousness. A static or a one-way analysis necessarily distorts social reality, and is therefore an inadequate basis for understanding industrial behaviour or predicting its development. The greatest potential for further progress in the sociology of industrial conflict (and the same is indeed true of sociology in general) must lie in the elaboration of a dialectical approach. . . .

The sociologist can therefore make sense of the social world only by taking account of the meanings which it holds for social actors and the motives which underlie their actions. This is not to say that the sociologist should be concerned only with their subjective viewpoint. Our actions do not always have the intended results, and often the unintended consequences of human activity are patterned by unrecognised structural determinants. Meanings and motives are themselves typically socially generated and sustained, in ways of which the actors themselves may be unaware. But a sociology which focuses—as much sociology has done—exclusively on the unrecognised determinants and unintended consequences of action is a one-sided and inadequate sociology. The proper concern of the sociologist should be the complex interaction of subjective meanings and objective reality. . . .

Until recently the Department of Employment listed nine 'causes of strikes': claims for wage increases; other wage disputes; hours of labour; demarcation disputes; employment dismissal questions (including redundancy); other personnel questions; other working arrangements, rules and discipline; trade union status; and sympathetic action. Only four of these categories of strike issues figure at all prominently: the two classes of wage disputes, employment and dismissal questions, and 'other working arrangements'. The remaining five categories have together accounted for only 10 to 15 per cent of stoppages in recent years, and often less than 10 per cent of striker-days.

Knowles has grouped these categories under three headings: 'Basic' causes (wages and hours), 'solidarity' (union status and sympathetic action), and 'frictional' causes (all the other categories). . . . It should be no cause for surprise that the grievances expressed by workers in strike situations centre primarily around wages. 'In a market economy, very many of the things that workers, and others, seek can be secured only through cash transations.' . . .

[1-6]See Bibliography

Glossary

<u>Fomented</u> stimulated, instigated.

<u>Machinations</u> the laying of plots.

<u>Propensity</u> inclination to do something.

<u>Heterogeneous</u> consisting of parts of different kinds.

<u>Unit and small batch manufacturing</u> craft or mechanised production technology, producing only individual items or small numbers.

<u>Mass production</u> assembly line technology.

<u>Process technology</u> automated production technology in which human workers do not intervene directly in the production process, merely monitoring and controlling it.

<u>Conducive to</u> leading to something.

<u>Conditioning</u> influencing (but not determining) the outcome of something.

<u>Technological determinism</u> the view that the nature of the technology employed determines other aspects of social life.

<u>Structural explanation</u> that form of explanation which emphasises the determining influence of outside forces on people's behaviour.

<u>Positivism</u> the view that societies operate in much the same way as the physical world and hence are amenable to the same sorts of methods of study.

Action frame of reference phenomenology, the sociological approach
which stresses an understanding of the motives and meanings of the
people being studied, seeing these as the important factors in
shaping social events.

Dialectic a clash of opposites to create a single new phenomenon, a
synthesis of them.

Questions

1 In your own words, sum up the 'structural' explanations of strike–
proneness.
2 What are 'the limits of structural explanation'?
3 What sort of explanation of strikes would Hyman like to see?
Illustrate this with examples.
4 Would you describe Hyman as a technological determinist?

**Questions on
all the
extracts**

1 Does Beynon's evidence tend to support or refute Blauner's ideas?
2 Compare and contrast Blauner's and Hyman's approaches to the
study of work.
3 Compare and contrast Blauner's and Beynon's view of the position
of the worker in advanced industrial societies.
4 Though production technology is undoubtedly an important factor
shaping the attitudes and behaviour of the worker, it is far from
being the only one. Explain and discuss.
5 Complete the following table, according to the views represented:

	Blauner	Wedderburn and Crompton	Beynon	Crompton and Jones	Hyman
Influences of technology on attitudes and behaviour					
Direction in which the nature of work is moving (if any specified)					
Factors other than technology which should be taken into account when studying attitudes and behaviour					
Most appropriate method for the study of the workplace					
Sociological perspective subscribed to					

Bibliography

Source of extracts

R. Blauner, *Alienation and Freedom*, University of Chicago Press, Chicago, 1964

D. Wedderburn and R. Crompton, *Workers' Attitudes and Technology*, Cambridge University Press, Cambridge, 1972

H. Beynon, *Working For Ford*, E. P. Publishing Ltd, Wakefield 1975, first published 1973

R. Crompton and G. Jones, *White Collar Proletariat*, Macmillan, London, 1984

R. Hyman, *Strikes* Fontana, Third Edition, London 1984, first published, 1972

Reference in the Introduction

H. Braverman, *Labour and Monopoly Capital*, Monthly Review Press, New York 1974

References in Hyman extract

1 C. Kerr and A. Siegel, *The Inter–Industry Propensity to Strike*, in *Industrial Conflict* (ed.) A. Kornhauser *et al.*, McGraw–Hill, New York, 1954

2 J. E. T. Eldridge, *Industrial Disputes*, Routledge & Kegan Paul, London, 1968

3 J. Woodward, *Management and Technology*, HMSO, 1958

4 J. T. Dunlop, *Industrial Relations Systems*, Holt, Rinehart & Winston, New York, 1958

5 K. G. J. C. Knowles, *Strikes: A Study in Industrial Conflict*, Blackwell, Oxford, 1952

6 M. Coulson and D. Riddell, *Approaching Sociology*, Routledge & Kegan Paul, London 1970

Further Reading

S. Clegg and D. Dunkerley, *Organisation, Class and Control*, Routledge & Kegan Paul, London, 1980

D. Gallie, *In Search of the Working Class*, Cambridge University Press, Cambridge, 1978

J. Goldthorpe and D. Lockwood, *The Affluent Worker*, Cambridge University Press, Cambridge, 1968 and 1969

R. Hyman and R. Price (eds), *The New Working Class? White Collar Workers and Their Organisations*, Macmillan, London, 1983

D. Lockwood, *The Blackcoated Worker*, Unwin University Books, London, 1969, first published 1958

S. Parker, *The Sociology of Industry*, Allen & Unwin, London, 1967

B. Turner, *Industrialism*, Longman, Harlow, 1975

S. Wood, *The Degradation of Work: Skill, Deskilling and the Labour Process*, Hutchinson, London, 1982

◪ The Sociology of Politics

Introduction

Political sociology covers a very wide range of topics. At 'A'-level, the sociology syllabuses cover areas such as the distribution of power in capitalist societies, the ways in which that power is legitimated, the nature of the modern state, the nature and role of pressure groups in western democracies, the origin and political philosophies of political parties and voting behaviour in Britain. The Bibliography suggests sources which the student may find helpful if he/she wishes to pursue these areas.

This chapter provides two recently published readings on voting behaviour, both concerned with the results of the 1983 general election and their significance in terms of trends in voting patterns. The first extract, from Butler and Kavanagh's *The British General Election of 1983*, gives a summary of the main points concerning the results of that election, comparing them in particular with the general election of 1979.

The second selection, from a newspaper article by Ivor Crewe, focuses in particular on where the support for the Labour, Conservative and Alliance Parties lay in that election. Crewe, a leading figure among psephologists (academic students of voting behaviour) and Professor of Government at Essex University, identifies five key factors in the decline of Labour's support in 1983. They are: the switch from Labour to the SDP among some ex-Labour voters; the switch to the Conservatives among others; support for the Conservative and Alliance Parties among many new (i.e. young) voters and, finally, the apathy and therefore abstention of many young unemployed people on polling day, a category of voters who might otherwise have been expected to vote Labour.

D. Butler and D. Kavanagh
The British General Election of 1983, 1983, pp. 289–91

1 Turnout fell from 76.0% to 72.7%. The level of abstention—27.3% of those nominally on the register—compares to the 28.0% of 1970, the post-war election with the lowest turnout. But allowances for holidays, postal votes, and inefficient registration renders exact comparisons suspect. There is no indication that local variations in turnout between 1979 and 1983 have any differential impact on party fortunes.

2 The slump in Labour support meant that 1983 marked a sharp departure from past voting patterns. The Conservatives won 60.6% of the combined Conservative and Labour vote. The previous post-war peaks in share of the two-party vote were 54.8% for Labour in 1945 and 54.3% for the Conservatives in 1979. Since mass suffrage came in, the Conservative lead of 14.8% over the second party has been matched only in 1924, 1931, and 1935. Labour's 27.6% was its lowest share of the vote since 1918.

3 The swing from Labour to Conservative fol-

lowed a well-established pattern, once again being lower in urban areas and the north and higher in rural areas and the south. Long-term unemployment was also a factor reducing the level of swing but the extent of increase in unemployment during 1979–83 had surprisingly little effect. The central areas of Britain's five largest conurbations behaved most distinctively, with swings to Labour in Manchester, Liverpool and North Birmingham. The political division between the Conservative south and the Labour north increased: in the 186 seats outside London in the area from the Wash to the Severn, Labour held only three.

4 The long term increase in polarisation between constituencies continued. There were only 80 marginal seats in 1983 compared to 149 in 1979. This means that in a normal election the gross exaggeration of majorities, the familiar 'cube law' effect, no longer applies to British elections. If the trend continues the leading two parties are likely to get a share of seats that is closely proportionate to their votes. In 1983 61% of the two–party votes won for the Conservatives 66% of the 606 seats that went to the two leading parties, while 39% of the two–party vote won 34% of those seats for Labour. On the other hand the 3½% of seats which the Alliance secured with 25% of the total vote had as its nearest analogy the 8% of seats that Labour won in 1931 with 31% of the vote.

5 The Alliance vote was very evenly spread. 546 of their candidates secured within 10% of their national share of 25.4% (compared to 296 Conservatives within 10% of their 42.4%, and 240 Labour candidates within 10% of their 27.6%). The variations in the Alliance vote are much more linked to political than social or geographic factors: the few exceptional results were mostly associated with the presence of SDP defectors or to a past Liberal history or to a strong Nationalist presence.

6 There was little difference between the performance of Liberal and SDP candidates; the SDP did not do quite so well as might have been expected when it took over a previously strong Liberal seat; on the other hand the SDP fared a bit above expectation in seats where the Liberal vote had fallen away to a very low level in 1979.

7 The nationalist vote was down in most constituencies—but it stayed strong in the handful of Welsh-speaking seats as well as in a few seats that had had SNP members from 1974 to 1979.

8 In Northern Ireland, uniquely, turnout rose. The Official Unionists reasserted themselves as the primary vehicle for the Protestant vote while Sinn Fein cut significantly into the SDLP hold in Catholic areas.

Behind all these figures lies one central fact. The Conservatives gained 61% of the 650 seats with only 42.4% of the vote and increased their majority from 43 to 144. In 1964 the Conservatives had lost office with 43.4% of the vote. The 23 seats won by the Alliance which received over 25% of the vote represented, in the words of the *Sunday Times*, 'a new order of unfairness'. In a fully proportional system Conservatives would have gained approximately 120 fewer seats, Labour 20 fewer and the Alliance 140 more. Such an outcome would have made relevant the earlier discussion of the political and constitutional repercussions of a deadlocked parliament. As it was, the electoral system produced the biggest one-party majority in almost 50 years. But the Conservative and Labour parties provided the top two parties in less than half of the constituencies. 57% of all votes were anti-Conservative and 72% were anti-Labour.

The high level of unemployment did not produce class polarisation of the electorate. There was a 3% swing to the Conservatives from Labour in the working class; the Conservative 12% lead over Labour among skilled workers was cancelled by its 15% deficit among the unskilled. There was also a 4% swing to the Conservatives among middle–class voters as Labour support fell. The decline in the link between class and party continued as the Alliance made inroads across the class divide. The BBC Gallup election survey found that, for the first time since surveys began, less than half (47%) of British voters supported the party of their class (non-manual workers for Conservative and manual workers for Labour). Even if we discount the growth of Alliance support and its erosion of the class base of party politics, nearly 40% (39.2% according to MORI) did not vote for the party of their social class.

Glossary

Turnout the proportion of those entitled to vote who actually voted in a particular election.

Abstention refraining from voting.

Suffrage being qualified to vote.

Constituencies geographical areas, each represented by one MP who occupies a seat in the House of Commons.

Marginal seats constituencies where there is no strong majority for one particular party.

'Cube law' a mathematical relationship between:
   (a) the percentage swing from one of the two major parties to the other and
   (b) the number of seats gained in the House of Commons.
     The latter was the cube of the former.

SDP Social Democratic Party, formed in 1981 by members of the Labour Party on its right–wing.

SNP Scottish Nationalist Party.

Sinn Fein Northern Irish party, supported by Catholics and usually referred to as the political wing of the IRA.

SDLP Social Democratic and Labour Party— a Northern Irish party supported by Catholic voters.

Constitutional repercussions of a deadlocked parliament refers to the problems which would be caused concerning who should form the next government if there were no party with an overall majority in the House of Commons after the next general election. This sort of result is more likely than it was with the growth of the Liberal/SDP challenge to Labour and Conservative dominance.

MORI an independent polling organisation.

Questions

1 What did the *Sunday Times* mean by the phrase 'a new order of unfairness'?
2 How has the formation and considerable popularity of the SDP/Liberal Alliance affected voting behaviour in Britain?
3 What reasons can you suggest for the fact that Labour held only three seats outside London south of a line drawn between the Wash and the Severn?

I. Crewe

'The Disturbing Truth Behind Labour's Rout', *The Guardian*, 13 June, 1983

All election results are deceptive. They are judged by seats won, even though seats do not switch in exact tandem with votes. They are judged by the national flow of the vote even though this masks a flux of underlying cross–currents. Nineteen hundred and eighty three is no exception. The Conservatives' net gain of 37 seats (over the BBC/ITN estimate of their 1979 position on the new boundaries) produced a landslide majority of 144, but came from a modest 42.4 per cent of the vote (and an even more modest 30.8 per cent of the total elector–ate). This is 1.5 per cent down on 1979, and markedly lower than when the Conservatives won a series of less spectacular victories in the 1950s, or indeed, under Mr Heath in 1970. The Conservatives' vote share was actually *higher* when it lost narrowly to Mr Wilson in 1964 (43.4 per cent) and virtually the same (41.9 per cent) when it lost so decisively in 1966.

The electorate did not embrace the Conservatives; it rebuffed Labour and flirted with the Alliance. At 25.4 per cent the Alliance's vote share was the best performance of the Centre for 60 years. The Labour vote was down by 9.3 per cent—the sharpest fall incurred by a majority party at a single election since the war—to 27.6 per cent. Labour's lowest share since 1918.

The real position for Labour is in fact grimmer still, since its low vote in 1918, unlike now, was partly caused by its failure to contest over a third of the seats. If performance is judged by the average share of the constituency vote going to Labour candidates this was Labour's poorest showing since the party was founded in 1900.

Thus what needs to be explained about the 1983 election is not why the Conservatives did so well, but why Labour did so badly, and the Alliance not quite well enough.

The flow of the vote

The change in the three parties' vote share (Con minus 1.5 per cent, Lab minus 9.3 per cent, Lib/SDP plus 11.6 per cent) leads to an obvious conclusion: the Conservatives owe their triumph, Labour its humiliation, to a direct switch of votes from Labour to the Alliance. But preliminary analysis of the BBC/Gallup survey suggests that Labour charges of an SDP 'betrayal' are, however comforting, far too simple. The real explanation is more complicated—and disturbing.

It is certainly true, as Table 1 shows, that Labour suffered massive desertions. Well over a third (37 per cent) of its 1979 support—itself reduced to what might have been regarded as a loyal core—switched. But by no means all Labour deserters went to the Alliance. For every three switching to the Lib/SDP one went to the Conservatives and one stayed at home.

Moreover there was less than unswerving loyalty among 1979 Conservatives (23 per cent switched) and 1979 Liberals (28 per cent switched). The impact of the movement from Labour to Alliance (22 per cent) was lessened by the 9 per cent of ex-Liberals moving back to Labour and—far more important numerically—the 13 per cent of ex-Conservatives moving to the Alliance. The overall effect of the two-way traffic between the Alliance and the major parties was a mere 1.4 per cent swing from Labour to Conservative—just over a third of the total swing.

The Alliance's differential impact on the relative fortunes of the major parties was only one of four components in the national swing albeit, the

Table 1

The flow of the vote from 1979 to 1983

(To see how supporters of each party in 1979 voted in 1983 read down the columns of figures)

	Con	Lab	Lib	Did not vote	Too young
	(1521)	(1252)	(382)	(357)	(396)
	%	%	%	%	%
Con	77	7	14	22	28
Lab	4	63	9	12	17
Lib/SDP	13	22	72	14	20
Other	–	1	–		2
Did not vote	6	7	5	52	32
	100	100	100	100	100

Percentages do not total to 100 because of rounding. The figures in parentheses are the number of respondents in each category. Votes for National and other parties in 1979 have been omitted.

single most important. Next in significance was the larger proportion of direct converts from Labour to Conservative (7 per cent) than vice versa (4 per cent). This added another 1 per cent to the swing.

Labour was also hit by <u>differential turnout</u>. Former non-voters gave the Conservatives a 10 per cent majority over Labour, equivalent to an extra 0.5 per cent on the national swing. However, the Labour official's traditional lament of differential *abstention* ('we failed to get our voice out') did not occur, despite the rise in non-voting since 1979. The abstention rates of those voting Conservative, Labour, and Liberal in 1979 were almost identical. Labour's supporters in 1979 did not stay at home on Thursday. They went to the polling stations and switched parties.

The fourth nail in Labour's coffin was hammered in by new voters. Until 1979 surveys consistently showed that, compared with the old, the young voted Labour in higher proportions and, in addition, swung more heavily against whichever party held office. Under Conservative governments, therefore, these two tendencies reinforced each other to produce substantial majorities for Labour among new voters, in fact sufficient alone to give Labour its knife edge majorities in 1964 and February 1974.

In 1970, for the first time, new voters divided equally between Labour and Conservatives. This

Table 2 Vote by social class

% of three-party vote in 1983 and change in that share since 1979

	Professional & managerial (AB)		Office & clerical (C1)		Skilled manual (C2)		Semi-skilled & unskilled manual (D)		Trade unionists		Unemployed		All	
	1983	1979–83	1983	1979–83	1983	1979–83	1983	1979–83	1983	1979–83	1983	1979–83	1983	1979–83
Con	62	– 5	55	– 3	39	– 7	29	– 3	32	+ 1	30	– 10	44	– 2
Lab	12	– 6	21	—	35	– 12	44	– 11	39	– 14	45	– 4	29	– 10
Lib/SDP	27	+ 12	24	+ 4	27	+ 16	28	+ 14	28	+ 12	26	+ 15	27	+ 12
Con maj over Lab	+ 50		+ 34		+ 4		– 15		– 7		– 15			
Lab to Con swing	0.5%		– 1.5%		2.5%		4.0%		7.5%		– 3.1%			
Lab to Lib/SDP swing	9.0%		2.0%		14.0%		12.6%		13.0%		9.5%			
Con to Lib/SDP swing	8.5%		3.5%		11.5%		8.5%		5.5%		12.5%			

Table 3: Vote by sex and age

	Men		Women		18–22		23–34		35–44		45–64		65 +	
	1983	1979–83	1983	1979–83	1983	1979–83	1983	1979–83	1983	1979–83	1983	1979–83	1983	1979–83
Con	46	– 1	43	– 3	41	– 2	45	—	47	+ 1	46	– 1	48	– 3
Lab	30	– 9	28	– 11	29	– 12	32	– 8	27	– 10	27	– 13	33	– 4
Lib/SDP	24	+ 11	28	+ 14	30	+ 13	23	+ 9	26	+ 10	27	+ 15	19	+ 7
Con maj over Lab	+ 16		+ 15		+ 12		+ 13		+ 20					
Lab to Con swing	4.0%		4.0%		5.0%		4.0%		5.5%		6.0%		0.5%	
Lab to Lib/SDP swing	10.0%		12.5%		12.5%		8.5%		10.0%		14.0%		5.5%	
Con to Lib/SDP swing	6.0%		8.5%		7.5%		4.5%		4.6%		6.0%		5.0%	

time the swing to the right has gone further still. Labour came third among new voters, taking a mere 17 per cent of their vote, 3 per cent behind the Alliance and 11 per cent behind the Conservatives. The result was another 0.7 per cent on the swing.

That Labour should fail so dismally among the young at a time of severe youth unemployment must seem a mystery. Ironically, unemployment was part of the reason. Among unemployed 18–22 year olds, almost half (47 per cent) did not bother to vote at all. Marching for Jobs (and a Labour victory) is a strictly minority activity. Many more stayed in bed—at Labour's expense.

The main explanation for the Conservatives' win, therefore, is Labour desertions. But it is not the whole story. We also need to know why some ex-Labour voters switched to the Conservatives rather than the Alliance, and why the Alliance could not retain more of the 1979 Liberal vote. And we need to remember that the Conservatives held onto their 1979 national vote not through the rock like solidity of former supporters but by compensating their losses through recruitment of former Labour and Liberal voters and winning the competition for the new vote.

Who moved?

Let us put flesh onto this skeleton of the electorate by asking: who moved? Differences between men and women and across age groups were slim. A permanent feature of all elections until recently was the higher Conservative vote among women than men. The gap disappeared in 1979 and has now gone into reverse. For the first time, and under Britain's first woman Prime Minister, the Conservatives drew less support from women than men. (A similar reversal of the 'gender gap' occurred in the United States and Scandinavia in the early 1970s). The Alliance, not Labour, benefited, taking 4 per cent more votes among women (28 per cent) than men (24 per cent).

Conservative support steadily increased from the young to the old, but along a gentler gradient than in the past. The odd group out was not the new generation of voters—the object of such disproportionate media attention in every election—but as happened in 1979, the old. Among the over 65s, the Conservative vote dropped by more than the national average, the Labour vote by less, resulting in a tiny 0.5 per cent swing to the Conservatives. Labour policy on pensions, and the Government's record, could be an expla-

nation, although only a fifth of the over 65s cited pensions as an important issue. An alternative explanation is that the over 65s are the generation of the 1930s and the Second World War: the majority will have first voted in, and contributed to, the Labour landslide of 1945. Some of the Labour loyalty induced in their formative years will have lasted until today.

The Alliance did best among new voters (29 per cent), worst among the over 65s (19 per cent), probably because party loyalties are least fixed in the young and most ingrained among the old. But the Alliance's campaign must have been particularly effective among first-time voters, since all pre–election surveys found a lower than average vote for the Alliance in this group.

It is not age or sex, but social class, however defined and measured, that continues to structure party choice (see Table 3). The partisan differences between manual and non-manual workers are still greater than those within the two groups. Yet the class basis of party choice has steadily weakened over the last quarter century. In 1959 there was a 40 per cent gap between Labour's share of the non–manual as against the manual vote; by 1979 that gap had fallen to 27 per cent; and on Thursday it was 21 per cent. Thus mass unemployment failed to produce a class polarisation in the vote.

In the middle classes there was barely a swing to the Conservatives at all. Among clerical and office workers the small Labour vote held up. Among the professions and management it fell by 6 percentage points, but was matched by a similar drop in the Conservative vote.

The pro–Conservative swing was confined to the working class (2.5 per cent among skilled workers; 4 per cent among the semi–skilled and unskilled). This was not because the working class Conservative vote rose, but because the working class Labour vote, which had already haemorrhaged badly in 1979, continued to bleed away—mainly to the Alliance.

Only at the very bottom of the economic ladder, among the unemployed, was there a hint of working class backlash. The Conservative vote—which had risen sharply in 1979—dropped by 10 per cent, Labour's by only 4 per cent, to produce what was technically a pro-Labour "swing" of 3 per cent.

Support for the Alliance was remarkably even across the class spectrum. There was not a trace of evidence that it drew disproportionately from the professions, or the middling, intermediate strata, or that its supposedly middle class image was anathema to the 'real' working class. The Alliance's vote was almost exactly the same among the upper middle classes (27 per cent) as among the unemployed (26 per cent).

As Table 4 shows, defection was widespread across the entire social spectrum of the Labour vote. But it was especially heavy on the periphery of its social constituency—among its middle class, non-union, private sector supporters of 1979. The largest-scale switching occurred among home-owners—working class owners as much as middle class owners. The Labour vote held up best—although still not very well—among council tenants, blacks, and the over 65s. But there is scant comfort for Labour here. Council tenants are a slowly diminishing group; blacks are a tiny minority; and the over 65s will rapidly depart from the electorate.

The continuing abandonment of the Labour Party by manual workers makes its claim to be the party of the working class look increasingly threadbare—sociologically if not ideologically. True, the Labour vote remains largely working class; but the working class has ceased to be largely Labour. On Thursday it split its vote

three ways, giving Labour a mere 5 per cent majority over the Conservatives.

Among trade unionists the Labour vote was only 7 per cent ahead of the Conservatives. Labour's share of the working class electorate, as distinct from those who voted, was down to barely a quarter (27 per cent). More than ever before it is the middle classes, not manual workers, whose vote reflects class consciousness and solidarity.

The decline in the working class Labour vote, moreover, is not simply an inevitable concomitant of a Conservative landslide. In 1959, when the Conservatives' overall majority was 100, 62 per cent of manual workers still voted Labour; last Thursday the figure was 38 per cent. The transformation of working class partisanship over the past quarter century must rank as the most significant post-war change in the social basis of British politics.

To be sure, Labour remains the party of a segment of the working class—the traditional working class of the council estates, of the public sector, of Scotland and the North (see Table 5). Among these slowly dwindling groups Labour was still the first, if not always the majority, choice. But it has lost the new working class.

Among private sector workers it ran neck and neck with the Conservatives. Among manual workers owning their house, or living in the South, the Conservatives had a commanding lead and Labour came *third* behind the Alliance. The small minority (9 per cent) who bought their

Table 4

Defection rates among different groups of 1979 Labour voters

	% of group switching from Labour		% of group switching from Labour
All Labour voters, 1979	31%	bought council house	59%
non-manual	38%	home owner	44%
manual	29%	working class home owner	42%
member of white collar union	36%	council tenant	21%
member of no union	33%	white	32%
member of blue collar union	27%	black	21%
private sector	33%	22–44	33%
public sector	29%	45–64	34%
		65 +	25%

Table 5

The two working classes: % of three-party vote 1983

	New working class			Old working class		
	Owner-occupiers	Works in private sector	Lives in South	Council tenants	Works in public sector	Lives in Scotl'd/ North
	%	%	%	%	%	%
Con	47	36	42	19	29	32
Lab	25	37	26	57	46	42
Lib/SDP	28	27	32	24	25	26
Con/Lab majority	Con + 22	Lab + 1	Con + 16	Lab + 38	Lab + 17	Lab + 10
Category as % of all manual workers	43%	66%	36%	45%	34%	38%

council house divided Con 56 per cent, Lab 18 per cent, Lib/SDP 25 per cent; and of those who had voted Labour in 1979 fully 59 per cent switched to the Conservatives or the Alliance.

The old working class is now too small to give Labour electoral victory; the new working class too big to be ignored. By 1983 twice as many manual workers were employed in the private than public sector. Almost as many were home-owners as council tenants; almost as many lived in the South as in the North and Scotland combined. The division of Britain into two nations is no longer between the classes but within the working class; and the more secure, more affluent of these nations is increasingly preponderant. To regain its old electoral strength Labour will have to find ways of appealing to both.

What moved voters?

The Conservatives' landslide by default, secured through Labour weakness rather than their own strength, is underlined by the sharp increase in negative voting since 1979 (see Table 6). Fifty nine per cent of all voters—and 73 per cent of those deciding during the campaign—disliked the other party(ies) more than they liked their own. This begrudged vote was lower among Conservatives than Labour or the Alliance, but up on 1979, the majority sentiment, and the overwhelming attitude of those only persuaded to vote Conservative by the campaign. None of this suggests a ringing endorsement of the Government's record, the Conservative manifesto or the Resolute Approach.

Although the Labour posters said 'Think Positive, Act Positive,' the Labour vote owed far more to the Government's record than to Labour's programme: 62 per cent of all Labour supporters, and 70 per cent of those persuaded by the campaign, voted against rather than for. By this token the Labour vote was no less a protest vote than that for the Alliance. Without the rise in unemployment and the cuts in public services, the Labour vote might have diminished further.

Table 6
Motivation of party choice

	Con	Lab	Lib/SDP*	All
	Vote in 1983			
	(Figures in brackets show differences from 1979)			
Positive	45 (−3)	38 (−21)	37	41
Negative	55 (+3)	62 (+21)	63	59
	Decided how to vote during campaign			
	Con	Lab	Lib/SDP	All
Positive	22 (−24)	30 (−17)	31	27
Negative	78 (+24)	70 (+17)	69	73

The survey question was: 'What would you say is stronger—your like of the Conservatives (Labour/Lib–SDP Alliance) or your dislike of Labour (the Conservatives/the Conservative and Labour parties)?' The small number replying 'both equally' are excluded.

*The motivation question was not asked of Liberal voters in 1979.

The survey was commissioned by the BBC, undertaken by Gallup and designed by the author. It consisted of 4,141 interviews, 3,174 in England and Wales and 967 in Scotland (which were weighted down for overall Great Britain figures), drawn from a quota sample composed of age, sex, and housing. The survey incorporated weighted, booster samples of 862 respondents in Lab–Con marginals and 738 in Lib–Con and Con–Lib marginals. Interviewing was conducted on June 8 and 9. Party support recorded by the survey was very close to the actual result in Great Britain (in parentheses): Con 43.9 (43.4), Lab 28.7 (28.2), Lib/SDP 25.6 (25.9), and Others 1.6 (2.5).

Glossary   Differential turnout refers to the fact that people who did not vote in the last election may vote in this one, and that this may happen predominantly among supporters of one Party in particular.

Differential abstention refers to the fact that potential voters of one Party might be more or less willing to actually go to the polling booth to register their vote than those of another Party. In 1983 the Labour Party suffered the effects of this.

Gallup an independent opinion polling organisation.

Preponderant being the most important in terms of power and
influence.

Quota sample a method of chosing a sample to interview based upon
the process of identifying the type of person who should be
questioned and then asking interviewers to go out and find those
sorts of people. Statisticians consider quote sampling to be
unreliable because there is an element of choice on the part of the
interviewer. This can affect the reliability of the results to a degree,
increasing the margin of error.

Questions

1 In Table 1:
(a) What percentage of Labour voters in 1979 voted Conservative
in 1983?
(b) From which other Party did the Liberal/SDP Alliance benefit
most, comparing votes in 1979 and those in 1983?
(c) What percentage of people who voted Labour in 1979 also
voted Labour in 1983?

2 In Table 2:
(a) Examine the relationship between social class and voting
behaviour as revealed by this table.
(b) What reasons can you suggest for the considerable amount of
'deviant voting' revealed in this table?

3 In Table 3, what changes are discernible between 1979 and 1983 in
terms of the voting behaviour of the different age groups and
sexes?

4 In Table 4, which sort of person was most likely to defect from
Labour?

5 In Table 5, what is the difference in voting behaviour between the
'old' and the 'new' working class?

6 In Table 6, did most people tend to vote because of positive
preference for one Party or in order to keep another Party out of
office?

7 Does the evidence provided in this extract lead you to believe that
the Labour Party is now finished as a force in British politics?
Support your answer.

**Questions on
both passages**

1 In what ways does the pattern of voting behaviour in 1983 differ
from that found in previous post–war general elections?

2 Discuss the view that social class is no longer important as either a
determinant or indicator of voting intention.

Bibliography

Source of extracts

D. Butler and D. Kavanagh, *The British General Election of 1983*,
Macmillan, London, 1983

I. Crewe, *The Disturbing Truth Behind Labour's Rout*, *The Guardian*, 13
June, 1983

Further reading

Pressure groups
M. P. Jackson, *Trade Unions*, Longman, London, 1982
D. Thomas, *Pressure Groups Under the Tories*, New Society, 9 February 1984
D. Wilson, *The A to Z of Campaigning in Britain*, Heinemann, London, 1984

Distribution of power and its legitimation
P. Bachrach and M. Baratz, *Power and Poverty: Theory and Practice*, Oxford University Press, New York, 1970
R. Dahl, *Who Governs?* Yale University Press, New Haven, Connecticut 1961
C. W. Mills, *The Power Elite*, Oxford University Press, London, 1956
P. Stanworth and A. Giddens, *Elites and Power in British Society*, Cambridge University Press, Cambridge, 1974
J. Urry and J. Wakeford, *Power in Britain*, Heinemann, London, 1973

Voting behaviour
I. Crewe, 'Can Labour Rise Again?', *Social Studies Review*, Vol. 1, No. 1, September 1985
H. Himmelweit *et al.*, *How Voters Decide*, Open University Press, Milton Keynes, 1985
D. Kavanagh, (ed.), *The Politics of the Labour Party*, Allen & Unwin, London, 1982
I. Maclean, *Dealing in Votes*, Martin Robertson, Oxford, 1982
B. Slarvik and I. Crewe, *Decade of Dealignment*, Cambridge University Press, Cambridge, 1983

General
L. Robins, (ed.), *Topics in British Politics*, The Politics Association, London, 1982
R. Rose, *Politics in England: An interpretation for the 1980s*, Faber, London, 1980

The Sociology of Education

Introduction   This section has two main parts:
1 *Perspectives on the relationship between education, the economy and society*
2 *Perspectives on underachievement in education.*

Two extracts are included under the first heading. In the first, Marxists S. Bowles and H. Gintis put the view that the relationships of dominance and subordination found in school correspond to those found at work (hence the term 'correspondence theory' given to this view). The pupil is prepared by his/her educational experience to become another passive member of the workforce exploited by the capitalist class. This extract is from Bowles' and Gintis' *Schooling in Capitalist America*. The second extract, from *Education in Society* by R. Fletcher, puts the classic functionalist view of education. The educational system is seen to be providing the necessary knowledge, skills and personal development to enable the individual to operate properly in the social system and hence contribute to its efficient functioning. There is no hint of exploitation by the capitalist class in this passage. Society is seen as a well-integrated set of social institutions founded on shared values.

The bulk of the work in the sociology of education has been concerned with the causes of the relative failure of some groups, particularly the working class, within the educational system. Underachievement by females and ethnic minorities has received increasing attention recently. There have been four main explanations for this failure. The second section of the chapter includes extracts representing each of them:

(a) *Material circumstances in the home and the school*
Inadequate space, too few resources, illness caused by malnutrition leading to time off school, and so on, are suggested factors here. The extract from J. W. B. Douglas' *The Home and the School* puts this point of view. This is a longitudinal study of 4,195 children born in various parts of Britain in the first week of March 1946. The study followed them to their eleventh year. Information was gained by interviewing teachers, examining health and attendance records, interviewing parents, gaining data from local education authorities and administering tests of mental ability and school performance. The purpose of the book is to relate school performance to home background, both in terms of physical circumstances and the attitudes of parents and peer groups. The extracts selected concentrate on the findings which relate underachievement at school to poor physical conditions at home and in the school. Douglas concludes that, 'much potential ability is wasted during the primary school years and misdirected at the point of secondary education'. A follow-up study *All Our Future* was published in 1968. This followed the same children

from their eleventh year to the time they were sixteen and a half. It found that social class differences in educational opportunity increased during the period of secondary education to include even working class pupils of high ability, though less so where schools were well-equipped and staffed. Early leaving and low job aspirations meant that perhaps 5% of the next generation of manual workers would be recruited from pupils who could, in other circumstances, have qualified for administrative or professional posts.

(b) *Cultural differences between social groups*

Differences in the use of language, parental attitudes to education and differences in the aspirations of members of different social classes, sexes and ethnic groups are key focal points for this perspective. The extract from B. Bernstein's article *Social Class and Linguistic Development: A Theory of Social Learning* illustrates this approach. Bernstein's work is more complex than might at first appear and there have been various interpretations of its meaning of which students should be aware. Critics first took Bernstein to be saying that the working class speaks an inferior form of English: 'public language'. The middle class, this interpretation of Bernstein ran, have a superior ability to express their thoughts because they speak the more subtle formal language as well. Thus they do better in the competition for qualifications. Bernstein has rejected this as a misinterpretation. He argues that what he was saying was not that one type of language is inferior; both classes have the same ability to express their thoughts. Rather, the working class child simply learns a *different* way of relating to the world and talking about it than that which is used in middle class dominated schools. To emphasise this, his later work uses the terms 'restricted' and 'elaborated codes'. Restricted code is a form of language use which is context-bound, linked to practical concerns and the here and now. Elaborated code is, on the contrary, oriented to universalistic orders of meaning. They are not different kinds of language, just of language *use*. Bernstein's work now goes into detail on the cultural relativity of schools and comes very close to the position adopted by M. Young in *Knowledge and Control*. Does Bernstein's earlier position point to the linguistic and cultural deprivation of the working class or simply to two inherently equal language forms and cultures which exist in a context where one dominates the educational institutions? Jack Demaine considers that:

> ... it is clear that his work (which now spreads over two decades) does not constitute a unitary discourse governed by a principle of coherence. Appearing within it are positions which are contradictory, and in particular, earlier arguments which Bernstein, with good reason, wishes to displace. Thus, some of the interpretations of his work which he designates 'misinterpretations' may well be legitimate, even though they are representations of positions he now rejects.

The extracts selected here are from Bernstein's early work and therefore tend to stress the linguistic deprivation side of the argument.

(c) *Interaction patterns in the classroom*

The effects of teachers' labelling of pupils, both individually and in groups, is the focus here. The working class, girls and blacks are particularly susceptible to this sort of labelling process. Interactionist theory suggests that pupils internalise the label given to them and begin to act in accordance with it. The extract from S. J. Ball's *Beachside Comprehensive* demonstrates this in operation. It follows in the tradition of D. Hargreaves' *Social Relations in a Secondary School* and C. Lacey's *Hightown Grammar*. Indeed Lacey was Ball's supervisor for the PhD on which the book is based. Ball spent three years, from 1973 to 1976, researching in Beachside school and writing up his findings. He observed lessons, taught some classes himself, did other tasks a teacher would do, interviewed pupils and teachers and 'carried out several small-scale questionnaire studies, sociometric and otherwise, and also worked through and analysed school records and registers'. The school was 'banded' into three ability ranges (with placement in the first year being based on primary school reports). The middle band was the one which created problems for the teachers; misbehaviour by bottom band pupils 'tended to be defined and dealt with in terms of emotional problems or maladjustment, rather than belligerence'. The two lesson notes quoted are from 2TA, a 'troublesome' second year band 2 class, and 2CU, a class in the top band (the letters merely denote the name of the class teacher).

(d) *The type of knowledge taught in the school*

This perspective argues that school knowledge is not equally accessible to all members of society. It is the knowledge of only one social group. Other groups, with different forms of knowledge, find it difficult to acquire and use. As a result they underachieve relative to those groups from which school knowledge originates. Two sets of extracts are included here. One from M. Young's *Knowledge and Control*, which deals with middle class knowledge, and one from D. Spender's *Invisible Women*, which focuses on the male–oriented nature of school knowledge. Spender also puts the point of view that because of the greater significance society gives to males and their knowledge teachers unconsciously ignore both the presence of the girls in the classroom and the distinctive contribution they could make to the educational environment. This knowledge-based perspective is commonly referred to as the 'new' sociology of education.

S. Bowles and H. Gintis

Schooling in Capitalist America, 1976, pp. 10–13

The motivating force in the capitalist economy is the employer's quest for profit. Profits are made through hiring workers and organising production in such a way that the price paid for the worker's time—the wage—is less than the value of the goods produced by labour. The difference between the wage and the value of goods produced is profit, or surplus value. The production of surplus value requires as a precondition the existence of a body of wage workers whose sole source of livelihood is the sale of their capacity to work, their labour power. Opposing these wage workers is the employer, whose control of the tools, structures, and goods required in production constitutes both the immediate basis of his power over labour and his legal claim on the surplus value generated in production.

Capitalist production, in our view, is not simply

a technical process; it is also a social process. Workers are neither machines nor commodities but, rather, active human beings who participate in production with the aim of satisfying their personal and social needs. The central problem of the employer is to erect a set of social relationships and organisational forms, both within the enterprise and, if possible, in society at large, that will channel these aims into the production and expropriation of surplus value. Thus as a social process, capitalist production is inherently antagonistic and always potentially explosive. Though class conflicts take many forms, the most basic occurs in this struggle over the creation and expropriation of surplus value.

It is immediately evident that profits will be greater, the lower is the total wage bill paid by the employer and the greater is the productivity and intensity of labour. Education in the United States plays a dual role in the social process whereby surplus value, i.e. profit, is created and expropriated. On the one hand, by imparting technical and social skills and appropriate motivations, education increases the productive capacity of workers. On the other hand, education helps defuse and depoliticise the potentially explosive class relations of the production process, and thus serves to perpetuate the social, political, and economic conditions through which a portion of the product of labour is expropriated in the form of profits.

This simple model, reflecting the undemocratic and class-based character of economic life in the United States, bears a number of central implications which will be elaborated upon and empirically supported in the sequel.

First, we find that prevailing degrees of economic inequality and types of personal development are defined primarily by the market, property, and power relationships which define the capitalist system. Moreover, basic changes in the degree of inequality and in socially directed forms of personal development occur almost exclusively—if sometimes indirectly—through the normal process of capital accumulation and economic growth, and through shifts in the power among groups engaged in economic activity.

Second, the educational system does not add to or subtract from the overall degree of inequality and repressive personal development. Rather, it is best understood as an institution which serves to perpetuate the social relationships of economic life through which these patterns are set, by facilitating a smooth integration of youth into the labour force. This role takes a variety of forms. Schools foster legitimate inequality through the ostensibly meritocratic manner by which they reward and promote students, and allocate them to distinct positions in the occupational hierarchy. They create and reinforce patterns of social class, racial and sexual identification among students which allow them to relate 'properly' to their eventual standing in the hierarchy of authority and status in the production process. Schools foster types of personal development compatible with the relationships of dominance and subordinacy in the economic sphere, and finally, schools create surpluses of skilled labour sufficiently extensive to render effective the prime weapon of the employer in disciplining labour—the power to hire and fire.

Third, the educational system operates in this manner not so much through the conscious intentions of teachers and administrators in their day-to-day activities, but through a close correspondence between the social relationships which govern personal interaction in the work place and the social relationships of the educational system. Specifically, the relationships of authority and control between administrators and teachers, teachers and students, students and students, and students and their work replicate the hierarchical division of labour which dominates the work place. Power is organised along vertical lines of authority from administration to faculty to student body; students have a degree of control over their curriculum comparable to that of the worker over the content of his job. The motivational system of the school, involving as it does grades and other external rewards and the threat of failure rather than the intrinsic social benefits of the process of education (learning), or its tangible outcome (knowledge), mirrors closely the role of wages and the spectre of unemployment in the motivation of workers. The fragmented nature of jobs is reflected in the institutionalied and rarely constructive competition among students and in the specialisation and compartmentalisation of academic knowledge. Finally, the relationships of dominance and subordinacy in education differ by level. The rule orientation of the high school reflects the close supervision of low-level workers; the internalisation of norms and freedom from continual supervision in elite colleges reflect the social relationships of upper-level white-collar work. Most state universities and community colleges, which fall in-between, conform to the behavioural requisites of low-level technical, service, and supervisory personnel.

Fourth, though the school system has effectively served the interests of profit and political stability, it has hardly been a finely tuned instrument of manipulation in the hands of socially dominant groups. Schools and colleges do indeed help to justify inequality, but they also have become arenas in which a highly politicised egalitarian consciousness has developed among some parents, teachers, and students. The authoritarian classroom does produce docile workers, but it also produces misfits and rebels. The university trains the elite in the skills of domination, but it has also given birth to a powerful radical movement and critique of capitalist society. The contradictory nature of US education stems in part from the fact that the imperatives of profit often pull the school system in opposite directions. The types of training required to develop productive workers are often ill suited to the perpetuation of those ideas and institutions which facilitate the profitable employment of labour. Furthermore, contradictory forces external to the school system continually impinge upon its operations. Students, working people, parents, and others have attempted to use education to attain a greater share of the social wealth, to develop genuinely critical capacities, to gain material security, in short to pursue objectives different — and often diametrically opposed — to those of capital. Education in the United States is as contradictory and complex as the larger society; no simplistic or mechanical theory can help us understand it.

Lastly, the organisation of education — in particular the correspondence between school structure and job structure — has taken distinct and characteristic forms in different periods of US history, and has evolved in response to political and economic struggles associated with the process of capital accumulation, the extension of the wage–labour system, and the transition from an entrepreneurial to a corporate economy.

Glossary	Expropriation taking property away from someone.
	Inherently a characteristic that exists in something.
	Empirically based on observation or experiment, not theory.
	Facilitating making easier.
	Ostensibly apparently, but not really.
	Intrinsic similar meaning to inherent. See above.
	Egalitarian consciousness awareness of the principle of equal rights.
	Perpetuation preservation from destruction.
	Simplistic too simple.
	Entrepreneurial economy an economic system based upon private enterprise.
	Corporate economy an economic system based upon control by a few organisations, i.e. multinational corporations, large trade unions, etc.

Questions

1 (a) How can surplus value be increased?
   (b) Why is capitalist production based on conflict according to Bowles and Gintis?
2 Give examples of the following educational functions and show how they might be useful to the capitalist:
   (a) imparting technical skills
   (b) imparting social skills
   (c) imparting 'appropriate motivations'
   (d) helping to defuse and depoliticise potentially explosive class relations.
3 Summarise correspondence theory in point form.
4 (a) Choose five of the points of correspondence between schools and the economy identified by Bowles and Gintis and criticise their portrayal of that correspondence.

(b) Would you agree that schools 'create and reinforce patterns of social class, racial and sexual identification among students'? Support your answer.

R. Fletcher
Education in Society: The Promethean Fire, 1984, pp. 43–7, 50

What are the *functions* of education in society? We can begin with a very straightforward analysis.

1 Vocational and specialist education

In any society, there must be some adequate provision for instruction and training in all the tasks and skills of the social order, and in the various qualities (of mind, character, physical abilities, etc.) required for their satisfactory performance. There must be an effective handing on of skills and related qualities if new generations are going to maintain and enjoy the previous achievements of their society, and if they are to have the opportunity of improving upon them. There must, in short, always be a practical, utilitarian, technical and specialist kind of education in society.

2 The allocation of education and recruitment to occupations

Every society, too, must employ some systematic way of *selecting* individuals in accordance with their merits, potentialities or, sometimes (as in a customary division of labour between the sexes), their traditional status. This is necessary so that *appropriate kinds* of education, instruction and training can be given. There is a selective *apportioning of resources*. In some way, too, all this must be connected with the method of *recruiting* individuals to those tasks in the social order for which they seem to be best fitted (by nature and ability) and best trained. The educational provisions of a society can therefore always be considered in terms of their *efficiency*: (a) in selecting, (b) in providing appropriate kinds of education for different capacities, (c) in allocating resources effectively, and (d) in recruiting accurately and satisfactorily to the tasks of the social system.

Let us note, however, before leaving this point, that there is no reason to suppose that *all* these functions need be carried out by one and the same institution—by the 'educational system', for example. It may be that many institutions—in education, government, industry, the professions, etc.—are involved. In one way or another, however, these things have to be done.

3 Moral and cultural education

Thirdly, every society must provide an adequate and effective inculcation—in the character of its individual members—of those moral and cultural values it believes to be important. In some way or other, every society seeks to *regulate* individual conduct in the light of certain standards of behaviour. It tries to have the young *realise* the qualities of the culture they have inherited, and tries to inculcate these values in order to sustain both the qualities of life in society and the qualities of character of the individual. . . .

4 General education

Just as every society must provide adequate instruction and training in all its special skills (and in this sense provide *specialist* education), so it must also provide at least a modicum of *general* education, so that those elements of knowledge which are a common basis for *all* skills are established throughout the population, and so that it can be seen and understood how all these specialisms are linked together in society as a whole. . . .

5 Differential education

(a) It follows quite definitely from what we have said that no educational system in any society can possibly be equal in its treatment of individuals. Since education has to be provided for various levels of potentiality and aptitude, and the fulfilling of tasks differing widely in their required degrees of skill and complexity, it is clear that no educational system can be a simple, uniform structure. It must provide different types of education and instruction for different levels of capacity with reference to different ends. At some point or other, soon or late, *different* levels, *different* capacities and responsibilities, *different* directions of inclination and occupation, have to be recognised and provided for. . . .

(b) Again, however, we have spoken so far as

though the 'functions' of education were almost entirely concerned with *society* and its claim upon individuals, but this, of course, is only one side of education. There are aims other than stability and efficiency in the social order. One of them is to cultivate the qualities of individuals so that they become capable of exploring and developing their own diverse capacities to the full—and this *for their own personal happiness and satisfaction,* not solely with reference to some social end. . . .

6 Improvement and research

A final function of education can be stated very briefly. In any society, if *improvement* in the qualities of individual and social life is to be achieved, its educational system must have two characteristics. First, it must be such as to be always *critical of itself;* always prepared to reflect critically upon its own assumptions; always ready to change its ideas, techniques and administrative organisation in the light of new problems and new advances. Its knowledge, and the criteria on which this rests, must always be openly available, self-critical, flexible. And, second, it must make provision for the undertaking of continual, exploratory research. . . .

Glossary	Utilitarian based on usefulness. Apportioning sharing out. Inculcation persistently pressing ideas upon a person or people. Modicum small quantity of something.

Questions

1 (a) Give examples of 'moral and cultural values' which are considered to be important in Britain and which are transmitted by the education system.
(b) Would you say that Fletcher supports comprehensive or selective education from the evidence in this passage?
(c) Functionalism is often said to be a politically conservative perspective. Is there any evidence of this here?
2 Is the British educational system successfully fulfilling all of these functions? If not, what should be done to improve its effectiveness?
3 Choose three of the points that Fletcher makes in this passage, e.g. that education systems recruit individuals to those tasks in the social order to which they are best suited and evaluate their validity.

Questions on Bowles and Gintis, and Fletcher extracts

1 Complete the following table, according to the views represented:

	Marxist	Functionalist
An ideal education system would be . . .		
Relationship between education and the economy . . .		
Effect of education on the individual . . .		

	Marxist	*Functionalist*
Relationship between the education system and the social structure . . .		
Criticisms of this perspective's view of education . . .		

2 While it is true that the Marxist and Functionalist perspectives are opposed to each other in many ways, they also have much in common. Discuss this statement in relation to their approach to education.

3 Do schools operate in the interests of children, a particular social class or society at large?

J. W. B. Douglas
The Home and the School, 1969, pp. 66–7, 133–5

The teachers say that the children from unsatisfactory homes tend to be poor workers or lazy and that the manual working–class children from these homes have poor powers of concentration in school. They also consider that children from unsatisfactory homes are less able to profit from grammar school education than children from satisfactory ones, and they say this when they are comparing children of the same measured ability. Perhaps their views reflect the attitudes of the parents themselves who, when home conditions are unsatisfactory, tend to have low educational ambitions, to wish their children to leave school early and, in the manual working classes, to expect them to go to secondary modern rather than to grammar schools.

When children of similar measured ability compete for grammar school places, those from satisfactory homes have an advantage over the rest which, though small, is consistent in each social class, whether the area be one of good or poor provision of grammar school places. . . .

There are many possible explanations for the deterioration observed between eight and eleven years in the test performance of children whose home circumstances are bad. In overcrowded homes they will be deprived of quiet and privacy. When they share their beds they may sleep badly, and through tiredness be unable to concentrate on their school work.

At the time when these children took the eleven–year tests of mental ability and school achievement, their headmasters or headmistresses were asked to give a detailed description of each school. They described the buildings in terms of their age, the extent of modernisation, the type of site and the amenities provided for staff and pupils. They gave the number of staff and the number of pupils and estimated the proportion of the latter who had fathers in the professions, in agriculture or in unskilled manual work; they also gave various other details including information about special conditions of entry.

Their answers show a familiar picture of crowded class rooms and of schools which are grossly lacking in amenities. Forty-five per cent of the children are taught in classes of 40 or more. Primary schools built in the nineteenth century accommodate 48 per cent of the children and of these old schools nearly half have not been modernised in any way since the war. Amenities such as electric light, hot water, efficient sanitation, an adequate playground, a separate dining hall, an assembly hall and a head teacher's study are lacking in many schools; 16 per cent of children are at schools which lack four or more of these amenities and only 24 per cent of them are at schools which have them all. Lastly, 28 per cent of the children are taught in schools built on noisy sites.

In addition to giving these material details, the heads supplied figures of the number of pupils who had been eligible to take the secondary selection examinations in the previous year, and the number of successful ones.

All this information refers only to the schools which had one or more of the survey children on their rolls in March 1957. We are only able to describe the last school attended by the 29 per cent of children who changed their primary schools between the ages of eight and eleven.

The middle–class parents are highly selective in the primary schools they choose for their children. They are the chief, almost the sole, users of private schools; when they do send their children to maintained schools they favour those that have a reputation for getting a large proportion of their pupils into grammar schools, and those that draw their pupils predominantly from the middle classes. There is a concentration of the best primary schools in the more prosperous residential areas, and to some extent the middle–class children go to these schools because they are the nearest ones; there is also an element of choice, for it is those middle–class parents who take a great interest in their children's work who are most likely to send them to schools that have a good record of grammar school awards.

The choice of a distant school that has a reputation for getting its pupils into grammar schools, rather than of a nearby one that lacks this reputation, is sometimes possible only because there is a family car. For this reason the opportunities of choice are less for the manual working than for the middle–class parents. In general the former send their children to the primary schools that have a poor record of grammar school awards; only 16 per cent of the lower manual working–class children go to schools that send 31 per cent or more of pupils to grammar schools, whereas 44 per cent of the upper middle–class children attend these schools. On the other hand the educationally ambitious working–class parents are more selective in their choice of schools.

Questions

1 What links between material circumstances and cultural characteristics does Douglas make?

2 What other material factors, not mentioned here, might affect a child's school progress today? You should consider the educational provision of all sorts in affluent areas, the hidden costs of school, material incentives for leaving school, and so on.

3 What educational policies would you recommend in order to overcome the problems identified here?

4 (a) Would you agree that the importance of unsatisfactory conditions at home as a factor in educational underachievement has declined since the 1950s when this study was done?
(b) Why, do you think, is there a connection between areas which have a large proportion of families in the manual working class and schools which are old, have crowded classes and lack amenities?

5 Comment on the quality of Douglas' evidence.

B. Bernstein

'Social Class and Linguistic Development: a Theory of Social Learning', in A. H. Halsey, J. Floud and C. A. Anderson (eds), *Education, Economy and Society*, 1965, pp. 291–93, 295–98

The evidence from … language studies indicates that the level of linguistic skills may be independent of the potential IQ, certainly independent of measured non–verbal IQ, and that grossly different environments affect aspects of language structure and vocabulary. It is also clear that linguistic performance is basic to educational success. It is suggested that the measurable interstatus linguistic differences between the lower working–class and middle–class, rather than simply reflecting differences in potential capacity, result from entirely different modes of speech, which are dominant and typical of these strata. It is proposed that two distinct forms of language use arise because the organisation of these two strata is such that different emphases are placed on language potential. Once the emphasis or stress is placed, then the resulting forms of speech progressively orient the speakers to distinct types of relationships of objects and persons. The role intelligence plays is to enable the speaker to exploit more successfully the possibilities symbolised by the socially conditioned linguistic forms. There are exceptions to this linguistic determinism, which arise under special limiting physiological and psychological conditions. It is suggested that the typical and dominant mode of speech of the middle class is one where speech becomes an object of special perceptual activity and one where a theoretical attitude is developed toward the structural possibilities of sentence organisation. This speech mode is one where the structure and syntax are relatively difficult to predict for any one individual and where the formal possibilities of sentence organisation are used to clarify meaning and make it explicit. This mode of speech will be called a *formal* language.

By contrast, the speech mode of the lower working class may be distinguished by the rigidity of the syntax and the limited and restricted use of structural possibilities for sentence organisation. Thus, these speech elements are *highly* predictable for any one speaker. It is a form of relatively condensed speech in which certain meanings are restricted and the possibility of their elaboration is reduced. Although any one content of this speech is not predictable, the class of the content, the structural organisation, and syntax are highly predictable. This use of speech will be called a *public* language. The individual, when he speaks a *public* language, operates within a speech mode in which individual selection and permutation are severely restricted; whilst in the case of a *formal* language, the speaker is able to make a highly individual selection and permutation. I am not arguing that a *formal* language speaker always does this. I am simply stating that the possibility exists. A *formal* language facilitates the verbal elaboration of subjective intent, sensitivity to the implications of separateness and difference, and points to the possibilities inherent in a complex conceptual hierarchy for the organisation of experience. It is suggested that this is not so for members of the lower working class, *who are restricted to a public language*, which, although allowing for a vast range of possibilities, provides a speech form that discourages the speaker from verbally elaborating subjective intent, and progressively

orients him to descriptive rather than analytic concepts. It limits the type of stimuli to which the speaker learns to respond.

Fundamental to this paper is the assertion that a middle–class child learns *both* these linguistic modes and uses them according to the social context, whereas a lower working–class child is restricted to a *public* language. A *public* language will occur in any social structure that maximises identifications with others at the cost of the significance of individuated differences. Thus, approximations to a *public* language will be associated with the peer group of children and adolescents (irrespective of class), combat units in the armed services, criminal subcultures and rural groups. . . .

. . . . When a middle–class mother says to her child, 'I'd rather you made less noise, darling,' the child will tend to obey because previous disobedience after this point has led to expression of disapproval or perhaps other punitive measures. The operative words in this sentence, which the middle–class child responds to, are 'rather' and 'less'. The child has learned to become sensitive to this form of sentence and the many possible sentences in this universe of discourse. The words 'rather' and 'less' are understood, when used in this situation, as directly translatable cues for immediate response on the part of the middle–class child. However, if the same statement were made to a child from the family of an unskilled worker it would not be understood as containing the same imperative cues for response. 'Shut up!' may contain a more appropriate set of cues. Of course, the last statement is meaningful to a middle–class child, but what it is important to stress is the fact that the middle–class child has learned to be able to respond to both statements, and both are differentially discriminated within a finely articulated world of meaning. . . .

One of the aims of the middle–class family is to produce a child oriented to certain values but individually differentiated within them. The child is born into an environment where he is seen and responded to as an individual with his own rights, that is, he has a specific social status. This early process of individuation is accomplished by two important factors: the scrupulous observation of the child by the parents so that the very fine stages of development and the emergence of new patterns of behaviour are the oject of attention and comment; together with recognition and communication in a language structure where personal qualifications are significantly used and which the child learns to use in response. The child's relation to the environment is such that his range and expression of discriminating verbal respones is fostered by the social structure from the beginning. A virtuous circle is set up which is continuously reinforced, for the mother will elaborate and expand the embryonic personal qualificatory statements that the child makes. It would follow that the greater the differentiation of the child's experience, the greater his ability to differentiate and conceptualise objects in his environment. This, of course, is part of the socialising process of any child, but it is the *mode of established relationships* that is of decisive importance, because the mode determines the levels of conceptualisation possible. Different children will be able to benefit more from this environment as a result of other factors, e.g., specifically psychological factors, but the means of utilising and exploiting formal educational facilities are provided.

The school is an institution where every item in the present is finely linked to a distant future, and in consequence there is no serious clash of expectations between the school and the middle-class child. The child's developed time-span of anticipation allows the present activity to be related to a future and this is meaningful. There is little conflict of values between the teacher and child, and even more importantly the child is predisposed to accept and respond to the language structure of communication. The school aims at assisting the development of consciousness of self and cognitive and emotional discrimination, and it develops and encourages mediate relationships. There is, in the child, a desire to use and manipulate words in a personal qualifying or modifying way, which together combine to reduce the problem of teaching of English—reading, spelling, writing. The middle-class child is predisposed toward the ordering of *symbolic* relationships and more importantly, *imposing order* and seeing new relationships. His level of curiosity is high. There is a conformity to authority and an acceptance of the role of the teacher, irrespective of psychological relationships to his personality. (This is not to say that at times feelings of rebellion will not appear.) The middle-class child is capable of manipulating the two languages—the language between social equals (peer groups), which approximates to a *public* language, and a *formal* language. This leads to appropriateness of behaviour in a wide range of social circumstances. Finally, the school is an important and socially approved means whereby the developing child can enhance his self-respect. Thus, the social structure of the school, the means and ends of education, create a framework that the middle-class child is able to accept, respond to, and exploit. . . .

In the lower working class, the linguistic relationship between mother and child is of a different order. It is essentially a verbal form, where, initially, personal qualifications are made through *expressive* symbolism; that is non-verbally, or through the possibilities of a limiting language structure. The child's relationship to the mother is of a direct, immediate nature. His strategic referent is not her language, for the personal qualification, the 'I' of the working-class mother, will primarily be signalled by expressive symbolism that has no reference other than that to itself. Briefly, *subjective intent is not verbally explicit or elaborated*. The child early learns to respond to, and make responses to, cues that are immediately relevant. Thus, it is a form of communication that maximises the direct experience of affective inclusiveness rather than verbally conditioned emotional and cognitive differentiation. The working-class child is sensitive to a form of language use quite distinct from the middle-class child's usage. The characteristics of the language use are:

1 Short, grammatically simply, often unfinished sentences with a poor syntactical form.
2 Simple and repetitive use of conjunctions (so, then, and, because).
3 Little use of subordinate clauses used to break down the initial categories of the dominant subject.
4 Inability to hold a formal subject through a speech sequence, thus facilitating a dislocated informational content.
5 Rigid and limited use of adjectives and adverbs.
6 Infrequent use of impersonal pronouns as subjects of conditional clauses or sentences, e.g., 'one'.
7 Frequent use of statements where the reason and the conclusion are confounded to produce a categoric utterance.
8 A large number of statements and phrases that signal a requirement for the previous speech sequence to be reinforced—'Wouldn't it,' 'You see,' 'Just fancy.' This process is termed 'sympathetic circulatory'.
9 Individual selection from a group of idiomatic sequences will frequently occur.
10 *The individual qualification is implicit in the sentence organisation: it is a language of implicit meaning.*

Glossary

Interstatus linguistic differences differences in language use between the social classes.

Linguistic determinism the determination of language use by other factors.

Syntax the grammatical arrangement of words in speech or writing.

Permutation a combination of things.

Verbally elaborating subjective intent putting intentions into words.

Imperative that must be obeyed.

Differentially discriminated selection based upon different characteristics.

Virtuous circle the opposite of a vicious circle.

Conceptualise comprehend something in the imagination.

Questions

1 Find passages in the extract which could be used to support the view that public language is inferior to formal language.

2 What is the nature of the language which is used in school lessons, according to Bernstein?

3 What educational policies would you recommend in order to overcome the problems identified here?

4 What arguments could be used against the idea that the language used in the classroom puts the working class at a disadvantage there?

5 (a) Would you agree that Bernstein is saying that one linguistic form is inferior to the other in this passage?

(b) Do you agree that class–related forms of language or language use exist?

S. Ball

Beachside Comprehensive, 1981, pp. 32, 27–29, 36–39

Table *Distribution of social classes across the case–study forms 2TA and 2CU*

	I	II	IIIN	Total non-manual	IIIM	IV	V	Total manual	Unclass
2CU	5	10	5	20	12	–	–	12	–
2TA	2	3	2	7	15	8	3	26	–

2TA English with Mrs Bradley: lesson notes

The pupils are arriving singly or in small groups while the teacher waits. The time between the first arrivals and the last is over four minutes. While the teacher waits for the last arrivals to sit down, the noise being made by the form is considerable. Corina Newnes is the last to come in.

Teacher 'Where you have been?'

Corina 'Mr Dawson kept me behind.'

Teacher 'What for?'

Corina 'To talk to me.'

Teacher 'Well, this is my lesson now. You should be on time.'

Corina sits down, the teacher addresses the whole class.

Teacher 'All right, let's have some quiet.'

This is shouted over the noise of the class: the teacher is standing at the front of the room with one hand on her hip; she looks displeased. '2TA,' she shouts more loudly; the noise is considerable reduced. 'Peter, I am waiting for you. [To the whole class] I told you last week that I wanted you here on time. It is nearly ten minutes gone now. If it happens next week ... Peter, I've told you once, what did I just say?'

Peter 'If it happens next week.'

Teacher 'Right, now stop talking to Sammy and listen to me ... if it happens next week we will stay behind at four o'clock to make up the time we've lost.'

Two of the girls at the back are talking and writing on a small book.

Teacher 'Dorothy, bring your books and sit here.' The teacher indicates the empty desk at the front, next to one of the boys.

Dorothy 'You moved me last week.'

Teacher 'Well, I'm moving you again, come on.'

Grudgingly, Dorothy gets up, making her chair scrape noisily on the wooden floor, and picks up her books slowly; she goes to the front and stands behind the empty desk.

Dorothy 'Ugh, I'm not sitting next to him.'

She gestures at Wally who is sitting next to the empty desk; several of the class laugh and the teacher looks angrily around the room; her gaze returns to Dorothy.

Teacher 'You sit where I tell you.'

Dorothy 'Not next to him.'

She pulls the empty desk away from Wally's until there is a six-inch gap, and sits down. The teacher seems to be about to say something to her and then changes her mind; she picks up a book from her desk instead.

Teacher 'We began last week to look at ...'

Teachers found it almost impossible to organise discussions in 2TA lessons, and even question and answer sessions tended to deteriorate into noisy shouted responses. Few members of the form would listen to their fellows' contributions, and many pupils took such opportunities to talk amongst themselves or to 'muck about'. In some lessons with young and inexperienced teachers, 2TA could get completely beyond control. In extreme cases the pupils would run around the classroom virtually ignoring the teacher's rebukes or threats or attempts to 'teach'. The maintenance of quiet and keeping the pupils working involved special effort in 2TA's lessons.

2CU Chemistry with Mr Baldwin: lesson notes

The lesson begins with twenty minutes of 'administration–talk' from the teacher. Books are returned and he comments on the homework, on writing up experiments, especially the method, and he explains the rationale of the marking. 'So if you got a bad mark for this homework it was not necessarily because the experiment or your conclusions were wrong, but that it was not written up correctly.'

The form is silent and attentive throughout the whole of this time. The teacher now begins some experiments with CO_2 to show its qualities as a fire extinguisher; the form is gathered round the bench at the front but are orderly, without pushing one another or talking. The teacher asks questions as he goes along, hands are raised, he chooses a respondent and the rest of the form listens to the answer given.

Teacher 'Why wouldn't I use water in this case?' He looks up. 'Chris ...' The lesson ends with the writing up of what was seen; the bell goes, but the class continues to work as if nothing had happened.

Teacher 'Off you go when you are ready.'

The pupils leave in ones or twos. Several remain for more than five minutes of their break–time to finish writing. ...

The fact that the pupils came to the secondary school pre–selected, sorted out into bands, may have been important in making the allocation 'real' to the Beachside teachers. As the band allocation of the pupils was 'given', a label imposed from outside prior to any contact with the pupils, the teachers were 'taking', and deriving assumptions on the basis of, that label, rather than 'making' their own evaluation of the relative abilities of individual pupils. Each band–label carries its own particular status within the school and the staff hold preconceived and institutionalised notions about the typical 'band 2 child', the 'remedial child', etc. To a great extent these typifications are based on what the teacher knows about the bands in terms of their status identity. From the teacher's point of view the behaviour of band 2 forms is 'deviant', contravening their expectations of appropriate classroom behaviour. These labels are consistent and embedded aspects of the system of meanings shared by all the teachers, and are not dependent upon the identification of particular forms or pupils. Once established, the typification 'band 2 form' or 'band 2 pupil' merely awaits the arrival of each new cohort in the school. I am not suggesting that the 'label' of being band 2 in itself creates a 'deviant' identity and is the cause of the 'deviant' acts described previously. But the label of being band 2 imposes certain limitations upon the sort of social identity that may be negotiated by the band 2 pupil. When persons are subjected to a process of categorisation, they are subject also to the imputation of various social identities by virtue of their membership of that category. In this case, it is an identity that involves a status–evaluation and allocation to an inferior position in the status–hierarchy of the school. Band 2 forms, as we shall see, are considered to be 'not up to much academically' and most teachers find them 'unrewarding' to teach. Certainly, by the beginning of the second year in the careers of the case–study forms, it is a label that denotes a behavioural stereotype. The teachers hold stereotypical images of band identity (which I shall refer to as the 'bandness' of pupils). That is, they tend to jump from a single cue or a small number of cues in actual, suspected or alleged behaviour, to a general picture of the 'kind of person with whom one is dealing'.

In one sense, stereotyping may be understood quite straightforwardly in terms of the demands of a complex interaction situation. The classroom involves one individual interacting in various ways with 35 other individuals, and stereotyping may be necessary for the teacher to be able to order his expectations of, and thus predict the actions of, the pupils. The reality of everyday life commonly involves stereotyping in terms of which others are 'dealt with'. That is, people apprehend others through patterns built up from previous experiences. But in regard to individual pupils in the banded classroom, stereotyping by the teacher may also be considered as a reaction that is based upon a selective perception or incorrect assessment of pupils, derived from preconceived notions of band behaviour. In their attempts to make sense of, and derive meaning from, social situations, people tend to organise data about other people in their environment. They tend to do so by making interpretations and inferences from what they 'know' and what they can see in front of them. Once such interpretations and inferences are made, further information is sought to confirm and strengthen them, and contradictory information tends to be overlooked.

The normal way of discussing pupils among the staff was in terms of singular and unitary characteristics, a categorical identification that tended to become a pejorative label. Thus, with regard

to projects: 'the band 1 child, who is intelligent, loves doing projects but the lower–band child will just copy chunks out of a book and cover about four sides.' (English teacher) The band 1 child is 'intelligent' and by implication here the band 2 child is not. Yet the discrimination between band 1 and band 2 in the original allocation of pupils makes no such distinction; these differentiating perceptions are socially constructed. The original sum–variable basis of allocation to bands, recommendations made by the primary school indicating pupils of more or less ability, is here transformed into a zero–sum perception: band 1 pupils have ability; band 2 pupils do not. Cohen (1972:12)[1] makes the point that: 'Society labels rule breakers as belonging to certain deviant groups and, once the person is thus typecast, his acts are interpreted in terms of the status to which he has been assigned.' In this way the band stereotypes were an important aspect of the shared meanings of the staff in their perceptions of and interactions with pupils. As Cohen indicates, 'the deviant or delinquent is always portrayed as a certain type'. As labels, the stereotypes of band identity provide a framework within which the pupil must negotiate his social identity in the school. Thus the band to which he is allocated is an important constraint upon the range of possible social identities available to him. For example, 'brilliant pupil' is an identity that is not normally available to the 'band 2 pupil' because of the sorts of notions that accompany that label. However, as we have seen, there is still the possibility that *some* pupils may negotiate identities that supersede these constraints, at least in the early stages of their band career.

The framework of identities which derive from the band–labels can be seen in the following composite band–profiles, constructed from teachers' descriptions. These are the stereotypical notions that the teachers hold about the bands. As such they are also situational–expectations, that is, expectations about 'what this form is going to be like'. These stereotypes are constraints which the teacher brings into the classroom and with which the pupil has to deal.

The band 1 child

'Has academic potential ... will do O-levels ... and a good number will stay on to the sixth form ... likes doing projects ... knows what the teacher wants ... is bright, alert and enthusiastic ... can concentrate ... produces neat work ... is interested ... wants to get on ... is grammar school material ... you can have discussions with ... friendly ... rewarding ... has common sense.'

The band 2 child

'Is not interested in school work ... difficult to control ... rowdy and lazy ... has little self control ... is immature ... loses and forgets books with monotonous regularity ... cannot take part in discussions ... is moody ... of low standard ... technical inability ... lacks concentration ... is poorly behaved ... not up to much academically.'

The band 3 child

'Is unfortunate ... is low ability ... maladjusted ... anti–school ... lacks a mature view of education ... mentally retarded ... emotionally unstable and ... a waste of time.'

It is apparent that by the beginning of the second year the majority of the teachers 'see', that is make sense of, the classroom in terms of these preconceived notions. They act as a 'filter' upon the teacher's perceptions of the pupils. And yet they derive from a fairly arbitrary line of demarcation between pupils; the importance of these stereotypes is perhaps best seen in terms of the borderline child who would be differently perceived in each band according to the point at which the allocation line is drawn. Keddie (1971:139)[2] also makes the point that 'what a teacher knows about pupils derives from the organisational device of banding or streaming'.

[1–2] See Bibliography.

Glossary

Typifications (here) classifications of a type of person.

Selective perception recognising only *some* aspects of reality, usually in accordance with some prior idea of what reality is like.

Inferences conclusions one comes to based on a limited number of facts.

Pejorative having negative associations.

Zero–sum either yes or no, black or white, with no possibility of a middle position. Sum variable is the opposite of this.

Questions

1 (a) Summarise Ball's argument in point form.
   (b) In what other occupations than teaching might the observations that he makes be of interest to the sociologist?

2 Have you any evidence to confirm or refute the idea that teachers see individual children in terms of stereotypes and ignore information which may challenge that stereotype?

3 Interactionists are sometimes criticised for seeing the individual as powerless to reject the label imposed on him/her by other people or to adopt forms of behaviour other than those which conform to that label. Could one level this criticism at Ball? Why or why not?

4 Ball argues that the staff hold stereotypical notions of the typical 'band 2' child, the 'remedial' child, and so on. What is the source of such notions and do you think that teachers are justified in using them in their interaction with children?

5 What arguments could be used against Ball's view that teachers' labelling of pupils strongly influences the outcome of the latter's school careers?

6 What educational policies would you recommend to overcome the problems identified here?

7 What problems may be associated with the research techniques adopted by Ball in this study?

M. Young
Knowledge and Control, 1971, pp. 24–6

Sociologists seem to have forgotten, to paraphrase Raymond Williams, that education is not a product like cars and bread, but a selection and organisation from the available knowledge at a particular time which involves conscious or unconscious choices. It would seem that it is or should be the central task of the sociology of education to relate these principles of selection and organisation that underlie curricula to their institutional and interactional setting in schools and classrooms and to the wider social structure. I want to suggest that we can account for the failure of sociologists to do this by examining on the one hand the ideological and methodological assumptions of the sociologists, and on the other hand the institutional context within which the sociological study of education has developed. However, perhaps as significant a fact as any in accounting for the limited conception of the sociology of education in Britain has been that in spite of the interest in the field reported by respondents to Carter's recent survey (Carter, 1967)[1], *very few* sociologists have been involved in research in education.

Much British sociology in the late fifties and the sociology of education in particular drew its ideological perspective from Fabian socialism and its methodology from the demographic tradition of Booth and Rowntree. They broadened the notion of poverty from lack of income to lack of education, which was seen as a significant part of working–class life chances. The stark facts of the persistence of inequalities over decades and in spite of an overall expansion do not need repeating, but what is important is that these studies and those such as Douglas and Plowden which followed, in their concern for increasing equality of opportunity, focused primarily on the characteristics of the failures, the early leavers and the drop-outs. By using a model of explanation of working-class school failure which justified reformist social policies, they were unable to examine the socially constructed character of the education that the working–class children failed at—for instance, the peculiar content of the grammar school curriculum for the sixteen-year-old in which pupils are obliged to do up to ten different subjects which bear little relation either to each other or to anything else. It would not be doing these studies an injustice to say that they

developed primarily from a sociological interest in stratification in the narrow sense rather than education. They were concerned to show how the distribution of life chances through education can be seen as an aspect of the class structure. Inevitably this led to an over-mechanistic conception of 'class' which isolated the 'class' characteristics of individuals from the 'class' content of their educational experience. It may clarify this point by looking at the implicit model more formally as follows:

Assumptions	Independent variable	Dependent variable
Criteria of educational success— curricula, methods and evaluation. What counts as 'knowledge and knowing' in school	Social characteristics of the success and failure groups	Distribution of success and failure at various stages—stream, 11+, 'O' level, etc.

Though the table illustrates the point in a crude and over-simplified form, it does show that within that framework the content of education is taken as a 'given' and is not subject to sociological enquiry—the 'educational failures' become a sort of 'deviant'. We can usefully reformulate the problem in a similar way to that suggested by Cicourel and Kitsuse[2] in their discussion of how 'official statistics' on crime are produced, and ask what are the processes by which rates of educational success and failure come to be produced. We are then led to ask questions about the context and definition of success and how they are legitimised. In other words, the methods of assessment, selection and organisation of knowledge and the principles underlying them become our focus of study. The point is important because what is implied is that questions have to be raised about matters that have either not been considered important or have been tacitly accepted as 'given'. How does the education that poor working–class children fail at come to be provided? What are the social assumptions that are implicit in the criteria used in the Crowther Report to delineate a 'second group' who 'should be taught a sensible practicality—moral standards and a wise use of leisure time'? One could raise similar questions about the Newsom Report's 'below average child', and in fact about much educational research. One can see that this kind of reformulation would not have been consistent either with the methods or with the ideology of most British sociological research, particularly that concerned with social class and educational opportunity. A similar point can be made about studies of schools and colleges as 'organisations'. They have either begun with 'models' from 'organisation theory' or have compared schools with mental hospitals and prisons as 'people processing organisations'. In neither case is it recognised that it is not only people but knowledge in the educational institutions that is 'processed', and that unless what is 'knowledge' is to be taken as 'given', it is the interrelation of the two processes of organisation that must form the beginning of such studies. An examination of the knowledge teachers have of children and how this influences the knowledge they make available to them would provide one way of tackling this empirically (Keddie, 1970).[3]

Turning to the institutional context, it does seem clear that most of the teaching and published work in the sociology of education has taken place in colleges, institutes and departments of education. It is only very recently that university departments of sociology have offered main options at either B.Sc. or M.Sc. level in this field. Thus sociology of education has developed in institutions devoted to the 'academic' study of education where ten to fifteen years ago it hardly existed. We can pose the question as to how did the new specialists legitimate their contribution to educational studies and justify their particular field of expertise—particularly when the ex-school subject specialists and the philosophers had defined their area of competence as covering the curriculum and pedagogy. Not surprisingly, the sociologists mapped out new unexplored areas. They started from the social context of education, with an emphasis on social class, relationships to the economy, the occupational structure and the family, and moved to the consideration of schools as organisations and pupil subcultures. Through an arbitrary division of labour which had no theoretical basis, this allowed the expansion of sociology of education with the minimum of 'boundary disputes'. Inevitably this is speculation, but it does suggest an explanation of what appears to have been a consensus among sociologists and non-sociologists alike that the curriculum was not a field for sociological research.

[1-3]See Bibliography

Glossary

Methodological being concerned with the methods used in an enquiry.

Demographic concerning births, deaths, etc., in the study of population and conditions of life in a community.

Tacitly understood without being stated.

Pedagogy the science of teaching.

Questions

1 (a) Distinguish between syllabus and curriculum.
 (b) What is Young's criticism of Douglas?
2 Explain Young's view of the nature of knowledge.
3 Summarise Young's argument in point form.
4 What educational policies follow from Young's perspective?
5 (a) Given that 'education . . . is a selection and organisation from the available knowledge at a particular time' and that the knowledge taught in school cannot claim to be better than any other form of knowledge, what *should* be taught in schools according to you?
 (b) What criticisms have you of Young's theory?

D. Spender

Invisible Women: The Schooling Scandal, 1982, pp. 17–18, 29, 54, 62–63, 68

From the position of subordination, women can see that men miss much of the evidence and can construct only poorly informed explanations: women know a great deal about the world that men do not, they know a great deal about men that men do not know about themselves, and until women's view of the world coexists with men's view of the world, our entire system of education will be limited, distorted, sexist. Women have a responsibility to describe the world from the position they occupy—for other women; and for men, who will not know unless they are informed. If we wish to describe and analyse *human* experience, and to formulate explanations of the world which take *human beings* into account, then we must include the experience and understandings of women, as well as men. . . .

While males control education there is no direct means for women to pass on their understandings. What women know frequently dies with them, until feminists periodically rediscover them and their writing and attempt to reconstruct women's heritage and tradition. Each generation of women forges understandings about subordination, within their own lifetime and from the circumstances of their own lives, but because these meanings do not become the general currency of the culture they are not passed on to the next generation with the result that neither women nor men know about the women who have gone before. . . .

Within education more knowledge is made about men, more importance is attached to their education and more significance given to their experience, and this is the discipline which influences and even determines the parameters of education in schools and colleges. In surveying publications in the sociology of education since 1960, Sandra Acker reports that 37% of them were concerned exclusively with males while only 5% were concerned exclusively with women, and this does not satisfactorily document the extent of the male 'bias', for among the 5% concerned with women were studies that focused not on women as autonomous individuals (as was the case with men) but as transmitters of a code to young children. And of the 58% of studies in which the sex of the subjects was

not specifically stated, it would be unwise to assume that both sexes were included; many of them could well have been about males, but so common is the practice of focusing on males that it was not thought necessary to make this explicit. . . .

It is not difficult to establish who gets the teachers' attention in class, and numerous studies report that boys get most of it in mixed-sex classrooms. But while it has been known for a long time that boys get so much more attention from teachers than do girls, not surprisingly, few attempts have been made to explain this phenomenon or to speculate on its significance: in a society where men are perceived as more important such statistics can simply serve to confirm what we already know about male 'supremacy' and are therefore taken for granted rather than made the subject of further enquiry.

Teachers themselves are very often unaware of the way they allocate their time and it is not uncommon to ask teachers whether they give more attention to one sex than the other, and to have them <u>vehemently</u> protest that they do *not* and that they treat both sexes equally. But when their next lesson is taped it is often found that over two thirds of their time was spent with the boys, who comprised less than half the class.

In general, boys take up more space, even when they are a minority. They take up more space on their chairs (legs frequently extended as obstacles to unwary travellers), their chairs and desks take up more space, they move around the room more. (They also frequently have more space outside the classroom in corridors and, of course, in terms of sporting facilities: it is not unusual to find large areas of school playgrounds reserved specifically for boys and if there is a division of the playground it is sure to be the girls who get the smaller allocation. This too can be seen as 'fair' in the same way that a smaller allocation of teacher time can be seen as fair.) . . .

That boys do not like girls, that they find them inferior and unworthy—and even despicable—is a conclusion hard to avoid when observing and documenting the behaviour of boys towards girls in schools. In the tapes that I have made in the classroom there is the evidence that boys frequently make insulting and abusive (often sexually abusive) comments to girls. There is also evidence that more often than not teachers do not take them to task for this behaviour.

More often than not such attacks are ignored, rendered invisible by the teacher who does not notice (or pretends not to notice) such outbursts. Rarely, it seems, do teachers seek to make an issue out of such behaviour, and when I have asked why it is that such abuse is allowed to persist, even to go unchecked, the response has usually been in the form of an excuse: 'All boys behave like that at their age, it's a stage they go through' and 'It's best not to draw attention to it, they grow out of it you know.' Apart from the fact that I have grave concerns over what they 'grow in to', I cannot fail to notice that such an evaluation takes only the boys into account. . . .

Greater significance is attached to the male and to male experience in our society and it is therefore reasonable to expect that this value judgement will make its presence felt in schools. In every facet of classroom life, from the curriculum to classroom interaction, it is demonstrable that more attention is paid to males with the result that teachers are more familiar with male experience and individual males. Teachers are behaving in a manner that is completely consis-tent with the values and beliefs of society when they favour males and this is probably one of the reasons that they perceive their behaviour as fair and non–discriminatory, even when empirical evidence can so readily reveal their bias.

But a crucial question arises—what are the consequences for girls of this favouritism? Both sexes are learning the daily lesson that teachers prefer to spend time with males, to discuss male experience and to know and understand the individual males in the class, and while one sex may thrive, may expand and develop as a result of this knowledge, the other sex surely will not. While the members of one sex are more likely to be treated as individuals, to have individual and idiosyncratic problems which require individual solutions, the members of the other sex are more likely to be seen as a group in which both the problems and the solutions are generalised.

No research studies have been undertaken on this topic: it is not a problem which presents itself to men, for while male students receive this preferential treatment the male educational ex-perience is undoubtedly positive and all is going well. But in the absence of research it is not difficult to speculate on the significance of this differential treatment for the girls.

Glossary

Vehemently done with strong feelings.
Idiosyncratic something which is peculiar to one particular person.

Questions

1 Summarise Spender's argument in point form.
2 According to Spender, in what sense do 'males control education'?
3 What educational policies would you recommend in order to overcome the problems identified here?
4 (a) Do you agree or disagree with Spender? Give evidence or argument to support your position. What criticisms (if any) do you have of her theory?
(b) In the book she uses secondary data, i.e. information from other studies, quotes from interviews and anecdotes about tape–recorded lessons. She gives no details of how and when interviews were conducted. Is this methodology adequate? If not, then what methodological techniques should she have used?
(c) Spender makes no attempt to be value free. Do you think she should? Why/why not?

Questions on Douglas, Bernstein, Ball, Young, and Spender

1 Complete the following table, according to the views represented:

	Douglas	Bernstein	Ball	Young	Spender
Most important factor in explaining under–achievement at school					
Groups which suffer most from under–achievement					
How to overcome their under–achievement					
How this is best achieved in practice					

2 How successful have policies designed to make the education system more meritocratic been? What have been their major failings?

3 In what different ways have sociologists attempted to explain educational under–achievement? Why have sociological approaches to the subject changed since the 1950s?

Bibliography

Source of extracts

S. Bowles and H. Gintis, *Schooling in Capitalist America*, Routledge & Kegan Paul, London, 1976

R. Fletcher, *Education in Society: The Promethean Fire*, Penguin, Harmondsworth, 1984

J. W. B. Douglas, *The Home and the School*, Panther Books, London, 1969

B. Bernstein, *Social Class and Linguistic Development: A Theory of Social Learning* in A. H. Halsey, J. Floud and C. A. Anderson, (eds), *Education, Economy and Society* Collier Macmillan, Toronto, 1965, first published 1961

S. Ball, *Beachside Comprehensive*, Cambridge University Press, Cambridge, 1981

M. Young, *Knowledge and Control*, Collier Macmillan, London, 1971

D. Spender *Invisible Women*, Writers and Readers, London, 1982

References in the Introduction

J. W. B. Douglas, *All Our Future*, Panther Books, London, 1971, first published 1968

J. Demaine, *Contemporary Theories in the Sociology of Education*, Macmillan, London, 1981

D. Hargreaves, *Social Relations in a Secondary School*, Routledge & Kegan Paul, London, 1967

C. Lacey, *Hightown Grammar School*, Manchester University Press, 1970

References in Ball extract

1 S. Cohen, *Folk Devils and Moral Panics*, MacGibbon and Kee, London, 1972

2 N. Keddie, *Classroom Knowledge* in M. F. D. Young (ed.) *Knowledge and Control*, Collier-Macmillan, 1971.

References in Young extract

1 M. P. Carter, *A Report of a Survey of Sociological Research in Britain*, British Sociological Association, 1967

2 A. Cicourel and J. I. Kitsuse, *A Note on the Use of Official Statistics*, Social Problems II, 1963

3 N. Keddie, *The Social Basis of Classroom Knowledge—A Case Study*, M.A. thesis, University of London, 1970

Further reading

N. Bisseret, *Education, Class, Language and Ideology*, Routledge & Kegan Paul, London, 1979

R. Dale *et al.*, (eds), *Schooling and Capitalism*, Routledge & Kegan Paul, London and the Open University Press, Milton Keynes, 1976

M. David, *The State, The Family and Education*, Routledge & Kegan Paul, London, 1980

R. Deem, *Women and Schooling*, Routledge & Kegan Paul, London, 1978

M. Hammersley and P. Woods, *The Process of Schooling*, Routledge & Kegan Paul, London and the Open University Press, Milton Keynes, 1976

N. Keddie, (ed.), *Tinker, Tailor: The Myth of Cultural Deprivation*, Penguin, Harmondsworth, 1973

I. Reid, *Sociological Perspectives on School and Education*, Open Books, London 1978

G. Whitty and M. Young, (eds), *Explorations in the Politics of School Knowledge* Driffield, Nafferton, 1976

M. Young and G. Whitty, *Society, State and Schooling* Falmer Press, Sussex 1977

◪ Acknowledgements

The author and publishers are grateful to the following for permission to reproduce copyright material: A & C Black: *Working for Ford* by H. Beynon; Basil Blackwell: *Decarceration: Community Treatment and the Deviant* by A. Scull; Bristol Classical Press: *Endless Pressure* by K. Pryce; CBS College Publishing: *Pygmalion in the Classroom* by R. Rosenthal and L. Jacobson; Cambridge University Press: *Beachside Comprehensive* by S. Ball, *The Stages of Economic Growth* by W. W. Rostow, *The Affluent Worker in the Class Structure* by J. Goldthorpe and D. Lockwood, and *Workers' Attitudes and Technology* by D. Wedderburn and R. Crompton; Century Hutchinson: *Girls and Subcultures* by A. McRobbie and J. Garber; Collins: *The Home and the School* by J. W. B. Douglas, *Strikes* by R. Hyman; Professor Ivor Crewe: *The Disturbing Truth Behind Labour's Rout*; Fontana: *The Politics of the Media* by J. Whale, *Welfare State and Welfare Society* by R. M. Titmuss, *Social Mobility* by A. Heath, and *The Wife's Marriage* by J. Bernard; Glencoe Publishing: *The Outsider* by H. S. Becker; Gower: *Black and White Britain* by C. Brown and *Racial Discrimination* by C. Brown and P. Gay; Heinemann Educational: *Making Redistribution Work* by J. Le Grand; HMSO: *Social Trends*, 1985 and *General Household Survey*, 1981; Hodder & Stoughton Educational: *Middle Class Unionism* by T. May; Hutchinson Educational: *The Empire Strikes Back* by the Centre for Contemporary Cultural Studies; Macmillan: *Women and Crime* by F. Heidensohn, *The British General Election of 1983* by D. Butler and D. Kavanagh; *Society and Social Policy* by R. Mishra; *Hooligan: A History of Respectable Fears* by G. Pearson, *The Family in Question* by D. Gittins; *White Collar Proletariat* by R. Crompton and G. Jones; *Class, Capital and Social Policy* by N. Ginsberg; *City, Class and Power* by M. Castells; *Policing the Crisis*, S. Hall *et al.*; Methuen: *Reading Television* by J. Fiske and J. Hartley; *The Observer: Exposed: JMB Multi-Million Swindle* by R. Hall, D. Leigh and A. Harris; Open University Press: *War and Peace News* by the Glasgow University Media Group; Penguin: *Poverty in the United Kingdom* by P. Townsend, *Asylums* by E. Goffman, *Education in Society* by R. Fletcher, *What is to be Done about the Family?* by L. Segal, *Family, Socialisation and Interaction Process* by T. Parsons and R. F. Bales, *Sanity Madness and the Family* by D. Laing and A. Esterson, *Endless Pressure* by K. Pryce, and *What is to be Done about Law and Order?* by J. Lea and J. Young; Pluto Press: *Farewell to the Working Class* and *Paths to Paradise* by A. Gorz, and *Crimes of the Powerful* by Pearce; Prentice-Hall: *Social Change* by W. E. Moore; Routledge & Kegan Paul: *The Rules of Disorder* by P. Marsh, E. Rosser and R. Harré; Sage Publications: *Cruising the Truckers* by J. Corzine and R. Kirby; Secker & Warburg: *Free to Chose* by M. and R. Friedman; Times Educational Supplement: *The Swann Report*; University of Chicago Press: *Alienation and Freedom* by R. Blauner; Verso/NLB: *Women's Oppression Today* by M. Barrett; Weidenfeld & Nicolson: *The State in Capitalist Society* by R. Miliband; M. Young: *Knowledge and Control*.

Every effort has been made to trace copyright-holders, but this has not proved possible in every case.